D1580305

MODERN SUSTAINABLE
RESIDENTIAL DESIGN

MODERN SUSTAINABLE RESIDENTIAL DESIGN
A Guide for Design Professionals

WILLIAM J. CARPENTER, PhD, FAIA

John Wiley & Sons, Inc.

Copyright © 2009 by John Wiley & Sons, Inc. All rights reserved

Published by John Wiley & Sons, Inc., Hoboken, New Jersey
Published simultaneously in Canada

No part of this publication may be reproduced, stored in a retrieval system, or transmitted in any form or by any means, electronic, mechanical, photocopying, recording, scanning, or otherwise, except as permitted under Section 107 or 108 of the 1976 United States Copyright Act, without either the prior written permission of the Publisher, or authorization through payment of the appropriate per-copy fee to the Copyright Clearance Center, 222 Rosewood Drive, Danvers, MA 01923, (978) 750-8400, fax (978) 646-8600, or on the web at www.copyright.com. Requests to the Publisher for permission should be addressed to the Permissions Department, John Wiley & Sons, Inc., 111 River Street, Hoboken, NJ 07030, (201) 748-6011, fax (201) 748-6008, or online at www.wiley.com/go/permissions.

Limit of Liability/Disclaimer of Warranty: While the publisher and the author have used their best efforts in preparing this book, they make no representations or warranties with respect to the accuracy or completeness of the contents of this book and specifically disclaim any implied warranties of merchantability or fitness for a particular purpose. No warranty may be created or extended by sales representatives or written sales materials. The advice and strategies contained herein may not be suitable for your situation. You should consult with a professional where appropriate. Neither the publisher nor the author shall be liable for any loss of profit or any other commercial damages, including but not limited to special, incidental, consequential, or other damages.

For general information about our other products and services, please contact our Customer Care Department within the United States at (800) 762-2974, outside the United States at (317) 572-3993 or fax (317) 572-4002.

Wiley also publishes its books in a variety of electronic formats. Some content that appears in print may not be available in electronic books. For more information about Wiley products, visit our web site at www.wiley.com.

Library of Congress Cataloging-in-Publication Data:

Carpenter, William J., 1962–
    Modern sustainable residential design : a guide for design professionals / by William J. Carpenter.
        p. cm.
    Includes bibliographical references and index.
    ISBN 978-0-470-12673-8 (cloth : alk. paper) 1. Architecture, Domestic—Environmental aspects.
2. Sustainable architecture. 3. Sustainable engineering. I. Title.
    NA7117.5.C37 2009
    728'.047—dc22

                                        2008036196

Printed in the United States of America

10 9 8 7 6 5 4 3 2 1

Designed by Jay Anning,
Thumb Print New York

Contents

Foreword

I T IS MY HOPE THAT WITHIN TEN YEARS, ideally less, green will not be the new black but will simply be *normal*.

This paradigm shift won't be easy to make. Currently, 50 percent of new construction is residential yet less than 5 percent is green building. That's a statistic that doesn't jibe with popular perceptions of green as the new black. Rather, it seems clear that it's not easy being green at all, as evidenced by the tragically small number of green homes standing today. Depending on your definition, there are as few as 592 (according to the U.S. Green Building Council) and as many as 750,000 (according to ENERGY STAR) or somewhere in between (around 100,000), if you're listening to the National Association of Home Builders.

Misperceptions of green building, whether related to perceived costs, complicated construction, or level of consumer interest, are legion. In a 2008 study by RCLCO Research and Development, fully 96 percent of builders surveyed believed that green building translates into increased costs; 63 percent believed that green was more "complicated" to build; and 71 percent cited a lack of contractors experienced in green buildings. Where builders had a grasp on basic green elements, such as low-flow fixtures or ENERGY STAR appliances, their familiarity with local, recycled, and salvaged materials was low, and their understanding of more complex systems like solar and natural HVAC was minimal at best.

The obstacles inherent in these stats are dismal but not insurmountable thanks to major cultural and economic shifts around the idea of sustainability. "Going green" is no longer a matter of altruism; it has become an economic necessity. Once the realm of wacky visionaries and yurt-inhabiting hippies, it's now the focus at exclusive summits like TED and Davos, and the pet project of celebrities, politicians, and policymakers. As the economy struggles and venture capital money seems to disappear, clean tech remains poised for explosive growth.

But the change isn't only about dollars. What's also changed is the framing of the debate. The pursuit of sustainability can help save the planet, true, but savvier messaging allows us to understand how organic, low-VOC, renewable, and so on are good not just for the world but, more specifically, for our communities and families. A focus on local—whether it's the decision to grow food in your backyard or to limit the miles construction materials need to travel before being used to build your new dwelling—literally brings the issue of climate change home.

Homebuyers are helping to drive changes and demonstrate demand through increased knowledge, awareness, and purchasing power. And more forward-thinking architects and builders are offering innovative and attractive options in green building. House labels that spell out the relative health and efficiency of homes, similar to the Food and Drug Administration mandates for food packaging, are under consideration by the

American Institute of Architects, and at least one architect has made them standard in the houses she produces.

The success of these new ways of thinking about sustainability have resulted in changes once thought to be out of reach both emotionally and economically. Higher gas prices and heating/cooling costs are rather quickly altering the way people think about the location and square footage of the homes they are living in. A bigger, less expensive house further from your workplace might have seemed a better deal until the combined costs of commuting and utilities cancelled out any savings you might have been enjoying on your mortgage, for example—a reality that has resulted in recent months to a swift exodus back toward city centers and into smaller homes.

The world of residential building is poised to do great things. The guidance, information, materials, and technology, while ever evolving, are in place. Now it's the hearts and minds that must follow. *Modern Sustainable Residential Design: A Guide for Design Professionals* is a comprehensive, user-friendly guide that can help. So let's get started.

—ALLISON ARIEFF

Preface

N MY PROFESSIONAL LIFE, I HAVE HAD the good fortune to work closely with two of the world's most talented residential architects: Norman Jaffe, FAIA, and AIA Gold Medalist Samuel Mockbee, FAIA. Under their guidance, I first realized the extraordinary opportunities that lay in the interconnections between design and construction, a realization that led to my first book, *Learning by Building* (Wiley, 1997). In my ensuing work as a teacher, as well as a practicing architect, I have been gratified at how stimulating such a book can be—both to students and to seasoned practitioners. I also have continued to explore design-construction interconnections, even as we all have increasingly recognized the need to step lightly on the earth. In the process, I have become aware of new needs and opportunities.

Books and articles celebrating so-called green design have become almost commonplace, yet I am unaware of any book written for design professionals that provides a how-to approach to the fundamentals of sustainable residential design. This book is an attempt to meet that need.

For the purpose, I recruited as contributors some of the most talented professionals in sustainable design. Each of the chapters in the book presents vanguard concepts for the creation of contemporary green houses, concepts that not only draw on historical principles but also illuminate new opportunities for further exploration. As such, this book is not only a record of the current best thinking in the field, it is also an invitation to our present and future colleagues to help us push the boundaries of our critically important professions, and provides a tool for doing just that.

Acknowledgments

I would like to thank the following people for helping on this book: Lee Cuthbert, Ric Nardin, Dana Ryan, James Burton, Laura Biering, Dana Topley, Mike McGrath, Wesley Thiele, Maria Sykes, Mario Knezevic, Rebecca Barnett, and Robert Soens. They were an integral part of the manuscript review and the research and writing of the case studies. Their interest in creating meaningful architecture through sustainable design, with focus and determination, helped immensely.

I was inspired by working for luminaries Samuel Mockbee, FAIA, and Norman Jaffe, FAIA. They informed my thinking, and I hope their profound spirits in some small way live on through this book.

I am grateful, too, for the support and encouragement of Gregory K. Hunt, FAIA, Jaan Holt, William Quatman, FAIA, Robert Fisher, Robert Ford, FAIA, Thomas Muir, RIBA, Will Draper, Michael and Donna Waterhouse, Alan Greene, Anne Brown, Dr. Bart Lester, Fisher Paty, Cathy and Bill Carpenter, and James Fausett, FAIA.

I greatly appreciate the enduring support of my editor at John Wiley & Sons, John Czarnecki, editorial assistant Sadie Abuhoff, and production director Diana Cisek.

A special thanks to Leah Pine Goldberg, landscape architect, for her guidance and her master's thesis "The Wild Garden in the Twentieth Century," University of Georgia (1990), which served me well as a resource of valuable historical content and inspiration.

And, finally, I'd like to thank my beautiful daughters Esme and Mirette Carpenter for always being there for me—you both always bring light into every room you enter.

PART ONE

The Sustainable Modern Home: Process and Design

Sustainable Modern Homes: Historical Context

AROUND THE WORLD THERE IS growing recognition that our lives are intricately connected with the natural world and that its fate and ours are inseparable. In response, we have begun to focus our attention not only on halting the damage we are causing to the environment but also on developing new ways of living in it, ways that may save us both. To borrow from Dylan Thomas, we have lit a green fuse. As it burns, it is igniting explosions of creativity that may prove to be the primary sources of a bright and sustainable future. And yet, if we allow this burning fuse to fizzle as an eco-chic fad, we will surely find ourselves in another dark age. At this critical point in the history of the earth and in the history of our built environment, it is encouraging to note signs that our green fuse is burning with increasing luminosity.

Many former antagonists in the ecology wars now agree that what is good for the earth can also be good for the economy, including the corporate bottom line. GE, Google, and even Shell are among what some call the "corporate greens," joining activists, innovative designers, and the so-called Green Glitterati in pursuit of a more ethical and earth-friendly way to live. This partnership is in its fragile infancy, and the debates will no doubt continue. But we have begun to explore a variety of paths leading away from the unacceptably wasteful habits of the past to an incompletely imagined way of living that can protect the future—that of our planet and ourselves. This book is about one of those paths, the process of designing the sustainable eco-modern house.

By "modern," I mean something not only current but also a collection of design strategies rooted in the Modernist principles of early twentieth-century architects. It is instructive to note how many of these principles support the basic tenets of eco-friendly design and how, in a largely unacknowledged fashion, they are being incorporated in the most successful approaches to a carbon-neutral residence. It may be that Modernist architecture, now relegated to the past, may find a celebrated and enduring place as the foundation of sustainable residential design. Indeed, the convergence of modernism and sustainability, what we may term Eco-modernism, is now emerging as one of the most important design movements in history.

I am not advocating a uniform look; nor am I saying that a sustainable house should be a green version of Mies van der Rohe's Farnsworth House or Pierre Koenig's Case Study House #22. What I am suggesting is that the blend of modern and green is a natural one. Modernist principles cohere to a remarkable degree with green design and can help guide our explorations of the varieties of expression possible in the evolving green house.

Frank Lloyd Wright has not been celebrated as an environmentalist, but the architectural record, so to speak, reveals him as the father of the modern house and a revolutionary pioneer in sustainable design. As early as 1935, Wright had promoted "an Organic Architecture" where "the ground itself predetermines all features; the cli-

The force that through the green fuse drives the flower
Drives my green age; that blasts the roots of trees
Is my destroyer.

DYLAN THOMAS
"The Force That Through the Green Fuse Drives the Flower"
(Modern Poetry, Volume VII, Prentice-Hall, 1961)

mate modifies them; available means limit them; function shapes them" (*Frank Lloyd Wright's Usonian Houses*, 1984). Modern sustainable design has its roots in his Usonian Houses, beginning in 1936 with the Herbert Jacobs House in Madison, Wisconsin. The Jacobs House and other Usonian homes incorporate thoughtful site planning and an elegant economy of means. They also offer innovative and enduring ideas within residential architecture as they combine affordability and functionality with low-tech energy-conserving strategies. These homes pushed the envelope of residential architecture in a way that had never been done, until recently not equaled.

With the first Jacobs House, we have a prototype for a sustainable modern house some 30 years before the first energy crisis; here was an instructive attempt to develop a low-cost, low-energy architecture deriving from a lyrical form. This gave clients comfortable and efficient homes where aesthetics were not forgotten. With Wright's second Jacobs House, we have a design that ushers in—however unacknowledged—the notion of sustainability with the first solar hemicycle home, accommodating the warming winter sun and screening out that of the punishing summer. Until recently, too few designers have tapped into the resources and strategies exhibited in these projects. With open planning, cost-efficient slab designs, and radiant heated floors, the Usonian houses comprised a model of efficiency and responsible design. The open plans blurred the line between indoor and outdoor space, and interior rooms flowed into one another. This universal spatial strategy not only created wonderfully

modern space but also brought in the natural landscape, seamlessly. The result was cool and comfortable indoor spaces that spilled out onto warm and pleasant exterior patios, even in the most extreme summer heat.

Wright, in his brilliant 1954 manifesto *The Natural House* (Horizon Press), noted, "If the dictum, 'form follows function,' has any bearing at all on building, it could take form in architecture only by means of plasticity when seen at work as complete continuity. So why not throw away entirely all implications of post and beam construction? Have no posts, no columns, no pilasters, cornices

or moldings or ornament; no divisions of the sort nor any fixtures whatsoever to enter as something added to the structure. Any building should be complete, including all within itself. Instead of many things, one thing. The folded plane enters here with the merging lines, walls and ceiling made one." Clearly this statement is alluding to a simplification of the building plan and envelope, a move toward a more universal space and a reduction of inefficient complexities.

Wright's attention to site brings to mind the work of Alvar Aalto, whose projects clearly have

site-specific characteristics in line with the Scandinavian architectural tradition. His Villa Maria, for example, blends a sod roof with corrugated metal and wood, design strategies now becoming increasingly familiar. Along with Aalto, Rudolf Schindler and Richard Neutra produced projects that explored the concept of universal space. With overlapping rooms and primary living quarters dissolving into a much more open planning strategy, both employed ideas they learned while apprenticing in Wright's office, and simplified them to a level he never achieved.

In one of Schindler's first designs, the Kings Road House, in West Hollywood, California, he created what some consider the world's first modern house. Known today as an architect of materiality and novel construction techniques, he crafted the home as a design for living. If ever universal space was present in design theory and in practice, this is the place. Sleeping quarters spill outside onto patios; sliding panels create spatial variety, while deliberate landscaping extends the spatial experience outside. Inventive construction methods reduced costs, and tilt-up slab construction reduced the need for excavation, thus limiting the impact on the site while significantly reducing the construction footprint. The house is rather large at just 2,500 square feet, but its open planning and passive cooling strategies make what would have been an energy glutton an early model of energy efficiency.

Neutra built on the notion of universal space with a West Coast regionalist attitude and aesthetic. His architecture emphasized the interpenetration of interior and exterior space, and his contributions to architecture were groundbreaking. Here we are particularly concerned with the availability of good design to people of modest means. These ideas made him an ideal contributor to the Case Study Houses of the 1940s, projects that emphasized thoughtful construction, passive cooling systems, and the flow between indoor and outdoor rooms. These designs were sparked by the challenge of introducing inexpensive and efficient homes to the masses, and the goal of their architects was to create quintessential models of the modern house. Along with Neutra, Alfonso Soriano contributed to the

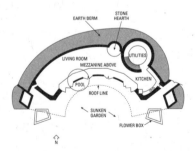

The second Jacobs House plan shows the berm and hemicycle incorporating passive solar principles.

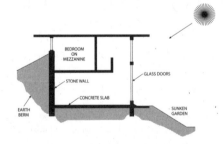

The section shows sun angles in winter and summer sun angles, allowing the home to respond to passive solar energy.

collaborative effort. The emerging designs became immensely popular, but they were largely unsuccessful in tapping into the mainstream market. The model was scrapped as a feasible approach to mass housing programs as inflation grew and prices soared while standardized elements did not reduce costs. At the same time these architects should be celebrated for their prescience it is important to note they did not recognize the need to forge relationships with industry, alliances that would have helped them to achieve their goal of economic efficiency.

Whereas Modernism championed simplicity in design, the Modernist design gods did not keep things simple. Or sustainable. A case in point is Soriano's 1950 Case Study house: Although beautiful, it was a model of inefficiency. Universal space and other Modernist principles were evident, but single-pane, western-facing glass and other inefficient strategies left fully half of the Case Study goals unresolved. Modernist icons like Mies' Farnsworth House or Philip Johnson's Glass House are other obvious examples—lacking overhangs, insulated glass, or operable windows. Other Case Study projects, such as the Lovell House, were also ridden with cost overruns, a factor that also made the designs unmarketable to the general public.

Today, these projects would be considerably cheaper to construct, with prefabrication becoming more widely used and markets shifting toward environmentally conservative designs with Modernist sensibilities. Notable architects such as Morphosis and Pugh + Scarpa have been influential in this shift, employing Modernist principles to promote green thinking. The latter's Solar Umbrella House, for example, uses both high-tech and low-tech solutions, including photovoltaic panels that double as a roofing system, shielding the interior from the harsh California sun. Not only do the panels reduce the heat gain within the interior, they enable the building's electricity meter to essentially run in reverse. The panels generate more electricity than the building uses and so actually supply power to the grid. Universal spatial strategies continue here, as Scarpa takes cues from other early California modernist architects like Neutra, conceiving of

exterior spaces as interiors. This blurs the line between indoor and outdoor space and combines flexible design with sustainable approaches.

Morphosis, too, has been on the forefront of environmental design with the San Francisco Federal Building, a daring approach in a large-scale building project with 70 percent of the building area naturally ventilated and cooled without the use of conventional heating and air-conditioning systems. The building's façade in essence breathes as computer monitoring systems track building temperatures and allow for mechanical windows to open at a moment's notice when the building begins to overheat. The building's narrow width also allows for it to be cooled by daily breezes and for light to filter into the entire space, negating dark interiors usually evident in typical office towers.

Energy conservation, energy generation, low environmental impact, and affordability are only a few of the goals of green design. The wise selection of materials is, of course, another. And by that I mean not only the use of eco-friendly and recyclable materials but also partnering with industry to create new materials. As noted previously, the Case Study projects tell an instructive tale in the failure of their designers to collaborate with manufacturers on materials and standards. Fortunately, a remedial tale became available in the 1960s with the evolution of the green movement.

Rachel Carson's 1962 best seller *Silent Spring* (Houghton Mifflin) is often cited as sparking the environmental movement. The book raised the consciousness of Americans and helped usher in necessary challenges to widespread industrial practices. Many now argue, however, that the resulting adversarial relationship between ardent environmentalists and defensive corporations created a model of activism that has, ironically, retarded change. While the movement blossomed, a lesser-known but more collaborative model of approaching industry also came into play. In the early sixties, Buckminster Fuller declared that the Bell Telephone kiosk was his archetype for the successful building, citing its prefabricated, sustainable nature and the varying locales in which it was effective. The prefabricated capsule provided equal comfort in the

We need a new industrial revolution.

WILLIAM MCDONOUGH
Vanity Fair, May 2008

The exterior street view of Beals' residence in Atlanta, Georgia, designed by Lightroom Studio, shows the entry trellis and roof overhangs, which protect the low-e glass during the harsh Atlanta summers.

coldest of climates and in the heat of the desert, giving it a wide array of practical applications. Until comparatively recently, however, designers have failed to follow his lead.

The failure did not stem from a paucity of complementary ideas. Environmental design books of the sixties and seventies featured passive solar and airflow logic to minimize the need for conditioned space. Victor Olgay analyzed regional physics with elaborate charts about thermal transfer and proper site analysis. His book *Design with Climate* (Princeton University Press, 1966), featured a concrete dome house by Paolo Soleri. David Wright produced *Natural Solar Architecture: A Passive Primer* (Van Nostrand Reinhold Co., 1978), easy to follow with diagram sketches. And the most thorough and popular book of this genre was *The Passive Solar Energy Book* by Edward Mazria. It remains a staple for any serious sustainable designer. These books now provide us with exceptionally useful ideas; but when they were published, readers failed to incorporate these ideas in practice. Most architects understood the principles, but their leadership abilities were weak, and they cashed in on what the mob was asking for.

Increasing numbers of architects have begun to heed the spirit behind William McDonough's injunction that "Designers must become leaders, and leaders must become designers." McDonough and Michael Braungart's *Cradle to Cradle: Remaking the Way We Make Things* (North Point Press, 2002) gives us an enlightening next step in green design, offering not only the ethos for environmentally successful collaborations with industry, but practical examples of how such collaboration has created eco-friendly and waste-free materials. Moreover, McDonough's recent projects demonstrate that damage wrought by the Industrial Revolution can be reversed on an unexpected scale and with unexpected partners.

Finally, this book, *Modern Sustainable Residential Design*, will be an informative approach to the design process while exploring the basic elements of modern sustainable housing. It is the first to recognize and articulate the design process of architects when approaching the development of a modern sustainable residence.

2

THE DESIGN PROCESS

For the purpose of developing a theory for ecological design, we can regard our building as a system that exists in an environment including both the man-made and natural environments. The general systems concept is fundamental to the ecosystem concept in ecology. The crucial task in design and similarly in any theory is therefore to pick the right variables to be included, which are those we find essential to our resolution of the design process.

KEN YEANG

THE PURPOSE OF THIS CHAPTER IS to describe the essential factors behind creating a model through the design process for the sustainable modern house. Outlined within this chapter are principles and guidelines that can be used to take the necessary steps toward a more sustainable approach to modern housing design. These guidelines offer insight into establishing a foundation for enhancing the overall quality of the architectural product with a focus on more environmentally aware designs. It is important to understand that while the principles outlined here may seem somewhat regulatory in tone, the architectural process is always ultimately about the individuality and unique nature of the architect or architectural practice. It is therefore the goal of this chapter to instill a basis for architectural growth based on more environmentally driven strategies and conceptions linking the design process to the final product.

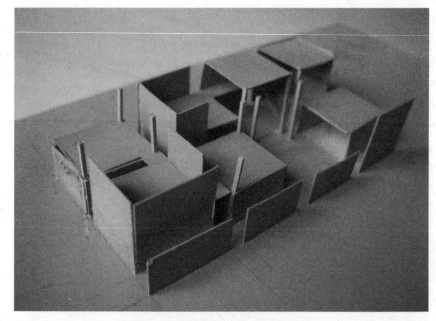

The Bush residence (Atlanta, Georgia) study model, completed by Lightroom Studio.

Overview of the Architectural Design Paradigm

The design process is a paradigm unique to architectural practice, one that sets it apart from a variety of other professions. For most artistic visions, intuition plays the primary role in governing the direction of a project. Architecture, in contrast, is more subordinate to its benefactors due to the nature of profession; still, as architects and designers, the role we play has a direct influence on the clients we serve. At the core of what we do is a process. This process, which has evolved over centuries, has become paramount in our effort to create architecture of purpose, beauty, and meaning. As part of that process, we had to learn to let go of our preconceptions and intuition. More recently, however, it has become apparent that we now have to rethink earlier tenets and convictions we held about architecture.

In general, practitioners modify the concept of their discipline as necessary to embrace new themes, concerns, and ways of practice; but in essence, the design process remains a process, an evolving conceptual basis or series of ideas to which the architect is striving to adhere. Sustainability is one more concept to add to this design process.[1] In recent years it has, in fact, become a governing criterion in the architectural practice of the future, as evidenced by the many firms and architects that have already effectively transitioned their practice to focus the process on "going green."

In the more traditional sense, there are two separate and distinct paradigms in the design process. First is the deductive reasoning pattern, which evolved out of the pragmatic approach developed during the Beaux Arts period. Proportioned and attractive floor plans, elevations, and space tended to lead to form over function, as seen in modern examples like the concrete monopoly house by Jacques Herzog and Jacques de Meuron. The second paradigm allows for an inductive process inspired by experimentation. The roots of this process emerged from Frank Lloyd Wright's *organasis* and the Bauhaus years and led by such innovative thinkers as Walter Gropius. Architects such as Michael Maltzan and Coop Himmelb(l)au have continued the inductive process by introducing phenomenological principles. They have also expanded and transformed the way architecture is conceived and produced with computer-aided design (CAD) and collaborative efforts, which Gropius promoted throughout his career. The Architects Collaborative was the manifestation of those efforts and helped spawn a revolution in modern architectural practice, which is now seeing a resurgence among architects such as Philadelphia-based KierenTimberlake Associates LLP.

While the modern design process, absent sustainability principles, was developing as a style generator for the rich, the New Age–inspired eco-design movement was merging into mainstream thought, linked to the cultural zeitgeist. Today, it is considered a noble cause to "be part of the solution not the problem" with regard to the creation of the built environment and fighting global pollution. Efforts are well under way now to reduce this pollution, as well as to increase awareness of energy conservation. The public has gotten involved in a variety of ways, pushing the cause far beyond the professional realm and proving that sustainability is, indeed, both a professional and public concern.[2] In a culture where trends tend to be short-lived, the realization that our environment is seriously endangered has led to a sea change in the public view. In architecture and the construction industry, architects and designers alike are helping to lead the charge to make the world more environmentally conscious. This is due in part to their deep understanding of how buildings contribute directly and substantially to the risk of environmental damage, caused by the large quantities of raw materials (and the pollutants they produce), energy, and capital involved in their construction.[3] It is also due in part to public pressure, which has called for a rethinking of architectural practice and design. Consequently, the process must continue to change and evolve to meet these demands.[4]

One of the main shifts in thinking with regard to sustainability, which can be traced back to the energy crisis of the early seventies, centers on how to balance environmental and aesthetic tactics in design. In that era, projects were primarily, if not completely, driven by environmental concerns, similar to the automobile production of the eighties, which showed little consideration for the look or styling of the product. Many buildings of this period resembled prisons, with interior spaces left dark and absent any natural daylighting. Building aesthetics resulted primarily from the derived vocabulary of environmentally driven exteriors. Certainly, these buildings often achieved the goals of reducing energy consumption and costs, but the negatives seemed to outweigh the positives, with comfort superseded by concerns for the efficiency of the building. Architecture seemed little more than an afterthought. This approach—to increase building efficiency—was a conscious decision made during the early stages of the design process, one that almost always precluded aesthetics.

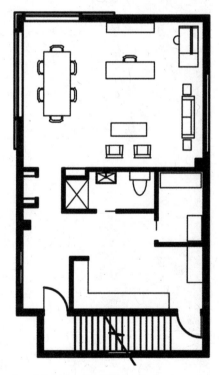

Second-floor plan of the Lightroom Studio.

INFLUENCE OF
NEW TECHNOLOGIES

Fortunately, over the last couple of decades, technology has advanced dramatically, bringing with it new possibilities for the design of sustainable architecture. Today, sustainable design practices and modern expression can be successfully blended. Buildings no longer have to reflect the planar orthogonal and repetitive processes of the traditional assembly line; they can respond to and express the nonlinear forces of nature. Going forward, such an approach will be central to designing effective and attractive buildings from a more environmentally aware perspective—the key to sustainable development.[5] It is also key to

changing the mind-set of the general public with regard to environmental design aesthetics, where the tendency often still is to relate anything associated with "green" building or environmental approaches as derivative of a New Age approach to "saving the world." Slowly but surely this is changing, as advances in technology steadily increase our ability to combine aesthetics with effective architectural practices.

New technologies are also enabling the design process to incorporate a much needed "pass-fail" approach. Programs such as Leadership in energy and Environmental Design (LEED) help to facilitate such an assessment by introducing building rating systems whereby a project can

accrue points for achieving a variety of different goals. Although these programs do not measure the success of the design rationale or the aesthetic treatment of the building, they do incorporate strategies meant to be used very early on in the design process and that maintain a strong emphasis on sustainability. This helps to ensure a commitment to integrated environmental design methodologies and strategies throughout the project. Architects such as Ed Mazria have been outspoken proponents of better tools, such as computer-aided software, for implementing design strategies to enable designers to evaluate every design decision at early stages to illustrate the consequences related to those decisions.

View of the new studio from the rear garden of the Carter residence showing the copper sunscreen.

THE IMPORTANCE OF COMMITMENT AND COLLABORATION

To ensure success in selecting design strategies and tactics to follow, a level of commitment must be established during the education phase. Creating the right process that will effectively blend modern and sustainable design is front-loaded now with information synthesis, which requires strong leadership by the designer. This leadership and vision will help keep the deductive process on track; and it will help during the inductive process, as well, to identify the most valuable paths of investigation.

The cumulative design process—deductive and inductive—will, of course, need to be customized to meet the individual level of commitment to environmental issues. Some people can afford to do more than others in implementing conservation practices while providing beauty in architecture; others may or may not have the resources or desire to make major sacrifices that make a difference in this regard. This is where the collaboration between the client and architect is essential, if the goals for the project are to be maintained. The architects at the KierenTimberlake firm are advocates of greater collaboration, not only with clients but with everyone involved on the project. Their efforts have slowly evolved into the concept of an emergent collective practice, with the objective of bridging the gap between architecture and construction, to create a more collaborative environment for design. The end goal of this extremely important idea in the design process is to develop a more efficient and informative approach to the process. Simply, when engineers, contractors, architects, and others involved in the project are on the same page, each becomes better informed about the entire process and thus better able to do a good job. Although this is not directly associated with an environmental approach to design, it makes it much more conducive to building efficiency and optimal results overall. This process results in a higher-quality project and allows for greater scope to be covered; it also reduces time and cost spent on each phase of the project, which is always an important consideration on any project, environmentally focused or not.

MAKING SUSTAINABLE DESIGN WORK

Defining the design principles inherent to the modern and sustainable house is at the heart of this chapter. A range of design choices, stemming from both the rational and the intuitive, are described, to ensure that the natural need for diversity and regionalism are addressed in tandem with universal design principles. Schools of thought aside, the pursuit of design that embraces sustainability will automatically provide a diverse range of design possibilities.

It is, after all, beliefs that drive process, and to define a process requires a decision as to where to begin a project. It is this decision, this choice, with which all designers and clients wrestle. Is it finding a "seed" from which all parts can grow organically, or is it more important to sort through a well-worked matrix of preconceived ideas to find one that is new and compelling? One thing is certain: These times of environmental awareness require an evolving, flexible, and thoughtful process. The outcome may be traditional or revolutionary, but it must work with nature, and nurture the human condition. More, the process must educate all parties involved and should ultimately establish the commitment needed to shift design toward an eco-modern way.

Studio 804's home is surrounded with numerous trees, providing an abundance of shading.

EDUCATING THE CLIENT

In the past 30 years, clients who could afford architects for the most part rarely concerned themselves with much more than how the project could best serve their own needs. Today, in contrast, educating clients, and learning from them, has become an active exchange that requires a shaping of ideas. Samuel Mockbee, founder of the Auburn University Rural Studio program, once said that designers should be subversive to ensure a better outcome in design. Clients do not want to be told how they are falling short on issues outside their immediate awareness. The aesthetic, cultural, and ecological outcomes of the design process have needed stronger leadership. To this end, Mockbee has implied this leadership need not be manipulative; rather, it should take a point of view that is informed at many levels. And if the discussion with clients does not cover all these levels, the designer must ideally achieve these things without compromising the clients' needs and wishes. The "servant versus leader" issue is one that has shifted back and forth with swings in the economy and changes in an architect's reputation. In step three of his "Eight Steps Toward a Solid Architecture"—"Diagnose the client's real needs and give him a consistent building"— Walter Gropius speaks of the difficult task of leading the client toward a consistency in the face of "whims" that may be requested. This is not to say that the client's ideas should be dismissed; they can in fact add richness to design and address the client's lifestyle more accu-

Sketch model—Lightroom Studio

rately. It is to say that the goal to achieve consistency not be sacrificed at the expense of trying to meet the changing requirements of the client. After all, design is a process and should always be seen as such.

First and foremost, the client must understand the role the architect plays in this phase of the project, the purpose for which he or she has been hired. Goals must be clearly identified and understood by both parties from the outset, with a level of commitment agreed on, to prevent them from being cast aside if monetary considerations become an issue down the road. This is especially true of environmentally driven projects. When clients are not completely committed to the sustainable design of the project, they will be much more inclined to discard it at the first sign of cost overruns. This reiterates the importance of a flexible design process. When the ideas and goals of the project are outlined at the beginning, and the client has signed off on them, the architect gains the ability to value-engineer the project and work these goals back into the project—ideally, under budget. It also makes the client more inclined to spend more when they are sold on certain aspects of the design.

The architect should never fall back on what Philip Johnson called design "crutches." One such crutch that designers with little confidence tend to lean on is "the client made me do it" or "it is not affordable" excuse. Allowing budget concerns to sway them is dangerous for designers because doing so gives the client all the power. Architects must keep in mind they have been hired for their creative thinking abilities, and it is in the best interest of all parties when they hold firm to their expertise, not only in regard to their creativity in the built form but also in regard to budgetary restraints. That is not to say, of course, that an architect should feel free to compromise the quality of the design or the budget to adhere to his or her artistic "vision." In terms of sustainable design, it is, in fact, rare for an architect to quit a job halfway through the design phase because the budget grew beyond the client's comfort zone to the point where the client felt forced to make "green" cuts over aesthetic choices, or vice versa. Ultimately, some compro-

mises are inevitable on most projects. This is why it is so important to get a grip of the full scope of the project early and follow the appropriate steps to control the checks and balances through completion. This is especially true for those with limited incomes.

ADDRESSING THE COST ISSUE

In the design process, the three main issues all designers and clients must juggle—size, quality, and price—usually break down at the price point where so-called sticker shock is far too common. Fortunately, as Americans come to realize they may not need as much living space as they once thought, this formula will begin to add up to a better outcome; and, more pertinent to the topic of this book, as green materials and systems become more affordable, the entire equation will become easier to balance. But until that happens on a wide-scale basis, reducing size usually will not be enough to cover the cost of raising design to meet the new green standards. Addressing the size issue alone does not take into account anomalies caused by restrictive sites, inaccurate estimates, or complex or structural gymnastics that must be performed. It is these types of hurdles that have made sustainable, modern design generally feasible only for the wealthy in recent years. There are, however, a number of exceptions to this generalize, exceptions we can study and learn from.

When the designer maintains proper control, many exciting possibilities become available. In defining a successful design process, there are several objective guidelines to follow:

1. Let the structure's design respect and be inspired by the site.

2. Enable the house to function so efficiently that a reduction in its size becomes a comfortable choice.

3. Use passive strategies to provide the highest limits of energy efficiency.

4. Choose reused materials to save money and resources; also, choose materials that contribute new efficiencies and expression without taxing the environment.

5. Design a house that contributes to the cultural significance of the built landscape and nurtures local trades, craft, and economies.

6. Provide flexible design that allows for both privacy and universal space, with an inside-to-outside spatial relationship that is at the heart of modern design.

7. Create a structure that blends new and reliable technologies to bring the design to the highest possible level of green standards, including a zero carbon logic.

This "totem" of green and modern issues can be used as an outline for the schematic process, which begins with predesign.

Predesign and Site Analysis

Designing a house or housing is of course a creative process, one that should be driven by a vision or strong ideas crafted by the designer and owner. The process can be clear from the beginning or one that evolves. The vision can be based on rational analysis or develop from an intuitive "leap" made based on understanding of the site, client, budget, technology, and place in time. Maya Lyn, best known for her design of the Vietnam Veterans Memorial in Washington, DC, described the beginning of her creative process as a three-month period of reading anything she could find that would feed her intuition for the assigned project. This period of open-mindedness prevents preconceived ideas from creeping in or rationalizing to defend irrational thought disguised as creativity.

To thoroughly understand the full scope of a project early in the process to prevent the loss of essential parts later, we find that the predesign (a.k.a. programming) and site analysis phases to be more important now than ever. In terms of predesign specifically, it cannot be overemphasized that the site not emerge as a surprise expense late in the flow of the decision-making process. In order to "hit all the marks" to make green and modern affordable within moderate budgets, the site must be an asset that is factored in from the beginning; it should never become a liability.

In other words, programming is the phase of fact-finding, leading up to design. To this end,

there are designers who move in with their clients for a period of time to learn how they actually live in a space. Other designers live on-site in order to imagine the issues it may present under construction. Still others employ questionnaires and long interviews. Sad to say, it is all too common for architects to start design before they are ready and make a premature diagnosis; or to push a personal agenda that they have been "testing out" on their clients over the years. Either way, it leads to the wrong beginning in many cases. From that point things can get out of hand quickly.

In terms of environmental considerations especially, whether on housing projects or other typologies, integrating these ideas must become intuitive to and inherent in the designer's repertoire. When not thought out and raised from the get-go, it becomes that much harder to persuade the client, and maintain a consistent, well-thought-out design. Glenn Murcutt, founding president of the Australia Architecture Association, has long understood this process. He adheres to four guidelines in creating sustainable and site-specific architecture that can be beneficial to every project. They are:

1. Use simple materials.

2. Touch the earth lightly.

3. Follow the sun.

4. Listen to the wind.

These four guidelines, so simply stated, are neglected in the design of housing, as well as larger commissions. If they were followed more closely, energy consumption would not be the problem it is today and the typical house would be much less dependent on artificial systems such as air conditioning. When incorporated in the design process, they not only help to ensure comprehensive site and design strategies but also lead later on to better communications with the client, even those negotiations about increasing the budget for features that increase energy savings once the project is complete.

Designers who are well known and have large bodies of work are, understandably, more likely

to be paid properly so that they may pursue much-needed research and budget analysis from the outset in order to simultaneously define the space, achieve tectonic materiality, and manage systems. Many firms present multiple design schemes in their first presentation meeting with the client, as a way to find direction. (This "service-oriented" approach also offers the opportunity for staffers to have input in office brainstorming sessions, thereby creating a team atmosphere.) The problem is that generating multiple ideas applies pressure to the bottom line, meaning that often it is not possible to go far enough in the development of each of the various designs, with the result that one has to choose from among less than optimal plans.

San Francisco-based SOMA Design believes that architects should be able to charge 50 percent of the fee up front to develop the "big idea" so that they are better positioned to lead with strength. This is, after all, the most important and valuable point in the process, when most of the money is earned. Keep in mind that architects are problem solvers as well as creative types. With thorough research and thoughtfulness, a designer can learn whether, for example, the owner has a rare disease or a food allergy, thus enabling him or her to balance the design "prescriptions" from the beginning when it is much less difficult and precludes numerous and expensive "follow-up visits." Such logic can justify the up-front fee, which also acts as a retainer.

This is even more important today, when programming and site analysis now also must incorporate sustainability analysis—for example, solar studies and energy modeling in diagram massing forms that show how to maximize energy efficiency. Such diagrams are used to investigate concepts about spatial relationships, which then enable a designer to present one or a few schemes that are more thoroughly thought out and, ideally, presented in three-dimensional form to help ease client comprehension. (Many clients have trouble visualizing spatial relationships from two-dimensional plans and elevations.)

Predesign requires a thorough site analysis, whether urban, rural, suburban, or exurban—of views, angles of sunlight, wind direction, incidence of storms, public versus private access, and more. All site analyses should start from the base of the design totem. From there the nuances of each site will either surface quickly or require a more thorough investigation. Sometimes it will be determined that demolition or excavation is necessary.

Obtaining accurate topographies, setbacks, site line paths, links, nodes, and buffers all are essential to laying a good foundation for design concepts and to enhancing or forging geometries. Likewise, mapping context will lead to an understanding of the natural rhythms and the human-made influences, to build additional layers of understanding. Just as important is to recognize how urban and suburban site design issues affect the built fabric, and that rural sites should respect the natural conditions or borrow from its raw assets (e.g., milling wood from fallen trees before it combusts and releases unwanted carbon gases). Ultimately, energy efficiency is the best reason to make a choice, keeping in mind, for example, that if a site's best views are toward the north, then compromises may need to be made with regard to passive solar strategies. Urban sites may naturally lead toward internally focused concepts. Using trees as wind or shade buffers requires the trees to be saved, nurtured, and integrated into design.

A Solmetric SunEye, a tool for assessing the total potential solar energy of a site, can be used to help study passive solar exposures. Diagramming, soils tests, and proposed grading make it possible to blend knowledge with abstract ideas in a scaled relationship. A team approach in concert with a landscape design strategy is important from the outset. In urban and suburban sites, a site plan review process can be lengthy and costly; but a proactive approach that is thorough and time-consuming up front can prevent delays when the builder is ready to start. Finding a balance and taking inspiration from a site allows the predesign and site analysis phases to flow and prevents costly false starts.

Schematic Design

The type of project will dictate the amount of time and numbers of meetings required for the schematic design phase. A standard design bid/build process that has been updated requires 20 to 30 percent of the time to get to the right Parti. A prefab project may have fewer options, limited either by transport unit sizes, a kit of parts, or plan options to choose from or alter. This could reduce the schematic design time by approximately 10 percent.

The best guideline for schematic design phase is a simple one: Work with the firm's strengths, whether that means relying on a strong single designer/signature product or taking a service-oriented approach. Blending approaches to attain a strong product is possible, but less common.

Using a firm with a "star" designer can save time and possibly money, but usually there will be a longer waiting list to work with the successful individual. An extreme example of this top-down process is Antoine Predock, the principal of Albuquerque-based Antoine Predock Architect PC who would work up a clay model that becomes the archetypal form from which all other decisions had to support. This deductive and subtractive method is an easy way to manage staff and clients in that it prevents false starts, which cost money. The designer's ability to process all aspects simultaneously will give clarity as long as there is no lack of critical thought. When there is a flaw in the sole practitioner's self-awareness, this process can lean to "misdiagnosis," resulting at the least in an almost placebo effect, and at worst an emperor's new clothes scenario. To nurture eco-modern design for more than the rich, it is essential to keep track of energy efficiency and full systems balancing, and this requires great depth of thought.

Simple plans and rich section or special designs can allow for efficient design and detailing. Enabling a design team to use BIN modeling early for energy and light analysis helps its members gain performance confidence. If, for example, a firm is pursuing the goals of Project 2030, the performance is a black-and-white process that needs validation throughout the design phases.

Gathering some estimates and soliciting initial builder feedback at the end of this phase will help test the waters for the project.

Design Development

This is the phase that requires reinforcing original thoughts or strategies with tactics that support the cause. Ultimately, any discrepancies may add richness of complexity. Energy and insulation calculations can be run while details begin to surface. Sun angles, airflow logic, and dynamic thermal mass temperature shifts should all reinforce the plan section and space plan. Material development that reinforces maintenance-free or natural and healthy logic will aid in developing proportion and choosing color, texture, and transparency.

Mechanical engineering can be integrated as a supportive concept, or it can take a leadership position in creating design revolutions. For example, buildings in cities could become the "lungs" that filter air pollution; and by using HRV units and filtering the air more often, houses could clean the air in cities. However, the extra energy needed to do the work would have to be solar powered and the disposal of the filters would be treated as nuclear power plant waste. Thus, this process would clean the air and ultimately clean rainwater and streams.

Construction Documents

Standard practice, whether design-build or mass customization, will affect how much effort and the level of detail required in this phase. Mies van der Rohe designs, for example, needed greater detail than that required in a design-build project. More specifically, a straw bale house would not require the same amount of thought as an Ando project. Construction documents are described in detail in Chapter 7.

Conclusion

As new technologies for creating, transporting, installing, and maintaining materials and systems improve and become more affordable, sustainable design will become more desirable and feasible. New design tools, for analyzing envelope performance, lighting calculation, and modeling, as well as context and special experience analysis, also are becoming more widely available.

The new designs may be defined by a physical difference or a performance difference, but there will be difference. Process now more than ever can give designers the ability to lead projects toward this new pass-fail logic with regard to both performance and beauty. At the same time, functional and aesthetic aspects must not be allowed to slip, in exchange for better material and energy strategies. With proper planning and a commitment from the owner, design, function, and green issues can all come together successfully. A new way of designing with a holistic understanding of the closed system called Earth requires all those involved to work together in harmony, with shared goals. Choices should always be based on context, local and global. A rock site should not be a place for a cut-and-fill earthberm house. A roof garden makes sense in an urban context. Solar power makes sense in America. Some decisions are local and some are universal. Ideally, we can blend the best of all there is to offer now in the architectural design field.

3

GREEN BUILDING: THE CONTRACTOR'S PERSPECTIVE

■ Robert J. Soens, Jr.

A S WITH ANY PROJECT, DESIGN, function, and budget are important concerns, and green building brings a new perspective and considerations to the many choices of materials and methods. The purpose of this chapter, to present the contractor's perspective on the green building process, starts by discussing some of the basics of what makes a project green and how the contractor will want to approach these.

The primary concerns of a green project revolve around the project's impact on the environment prior to construction (development and acquisition of materials), during construction (site development, materials, and methods of construction), and throughout the life of the structure (minimized use of natural resources and creation of environmental pollutants).

A new discipline, called Design for Disassembly, examines these concerns further, considering options in materials, methods, and design that help maximize the ability to reconfigure, reuse, and recycle the various components of a structure. Design for Disassembly also prolongs the usable life of the structure and minimizes the contributions to landfills when structures become obsolete.

While the owner of a project and the architect will have their own set of concerns and their own vision for the final product, much of the success of a green building project depends on the proper execution of the building process by the contractor and the buy-in to that process by the owner and architect. That makes the team approach to building the most effective one, and contractors appreciate being brought in during the design process so that their viewpoint on ma-

In the Dominey residence in Atlanta, Georgia, designed by Lightroom Studio, the exterior hearth creates an outdoor room, extending interior and exterior space. The existing water oak was carefully preserved with a porous concrete slab.

terials, methods, and budget may be taken into consideration. This is particularly helpful in green building, because there are so many choices to make and priorities to be balanced. Many green building programs put a premium on the involvement of the building contractor in the process, and some programs, such as LEED for Homes, require it.

There are now numerous organizations around the United States that have designed green building programs and have developed tools that help guide the decision-making process on materials, methods, equipment, design, and even location of a project. Two of the most important are the ENERGY STAR and LEED for Homes programs:

- The ENERGY STAR program is fundamental to almost every green building program in America, and anyone "building green" should become familiar with the program, the methods it endorses, and the products it approves. The energystar.gov Web site provides important and helpful information.

- The LEED for Homes program, as created by the United States Green Building Council (USGBC), has providers that administer the program in many markets around the country. There are also numerous organizations that provide program services in specific regions of the country. In the Southeast United States, Southface Energy Institute, located in Atlanta, Georgia, has created the EarthCraft program in partnership with the Greater Atlanta Home Builders Association, a member of the National Home Builders Association.

Later in the chapter the details of these programs are described, including how they can help guide you through the decision-making process of putting together a green building project. These organizations also provide verification, testing, and certification of projects. Extensive information is also available from a number of other sources and organizations, which have compiled databases of information on both methods of construction and products available. Two very helpful resources on methods are the Energy and Environmental Building Association, commonly know as EEBA, based in Bloomington, Minnesota, and the Building America program, created by the U.S. Department of Energy. Resources on green materials and products include The GreenSpec Guide to Residential Building Materials, produced by Building Green, and Web sites such as 4specs.com and greenguard.org. These resources and organizations are covered more thoroughly later in the chapter as well.

Objectives of a Green Building Process

This section elaborates a little on the early objectives of the process of putting together a green project. To begin, it's important to define what it means when we talk about *environmental sensitivity and responsibility.*

In brief, this means minimizing any negative effects on the environment caused by any part of the building process, whether that be at the site or off-site, such as during the manufacture of some building components or materials. It also means wisely using our natural resources in the building process and creating homes that are both energy and water efficient and nonpolluting.

Natural materials that are harvested in ways that are not detrimental to the environment, are renewable, are used efficiently, possibly contain recycled content, and can be reused or recycled are typically preferred. (An exception to this rule would be in the use of engineered or synthetic materials that are produced in an environmentally sensitive way, that provide wise use of the resource and superior performance, and are exceptionally durable.)

For example, vinyl siding has not been a popular choice of materials in green building for several reasons, including the negative effects of its manufacturing process involving the use of nonrenewable resources, the amount of energy required for its manufacture, and problems in disposing and recycling. A more popular choice in exterior finishes has been Hardi-board siding, which is considered greener in its manufacturing, seems to be highly durable, and creates job-site waste that can be ground and used for soil remediation and mulch.

Another example of products that are popular are gypsum board made of recycled content, or the new fiberglass-faced gypsum board, due to its apparent durability and resistance to mold, a factor in both durability and indoor air quality. Engineered lumber products, too, represent both a wise use of resources and are highly durable materials.

Products and materials should be chosen that are not only renewable and recyclable, but that are local, to eliminate the expenditure of energy in transporting over long distances.

Every green building project should also strive to minimize environmental impact at the site, by minimizing waste and recycling waste. Products chosen for job-site purposes, such as form release, sealers, paints, caulks, cleaning agents, adhesives, and the like should be nontoxic and handled and disposed of in a way that minimizes any detrimental effects on the environment. Job-site practices should minimize disturbance to the site, including tree protection and proper installation of silt fencing to minimize runoff.

A major concern in green building is *energy efficiency.* This is important for two reasons. The most obvious to most people is the waste of nonrenewable resources. The other, which we hear of more everyday, is the production of greenhouse gases. While many people understand the waste of resources and the environmental pollution created by a gas-guzzling, poorly performing automobile, few realize that the average house, built to minimum building codes, performs just as poorly and is energy inefficient and polluting.

Another primary concern of green building is *durability.* Building homes that make the most of our resources should be durable. To that end, clients need to be informed that building codes are a minimum standard, and encouraged to build their houses to a higher performance standard, using the latest in building technologies. Many advances have been made recently in producing materials that are durable, and the methods for installing these materials have advanced, too. House wrap and modern flashing systems, for example, when installed properly, do an excellent job of producing a house that more effectively minimizes water infiltration. Shading systems and glass coatings on windows decrease the damage that UV rays cause to interior finishes.

A green house should also be a very *comfortable* place to live. When the heating and air equipment and ductwork have been properly sized, the building envelope has been caulked, sealed, and insulated, capillary breaks have been installed in the foundation, and proper shading has been provided, the result should be a very comfortable home, free of excessive humidity and achieving constant, even temperatures throughout the space year-round.

Every bit as important as any other aspect of any green building program, *indoor air quality* is fundamental in providing a healthy environment for the occupants. All of the other aspects of the program, properly sealing the crawlspace, air-sealing the building envelope, excellent insulation, tight ductwork, use of materials such as low VOC paints, and good design of the HVAC system with fresh air intake, help to provide a healthy indoor air quality. This is one of the essential personal payoffs for the owner.

Getting Started

Preliminary design and site selection is typically complete by the time a contractor becomes part of the design process. As the design is refined and the process begins in selecting materials and equipment, the contractor can be a valuable resource in the process, offering knowledge of supply resources, methods of installation, and current costs. The contractor should also play a major role in making sure that the house as designed works well as a *system*, helping to determine that flashing systems work well with exterior finishes, that insulation is adequate, that the HVAC system is sized correctly, and so forth.

BASIC CONSIDERATIONS

If preliminary design decisions have already been made by the time a project gets to the contractor, meaning the contractor did not have an influence in these decisions, the contractor should at least understand their consequences. To address this possibility, this section addresses a number of fundamental yet very important basics to keep in mind:

1. Climate zone

2. Placement on site

3. Orientation

4. Foundations

5. Insulation

6. Exterior finishes

7. Roofs

8. Windows and doors

9. Systems compatibility

Climate Zone

As mentioned earlier, several very good information resources in green building are reference materials produced by the Energy & Environmental Building Association (EEBA), and Building America, a program of the U.S. Department of Energy. These are databases of best building practices and the latest technologies in building science, and each has a program specifically designed to work well within a particular climate.

It is extremely important to understand the climate within which you are building and which techniques or technologies work best there. Accordingly, both Building America and EEBA produce different guidelines for different climate zones.

Building America divides the United States into five different climate zones:

• Cold/very cold

• Hot-humid

• Hot-dry/mixed-dry

• Mixed-humid

• Marine

EEBA divides North America into four different climates, similarly designated:

• Cold

• Hot-humid

• Hot-dry/mixed-dry

• Mixed-humid

Make sure that you have the guidelines for your climate, and study the best practices for your region. These differences will cover a number of important construction concerns, including grading, foundations, waterproofing, framing, flashing, roofing, insulation, HVAC, plumbing, and so on.

Placement on Site

Many municipalities and counties, along with state and federal laws, already regulate such concerns as proximity to rivers, streams, and lakes, as well as disturbance of trees and adverse effects on neighbors. These considerations should be factored in along with a number of other possible concerns, such as minimizing disturbance of the site, achieving proper drainage of water away from the structure, location of geothermal loops or wells, orientation, type of foundation, and proximity to the flood plain.

Orientation

Understanding the ramifications of the orientation of the structure is vital in several areas, including heating and cooling loads, durability, and daylighting.

An orientation to the south, with large amounts of glass, may be desirable in some situations but not in others. For some areas, it would create a tremendous heat load to be overcome and would also create a need to protect the structure from damage by UV rays. But if properly done, this same orientation can provide good daylighting and warmth during winter months. When addressing these concerns, you should also make a point to study the micro climate, paying attention to placement and height of shade trees and use of proper roof overhangs.

If you are considering the use of either solar heating or photovoltaic power, proper orientation of the roof, along with the size and slope of the roof, become even more important.

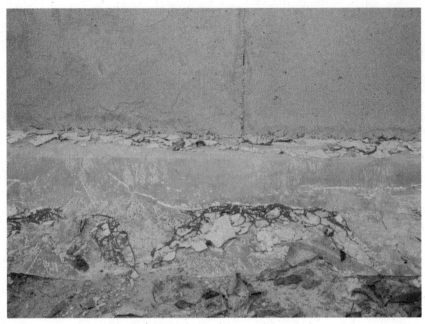

Insulating scabs add greatly to the energy efficiency of the Dominey house.

Plastic is used as a capillary break between the footing and wall of this foundation.

Foundations

One of the most important considerations in durability, indoor air quality, and comfort is keeping water out of the house. A primary building component in that endeavor is the foundation.

Typically, the best way to achieve that overall goal with the foundation is to use a properly constructed slab-on-grade. Important considerations with proper use of a slab-on-grade foundation include contouring the surrounding grade so that you provide positive draining of any water away from the house, with gravel below; a capillary break in the form of heavy plastic sheathing underneath; and good insulation. This assembly tends to be very stable, and with good construction on a well-graded site, it minimizes the chance of moisture being introduced into the house through the foundation. Remember that even in dry climates, placing plastic under the foundation slab and footings provides an essential capillary break, preventing moisture from wicking up through the concrete and into the house.

Because not all building sites best accommodate a slab-on-grade, it has become considered best practice to build a crawl space as a sealed, insulated, semiconditioned space in which the HVAC system and ductwork can be housed. As with the slab-on-grade, a capillary break should be used, either under the footing or between the footings and foundation walls. This measure prevents water from wicking up through the foundation walls, introducing moisture into the house. The entire crawl space area should be sealed for moisture with heavy plastic, covering a gravel base. The exterior of the foundation should have waterproofing with drainage plain and drainage at the footings installed. The interior of the foundation walls should be insulated.

Both the EEBA and the Building America manuals have excellent illustrations on how to properly build with either of these foundations. There are also several variations available to these two basic foundation types: the insulated concrete form, and the premanufactured steel

and concrete, insulated, foundation wall system. The systems should be installed with the same considerations as the others, with proper waterproofing, capillary break, and drainage provided.

Insulation

A well-insulated structure is critical for energy efficiency. Currently, many contractors are moving away from using fiberglass batt insulation in favor of using spray foam insulation. There are several advantages to the spray foams, including higher R-values, air-sealing of the structure, and the ability to more efficiently insulate foundation walls and roof structures.

If the project budget allows, use of an insulating sheathing, such as Dow Blue Board, rather than plywood or OSB, provides a thermal break in the framing of the structure, further adding to the effectiveness of the insulation system. At minimum, use insulation board to provide insulation and a thermal break at headers in exterior walls. The insulation board is typically sand-

A wall and roof system insulated with foam Icynene. Note the plastic seal used to protect the duct outlet in the ceiling during construction.

Even after the foam insulation goes in, adding a final detailing of air sealing around any penetrations is important.

wiched between the two structural members of the header, or added to the exterior face.

Modern framing techniques aim to provide the ability to maximize the effectiveness of the exterior insulation of the structure and to eliminate areas that are not able to be insulated, or create large areas of thermal transfer.

You may also want to consider providing a layer of foam board insulation over the exterior sheathing. This provides both the thermal break and added insulation, without compromising the structural strength of the exterior assembly. Some exterior finish systems, such as Dri-vit, now include foam board, which will provide both an insulation factor and thermal break.

It is now recognized that in addition to properly insulating a structure, two additional steps greatly add to the energy efficiency of the structure: air-sealing the envelope and creating conditioned spaces within which the HVAC systems and ductwork operate. Spray foam insulations help to achieve all three of these goals.

Exterior Finishes

As with foundations, water is a major concern in making the proper choice of, and installing, the exterior finish. While exterior finish systems are designed to shed water, it's important to realize that that does not mean completely sealing the house. On occasion, water will penetrate the exterior, and it must get back out. Exterior assemblies should include the capability to both shed water and breathe, so that moisture is not trapped in the wall.

In modern architecture today, three exterior finish systems are popular: stucco, metal, and wood. Each of these systems requires its own special attention to detail in installation, particularly in proper flashing at doors and windows. Each should also be installed with a proper drainage plain behind it.

Roofs

Roofs can perform several functions: They provide a way of protecting the structure from rain,

shading, and a way of collecting rainwater, and are an important assembly in insulation.

Flat roofs may provide a way of collecting water, as well as creating additional living area for the house, as rooftops can provide a popular garden area in cities. When making use of the rooftop, it is advisable to use a paver system to protect the surface of the roof.

When using a sloped roof, incorporating an overhang helps to provide shading, both helping the energy efficiency of the house and protecting the interior finishes of the house from UV rays, enhancing the durability of the structure.

Windows and Doors

As with any house, proper placement and flashing of windows and doors is critical. One of the greatest challenges to maximizing the durability of a structure involves minimizing water infiltration. Proper placement of the windows and doors, with protecting overhangs and proper flashing, are critical in achieving these goals. As with any penetrations in the building envelope, the proper caulking and sealing of doors and windows is also critical. No matter how structurally sound the house may be, if the building envelope is leaking, energy efficiency will suffer.

Many structures of contemporary design use large quantities of glass. While this adds in daylighting the interior, often it generates higher heating and cooling loads that must be accommodated; thus, proper sizing of the heating and air systems becomes even more critical. When using large amounts of glass, be careful not only to size the HVAC system equipment correctly, but to deliver adequate cubic feet per minute (cfm) of air to the proper areas for comfort.

Careful selection of the glass is extremely important. The glass for each area of the house should be chosen according to climate zone, orientation, and microclimate factors such as shading. As the amount of glass in the house increases, the importance of selecting the right glass does too, as it affects the energy efficiency and comfort of the home.

Building wrap and compatible window and door flashings are critical to protect the structure from the destructive effects of water and moisture after the siding is applied.

Systems Compatibility

As contractors, architects, and clients look for ways to create greener, energy-efficient, and durable structures, it is important that all the various technologies and systems work well together. This is particularly critical for the contractor, who is typically the one required to warranty the construction of the home, and the one typically blamed when things don't work as planned. This process requires being willing to try new materials and methods; it also requires doing the research to make sure that it's all going to work. Although many of these systems have been in use for years, sometimes new combinations of systems are in order, and making sure that they work well together takes some effort.

For instance, when building a house combining large amounts of glass, walls insulated with a spray foam insulation, and a geothermal heating and cooling system, great care must be taken to properly size the HVAC system and ductwork to properly heat, cool, regulate indoor humidity, and provide regular changes of fresh air. These considerations come to play in any structure, but in this situation, two items complicate it further: the large amount of glass and the geothermal system.

Large amounts of glass complicate things for several reasons. Glass has poor insulation qualities, allows transmission of UV rays and solar energy, and in tall windows and doors, tends to create convection loops. Care should be taken during the design phase to address concerns in the quantity and the orientation of glass in the exterior, and it is advisable to include the mechanical contractor in the discussions.

If you are going to use a geothermal system, pay close attention to the fact that these systems do not produce the differential in air temperatures that more conventional systems do. Under many circumstances, this is not a problem, particularly in a well-insulated, well-sealed house. But the introduction of large amounts of glass makes these considerations very important, especially when it comes to comfort.

In regard to the aforementioned importance of climate zone and orientation, the consideration of glass is a perfect example of how critical

this can be. The various factors that go into selecting the right glass have a lot to do with both climate zone and orientation. For example, a builder in the North may desire solar heat gain in that region, whereas a builder in the South almost certainly will not. And a room facing south will have considerations that a room facing north will not.

There are systems that may work well in one climate zone and yet be quite inappropriate in another region. A good example of this is radiant-floor heat systems. If you are building in the Rocky Mountain region or any region experiencing long periods of cold weather, where the temperature tends to be cold the entire day and requires steady heating of the house, radiant floor heating may be appropriate, for these systems tend to take time heating and then hold their heat for long periods of time. In contrast, in the South, which does not have long winters, or in many other areas where it may be cold in the morning but warms up considerably during the day, this type of heating system is ineffective and inefficient.

It is sad to note that with the current climate changes, builders in some areas are being forced to consider changing to systems that may have been unneeded earlier but are now necessary. In Canada, for example, a builder was renovating a beautiful vacation home, primarily of log construction, in the ski town of Whistler, British Columbia. The home had a radiant floor system for heating, which had proved adequate and worked beautifully for years. But two things had changed recently: the use of the home and the climate. Mountain biking began drawing people to the area during the summer, and winters there tend not to be as long or as cold as they had been historically. So although the radiant floor system continued to work well in the winter, the builder had to find a way to retrofit the house with a forced air cooling system, made all the more challenging by the log construction.

This is a good example of something occurring more often in many areas: builders mixing modern architecture with a number of building systems and exterior finishes that are more rustic in nature, creating beautiful homes that take a good deal of thought and care to do properly. These homes, which may combine log, timber frame, conventional framing techniques with stone, and lap siding, or stucco, and glass, require special attention to flashing details, thermal expansion characteristics of each component, and other ways in which these components relate to one another.

No matter which climate zone you are building in, and what types of building components, finish systems, insulation materials, amounts of glass, or mechanical systems you are working with, great care should be given to understanding how well the building system will perform, and how these factors will affect energy efficiency and comfort. One valuable resource for addressing such issues is the database of Home Energy Rating System (HERS) raters listed on the Web site RESNET.com. RESNET, the Residential Energy Services Network, is an organization representing qualified and licensed raters who have expertise in analyzing the building envelope of the house, its airtightness, insulation, and heating and cooling loads, as well as various other components, such as the R-value of the windows and doors.

Other systems that require consideration include combinations of various ways of heating domestic water, and different systems such as geothermal, solar, and conventional, whether gas or electric, and the new tankless hot water systems.

Still other factors to take into account include choosing between looped systems, for delivery of hot water, and a manifold system. The manifold system tends to be very efficient, but a more conventional piping system, looped or not, is easier to insulate, helping to eliminate issues of condensation.

Selection of Materials

A major consideration in green building is the selection of building materials. These decisions involve several major aspects of sustainability, durability, and energy efficiency.

- **Sustainable:** When we discuss sustainability in materials, we are primarily thinking of the resource from which the materials are drawn. During the building boom in Japan during the 1970s and 1980s, it was reported that it was common for Japanese construction crews to use plywood made of mahogany, harvested from the rain forests of Southeast Asia, to build concrete forms, which would be used once, then disposed of. This is a precise example of what we are attempting not to do. Wise use of resources is the objective. An outstanding example of that today is engineered lumber products, such as LVLs, OSB, even finger-joint 2 x 4 studs.

- **Recycled content:** Products made from recycled materials are popular for several reasons: Often, they require less energy to produce, eliminate the need to harvest more of the original raw materials, and save waste materials going to landfills.

- **Durable:** Products that are durable offer many of the payoffs of recycled materials in the effort to reduce waste. Houses that are more durable last longer, need less maintenance, and are replaced less frequently, reducing landfill waste and the need to harvest and process more raw materials, thereby saving energy.

- **Source location/distance:** Choosing materials that are available locally reduces energy spent in transporting materials over long distances. (Note: LEED for Homes currently considers "local" to mean within 500 miles of the job site.)

- **Reclaimed:** Having many of the same qualities as recycled materials, reclaimed materials save waste by finding other purposes for products not used on a project, rather than sending them to the landfill. A good example is milling old heart pine framing members into heart pine flooring. It's sad to imagine the amount of old heart pine framing that has gone to landfills, which could have been remade into flooring or trim.

- **Ability to recycle:** Many products, due to their core components or structure, lend themselves to reuse and recycling, while other materials do not. Many times old concrete can be recycled into aggregate for new concrete; gypsum can

be ground up and used to help amend soil; and lumber that has not been painted or pressure treated makes great mulch. Other products, such as old plaster, painted materials, and fiberglass insulation, currently do not recycle well. We must look forward to the day when some of these materials find a new purpose instead of going to the landfill.

- **Energy efficiency:** When considering products in terms of their energy efficiency, three different questions must be answered: How much energy does it take to produce the product? How much energy are we consuming to transport it to the job site and install it? And how does its use on the project contribute to the energy efficiency of the structure?

- **Indoor air quality:** The proper selection of materials has a profound effect on the indoor air quality of the house. Obviously, properly designing the building envelope and HVAC system are fundamental to the indoor air quality, but so is proper materials selection. Many people are affected in a variety of ways, some more seriously than others, by the chemical components released into their living space by the materials and products used in the house. Most people are familiar with the problems caused by paint fumes and the formaldehyde contained in plywood and insulation; fewer may be aware that offgassing from carpeting or other fabrics, for example, can cause discomfort as well, such as headaches and allergic reactions. More and more products like these and others are now manufactured to standards that greatly reduce or eliminate offgassing; they are labeled as "low VOC" (volatile organic compounds). Products of concern include everything going into the home, including paints, adhesives, carpet, wallcoverings, plywood, and other manufactured products. That is why it is important to read labels carefully, conduct research on the Internet, and visit Web sites like buildinggreen.com, featuring GreenSpec® products. And even after taking all these precautions, LEED for Homes still recommends airing out the house for a minimum of two weeks after the completion of construction before allowing move-in.

Methods of Construction

This section addresses several of the major issues in green building as they relate specifically to methods of construction.

MINIMIZING ENVIRONMENTAL IMPACT

Careful planning of the site, including placement of structures and the driveway and other impervious surfaces, is important. The objective is to minimize disturbance to the site during construction, which should include drawing up a specific plan for guarding trees and streams and carefully implementing and maintaining erosion control measures.

ENERGY EFFICIENCY

It has been said that you can never use too much insulation; and, of course, you must install it properly. It is possible to get good R-values with fiberglass batt insulation, but if it is not installed properly, it is rendered almost worthless. For fiberglass to work well, it must be contained within an airtight, sealed space. If air can move through the insulation, its effectiveness is lost. Using either a caulk or an adhesive to seal the gypsum to the wall framing helps to create this airtight space. The insulation must also be installed without any gaps, tight to the framing. This is possible to do, but it takes some time and effort on the part of the installation crew—which is why so many contractors are moving to other types of insulation.

The insulation that makes the job easy to get right is spray foam. This is because the foam not only insulates the wall, but it seals it airtight, too. This makes a huge difference in how effective the insulation really is.

This is why structural insulated panel (SIP) construction and insulating concrete form (ICF) construction have become so popular. You combine high R-values with building envelopes that are constructed properly and sealed airtight; the result is a very effective combination.

AIR-SEALING

As just noted, making the building envelope airtight is essential. Consider, for example, that an older, 1200-square-foot home, even when built to code, may have the equivalent of a 4-foot by 4-foot hole in the exterior wall due to all the cracks and leaks around doors, windows, pipe, wire penetrations, and so on. That's a tremendous amount of air passing the building envelope. To turn a house that "leaky" into an energy-efficient structure is difficult, no matter what insulation you use.

The guidelines thus are to caulk around any penetrations, windows, doors, sill plate, and other entry points for air. The EEBA and Building America books are excellent resources in this area. Also reference the ENERGY STAR recommendations and consult a HERS rater on the RESNET site. There are ways to test the house to see how well the envelope is performing.

DURABILITY

A well-constructed, energy-efficient home with a tight envelope should be a durable structure. There are a number of ways to achieve that goal, paying particular attention to keeping water out (more on this in a moment) and letting water vapor get out, rather than being trapped with the exterior wall assembly. Moisture within the house in the form of humidity should be taken care of by the HVAC system.

When we talk about durability, we're talking about designing a building that's going to last, specifically, longer than a typical house built to code. The life expectancy of a house built to code has been estimated at 50 years; the goal should be to build for at least twice that, 100 years. This section describes some simple, straightforward ways to help make that happen.

Obviously, you don't want any raw wood on the exterior of the house. In fact, you may want to limit the amount of wood on the exterior of the house in general. When you do use wood, choose it carefully for its durability and sustainability, and protect and install it properly. Many modern building materials, made of synthetic, engineered components withstand water and UV rays very well. Many are also composed of recycled material. Several of these products are superior to wood in durability when properly installed.

If you are going to use wood on the exterior of the house, make sure that it is a species of wood that is durable. As seen on the West Coast and in the Rocky Mountain region, log and timber frame construction is popular; some wood, when chosen carefully and treated properly, stands up very well. Western hemlock, fir, and cedar are good examples of wood used in these types of structures. Any wood trim pieces should be back-primed and sealed at cuts before installation. It is extremely important that it be installed in such a way that enables it to dry if it does get wet, and that it does not hold standing water. Installing lap siding over furring strips is a good way to achieve this.

Any area inside the house that is subject to a wet environment, such as kitchens, laundry rooms, and baths, should use materials that do not hold water and will not allow molds to grow. Rather than using a moisture-resistant gypsum board, use fiberglass-faced gypsum, a durable backerboard behind the tiled areas, and flooring materials that work well in wet areas, like tile.

These wet areas should always be exhausted with a fan ducted to the outside of the house. These fans should run for a minimum of 20 minutes after any activity that raises the humidity in the room—best achieved by putting the fans on a timer.

Insulating hot and cold water lines in the house is another good way of keeping condensation to a minimum and helping with durability; it is also good from the energy efficiency standpoint.

Walk-off mats at all exterior doors, or areas specifically used for shoe storage, also are advisable, and not just for northern climates where there's bound to be snow in the winters; they're effective at keeping rain-soaked wet shoes out of the house, too.

As you can see, a great deal of concern around durability has to do with water, so the next section covers other water issues.

WATER INFILTRATION, WATERPROOFING, FLASHING, AND DRAINAGE PLAINS

Water is not just the most important concern in durability; it also relates to the issues of indoor air quality and comfort. Since humans first started seeking and building shelters, a central purpose has been to prevent rain from getting in. We're still working on perfecting that science today.

In the most basic form of water prevention, we use roofs, walls, foundations, and the various other components of the exterior to drain water off and away from the structure. We extend that endeavor with the drainage system and grading of the site around the house. Complicating this effort are factors such as capillary action, wind, temperature, momentum, gravity, and surface tension. The level at which we address these concerns, and the best way to do so, have to do with the climate and the amount of rainfall of the locale where we are building.

We've come a long way in understanding how these various forces work, and what we can do to minimize water infiltration. The basics include: a roof that drains well, gutters and downspouts that collect and carry the water away from the house, a roof overhang that minimizes water on the exterior walls, an exterior wall that drains water with a minimum amount of infiltration and that can breathe to dry, a foundation that keeps water out, and site drainage and grading to carry the water away. Today, we have materials such as house wrap, window and door flashing systems, and drainage boards that were not available just a few years ago; likewise, we more fully understand the need to allow wall assemblies to breathe instead of trapping water in them.

To learn the technical details of how these various systems work, study the EEBA Builder's Guide for the climate where you are building. These books are excellent technical references and do an excellent job of explaining all the design considerations that are required, and include maps showing annual rainfall and the recommended design strategies for each area.

Properly constructing the rainscreen and drainage plane behind different exterior finishes is critical.

FRAMING TECHNIQUES

A central aspect of the green building movement is resource efficiency, or the wise use of resources. Many builders can remember the day when lumber was cheap, and little thought was given to wasting wood, particularly if it was a cold day and the carpenters needed fuel for the fire burning to help keep them warm. These days, we're working hard on the job site to eliminate that kind of waste.

As much as possible, we start by designing the house on 2-foot rather than 16-inch centers. This allows us to purchase materials and frame the house with less waste. We are also able to use more efficiently the materials we bring to the job site.

Modern framing techniques stress several objectives: reducing waste, building a structurally sound house while using a minimum of materials, and making sure that the entire building envelope is properly insulated.

Traditional framing of walls with dimensional lumber using stack framing, eliminating unneeded components such as the second top plate, headers in nonstructural walls, and building corners using just two studs are typical of modern framing techniques. Here again, the EEBA builder's guide is an excellent reference.

ENGINEERED MATERIALS

Outstanding advancements in building technology have been made in the recent past. The first of what many would consider a modern, engineered building material is plywood. It is a fine example of the ongoing attempt to find ways of producing a superior product while making use of something that previously had been an unused by-product of the manufacturing process. There are many examples today of products that carry on that tradition and take success to the next level. OSB is an obvious example, as it has replaced plywood as a best product for many applications.

We are now striving to refine many of these types of products by increasing their strength, including as much recycled content as possible, as well as taking out components to help reduce offgassing.

MINIMIZING WASTE

Proper design, planning, and material procurement go a long way in reducing job-site waste. With a house designed on 2-foot centers, engineered materials cut to length at the lumberyard, and modern framing techniques, we can eliminate a substantial portion of the waste produced in the past.

On a typical project, along with the design, planning, and procurement, we set up waste recycling areas on our job sites: one for debris that cannot be recycled, such as painted or pressure-treated wood; another for items that will be removed from the job site for recycling, such as asphalt roof shingles, concrete, and concrete block; a third for items that will be recycled on the job site, such as lumber to be ground into mulch, or gypsum board to be ground and used to amend soils on the property. We also set up containers for glass, plastic, aluminum, and paper, which we take to a local recycling center.

In addition to these recycling activities, we are also now attempting to reduce waste generated during the demolition process on our remodeling projects. A committee of the local National Association of the Remodeling Industry (NARI), called the Circle of Good, is working to formalize practices that contractors can put into place during the demolition phase of the project, carefully deconstructing materials to be recycled or reused. We are also establishing practices of taking reusable items such as kitchen cabinets, windows, doors, plumbing and lighting fixtures, and the like, and donating them to reuse centers, such as those operated by Habitat for Humanity, in exchange for a receipt of charitable donation, given back to the client.

As mentioned early in this chapter, there is also the design discipline know as Design for Disassembly, which looks at how we can design structures so that they are more flexible in their use and assembly, allowing for a lower operating cost during the life of the building, disassembly when the building use becomes obsolete, and recycling of the building and its components.

Scrap waste from various trades is stockpiled for recycling on-site.

Scrap wood materials.

Budget and Cost Considerations

Budget and cost considerations fall into three categories: construction, operational, and life-cycle.

CONSTRUCTION COSTS

There is a lot of discussion concerning the cost of going green, with clients raising a lot of questions in that regard. A good place to start to answer those questions is to remind clients that building to code, while fairly easy to do, is building to a minimum standard and so not a very good one when it comes to achieving energy efficiency or durability. Moreover, there are no real provisions in modern building costs for a consideration such as indoor air quality.

Experience has shown that the two most important aspects of building a greener, more energy-efficient house, once you have met the basic building code, is superior insulation and creating an airtight building envelope. Add to those two items an efficient HVAC and tight ductwork, and you've gone a long way to substantially improving the performance of the house. The least expensive way to achieve this is to properly—with emphasis on the word *properly*—install your insulation. This can be accomplished by using fiberglass or cellulous, but is much easier to do with foam. Yes, foam is more expensive, but it produces a superior result and certainly pays for itself in the long-term operating costs of the house. Caulk is relatively inexpensive, and thoughtful use of it to create an airtight building envelope will easily pay for itself in reduced heating and cooling costs.

Many aspects of green building—whether it be wise use of resources and materials through modern framing techniques or recycling—either add no real cost to the project or will actually save money. The only cost is training the construction crews to think and work differently than they have in the past.

Systems such as insulating concrete forms (ICF), structural insulated panels (SIPs), geo-thermal HVAC systems, and solar hot water heating systems have a larger up-front cost, hence have a longer payback period. Photovoltaic solar panel systems for generation of electrical power have the longest payback period.

There are various state and federal tax credits available to help offset the initial costs of some of these systems. It's also important to point out that at the time of this writing, 2007, in today's dollars with today's energy costs, which are fairly cheap, the additional up-front costs of going green and building energy-efficient structures more than pays for itself now, and will only make more sense in the future, as energy costs continue to rise.

OPERATIONAL COSTS

While it is true that building a green home may have some higher up-front costs than a lower-quality home, the returns gained in lower operational costs and higher value to the client more than make up for them.

A pertinent question to ask clients is where they would rather spend their money: investing it in a higher-quality, more durable, energy-efficient, comfortable, healthy home, or essentially giving that money to the power company. It really is that simple. Once that money is spent with the power company, it's gone forever. Instead, by paying a slightly higher mortgage payment, clients are investing money in a home that will return it to them in many ways.

In Atlanta, Georgia, Habitat for Humanity builds all its homes to the EarthCraft program standards. This program demonstrates that while it requires some extra effort and money in the beginning, doing so is well worth it in the long run. Someone said that a home is not an affordable home if you cannot afford to heat and cool it. To that can be added that a home is not affordable if living there is making its inhabitants sick, and they're spending their money at the doctor's office.

A well-constructed, energy- and water-efficient home should reduce monthly operating costs significantly. ENERGY STAR standards call for a minimum gain in energy efficiency of 15 percent over current codes, with 20 to 30 percent being more typical. Experience has shown that the gain is closer to the 30 percent range; and with more clients choosing higher-efficiency HVAC systems, supplemented with solar water heating, that number is destined to grow, closing in on a 50 percent reduction. More dramatically, use of systems such as geothermal, solar, and photovoltaic can eliminate those costs completely, and potentially turn the home into a net energy *producer*, making it possible to sell back to the power company more energy than is consumed.

LIFE-CYCLE COSTS

With the use of proper materials and methods of construction, the green home, which is a more durable home, reduces significantly the life-cycle costs of the structure.

As noted earlier, water is the primary destructive element that homes face, with ultraviolet light being a close second. Many of the synthetic materials used today, when combined with proper installation of all materials on the exterior, proper flashing, and establishment of the exterior drainage plain, will keep water infiltration to a minimum and allow the water that does get in to get back out. This should greatly increase the life of the structure while also reducing the need for maintenance, therefore lowering life-cycle costs. Choosing water-resistant, durable materials for inside the house is just as important, especially in high-moisture areas such as bathrooms, kitchens, and laundry areas. Equally important is properly conditioning the air inside, to reduce moisture and humidity inside, and vent it out.

Proper shading, including window treatments and high-performance glass in the windows, helps to minimize damage caused by ultraviolet light.

These measures, taken together, should contribute to a house that is more durable and incurs markedly lower life-cycle costs. A house that is durable helps to reduce contributions to landfill waste and the use of resources.

Programs and Providers

All contractors should familiarize themselves with the details of the green building programs and providers described in this section.

ENERGY STAR AND HOME PERFORMANCE WITH ENERGY STAR

The ENERGY STAR program was created by the U.S. Environmental Protection Agency (EPA) in 1992 to promote the use of energy-efficient products. Since then, its appliances, lighting, and HVAC equipment, identified by the ENERGY STAR blue label, have become well known to a growing number of people. The program, now run jointly by the EPA and the U.S. Department of Energy (DOE), encompasses a number of important programs; the most relevant to this discussion are those designed for both new and existing homes.

The ENERGY STAR program for homes emphasizes five major aspects of home construction:

- Effective insulation

- High-performance windows

- Tight construction of the building envelope and ductwork

- High-efficiency HVAC equipment

- Use of energy-efficient products such as lighting, appliances, and ventilation fans

Verification of the quality of construction according to the program's standards is provided by the independent Home Energy Raters (HERS). For information about how to proceed with the standards verification process, go to www.RESNET.com.

Visit EnergyStar.gov for information regarding federal tax credits available to homes that meet the ENERGY STAR requirements.

USGBC AND LEED FOR HOMES

The U.S. Green Building Council (USGBC), an independent nonprofit organization based in Washington, DC, is widely known for its Leadership in Energy and Environmental Design (LEED) program for commercial buildings. LEED for Homes, which began as a pilot program in August 2005, is now available through providers throughout the country.

LEED for Homes raises the bar of excellence in construction and achieving energy efficiency in homes. It is a comprehensive program that looks at many of the fundamental ways in which the construction and operation of a home affect the environment and the surrounding community, taking into account such factors as access to public transportation, contribution to sprawl and light pollution, and other concerns that many green building programs, including ENERGY STAR, do not cover.

The program primarily involves the documentation of the construction process, using the building technologies and guidelines developed by other organizations and programs such as ENERGY STAR, EEBA, and Building America. Certification of the home, at several different levels, is offered by providers located around the country.

NAHB NATIONAL GREEN BUILDING PROGRAM

The National Association of Home Builders (NAHB) has been sponsoring green building conferences for a number of years, typically offering classes and instruction given by knowledgeable professionals associated with the EEBA, Building America, and ENERGY STAR organizations. As the program continues to develop, it promises to offer ongoing high-quality and relevant help to professional home builders and developers in their efforts to bring to market homes that are both green and affordable.

GAHBA/SOUTHFACE AND EARTHCRAFT

The Greater Atlanta Home Builders Association (GAHBA) and Southface Energy Institute, located in Atlanta, Georgia, teamed up to create the Earth-Craft House program. Classes in the art of green building are taught to builders, developers, subcontractors, and homeowners alike. It is also one of the first to have also developed a complete, first-rate program for renovations of existing homes.

This very successful, high-level program promotes the basics of green building, emphasizing energy efficiency, durability, indoor air quality, and environmental responsibility in home construction. As a provider of the program, Southface offers classes, coaching, inspections, and certification (at several different levels) of completed projects. The building technologies and requirements are similar to those taught by EEBA, and ENERGY STAR certification is considered a minimum standard of achievement. EarthCraft has been held as a model for others around the country.

One of the commendable features of EarthCraft is its straightforward, stick-to-the-basics approach that makes it easy to understand and implement the program, which also eases its applicability to any architectural style and budget. As mentioned previously, Habitat for Humanity has adopted the program for the houses built by the group in Atlanta, based on the belief that an affordable home should be one that inhabitants can also afford to heat and cool, as well as be healthy to live in.

EEBA/HOUSES THAT WORK

Formed in 1982 as the Energy Efficient Building Association, the organization changed its name in 2001 to the Energy and Environmental Building Association. EEBA proudly regards itself as the group that got the ball rolling on energy efficiency and building technology. Original members included building professionals from the United States, Canada, and Sweden.

With the objective of helping others to build better houses that are durable and energy-efficient, EEBA teaches its Houses That Work classes around the country, sponsors conferences, and publishes some of the best guides available on building green.

Like those of ENERGY STAR, the technologies developed and promoted by EEBA and its Houses That Work program should become the basics of any green building program; and like the EarthCraft program, they are applicable to any architectural style and can be tailored to any climate.

BUILDING AMERICA

The Building America program is a private/public partnership sponsored by the U.S. Department of Energy that conducts research in creating energy-efficient housing. Technologies developed by the program are published for the use of builders, developers, and consumers. A number of its excellent publications are available for free download on the organization's Web site, www.eere.energy.gov/buildings/building_america.

CANADIAN MORTGAGE AND HOUSING CORPORATION/ EQUILIBRIUM HOUSING

In Canada, the climate is often cold and rainy, and so energy efficiency and durability in home building are major concerns there. Consequently, Canadians have been instrumental in leading the way in related technologies for years. They played a major role in the work of EEBA, and created the Healthy Housing program in the 1990s to examine issues of energy efficiency and resource conservation; more recently, they launched the EQuilibrium Housing program.

The EQuilibrium Housing program is an extensive, high-quality program that, like LEED for Homes, examines thoroughly how the house relates to and affects the environment. In addition, it addresses the issue of affordability.

The five primary areas of the program are health, energy, resources, environment, and affordability. The Canadian Mortgage and Housing Corporation has an excellent Web site, and as this program develops, it will be well worth learning the lessons taught there. Go to www.cmhc-schl.gc.ca.

The Construction Process: Managing the Details

The details involve proper installation and documentation.

PROPER INSTALLATION

Once you have chosen your methods for achieving the level of energy efficiency and green certification you are working toward, the major challenge is attending to the details during con-

struction. Experience has proven that the most difficult aspect here is getting the entire team of carpenters, subcontractors, and suppliers to buy in to the process and work as a team to ensure that the many new details are addressed and coordinated. Each trade tends to have its own challenges, requiring workers to adhere to the new standards on every job, whether a green project or not, in order to keep everyone on task.

For green projects, specifically, however, a number of guidelines will help ease the way:

1. For every project, set up a recycling center on the job site, and aim to have as little go into the landfill as possible. Order framing material carefully, to keep waste to an absolute minimum; and grind what scraps are left into mulch for ground cover.

2. Remind the framer not to build structural headers unless needed, keeping in mind that insulating the headers on the exterior and building the two stud corners takes time. Instruct your project manager to review those types of items with the sub at the start of the job.

3. Instruct the HVAC contractor to ensure that ductwork gets all the detail and sealing required, with the fresh air intakes, paying attention to supply and return locations.

4. Even when crews have been thoroughly trained, it's a good idea to assign several carpenters the responsibility of making sure that all the caulking and sealing of the exterior shell of the house is done on every job. This gets them accustomed to learning all the details and tricks of the trade to get it right.

5. Put the superintendent in charge of ensuring that building wrap and window and door flashings are all installed correctly.

DOCUMENTATION

Documenting the requirements of the project is primarily the responsibility of the architect, through the plans and specifications; nevertheless, many times it is the contractor's job to document that certain work items were properly completed.

Some green building programs provide a checklist to be completed as the job progresses, and there will be inspections during certain phases, such as predrywall. There are certain items, such as the placement of the capillary break at the footings or foundation, that will be covered by the time the certifying organization reviews the job. For situations such as these, the best recommendation is to provide the project manager or superintendent with a digital camera to visually document the covered items.

Wrapping It Up: Testing and Certification

One of the great strengths of a number of the green building programs available today is to give the builder the opportunity to earn independent verification of the performance of the house. This can be achieved through either an independent HERS rater or through the sponsoring organization or program provider. Along with the testing of the house, there may be a certification worksheet that needs to be filled out and scored. Here are three programs that offer these services:

ENERGY STAR/HERS: In the case of ENERGY STAR, you will typically be consulting with an approved, independent HERS rater or a local green building organization, who will guide you through some of the decisions to be made during the construction process, but most importantly, who will test the house and the HVAC system and ductwork for airtightness and the performance of the building envelope, using the duct blaster and blower door tests. Visit www.natresnet.org to find a local HERS rater.

LEED for Homes: USGBC has organizations around the country that work as LEED for Homes providers. Visit the LEED for Homes section of the USGBC Web site at www.usgbc.org where you will find a wealth of information about the program, checklists, names of providers, and the worksheet. If you plan on doing a LEED for Homes project, it is very important to work with the local provider from the start. Review the worksheet with the provider to map out how you are going to earn the points that you will need for certification, and work through the plan review. Be aware there is an extensive amount of documentation and planning to do before you even begin construction, as well as a large amount of paperwork along the way. Also keep in mind that all of the work items involved in earning points have to be documented, and, as noted previously, taking pictures of completed items is a good way to do that. There are also intermediate inspections to be planned for; and at the end of the project, you will go through a testing of the house very similar to the tests conducted by the HERS rater for ENERGY STAR.

EarthCraft: The EarthCraft program run by the Greater Atlanta Home Builders Association and Southface Energy Institute is an excellent green building program that has been modeled by other groups around the country. Getting a project EarthCraft certified also involves being certified as ENERGY STAR, so you'll be doing the duct blaster and blower door tests at the end of the project, along with working through a scoring sheet not unlike the one used for LEED for Homes. It is wise to get started with the worksheet and the staff at Southface before beginning construction; and you'll want to be documenting certain work items along the way and scheduling a predrywall inspection. Visit the program Web site at www.southface.org and www.earthcrafthouse.com. And, note, Southface is also a local LEED for Homes provider and so can help you with that program as well.

HOUSE AS A SYSTEM

■ Sydney G. Roberts, PhD, Southface Energy Institute

G REEN BUILDING REQUIRES DESIGN-ing and building a home that is energy, water, and resource efficient; a home that is respectful of site and works with the natural resources of sun, shade, and wind. But these are not your grandfather's hobbit holes. Quite the opposite. Designers and builders of green homes use the most state-of-the-art techniques and technologies coupled with proper installation to create energy-efficient, comfortable, and durable homes that are cost-effective and approachable from any design style.

It is estimated that 52 percent of residential buildings that will be standing in 2025 have not yet been constructed or will undergo major renovation. Today, buildings consume 48 percent of total energy in the United States, compared to 27 percent for transportation and 25 percent for industry.[1] Sixty-six percent of all electricity generated in the United States, largely from fossil fuels, is used to power buildings. Water is a limited resource in most parts of the country, and the link between water and energy is very strong. In the Southeast, three gallons of water are used to produce each kilowatt-hour of electricity.[2] Conversely, it requires vast amounts of electricity to purify, deliver, and treat potable water. Therefore, both the need for immediate action and the opportunity to affect significant change are large.

Design solutions are as varied as each design problem and client, but can be found using a systems engineering approach and treating the house as a system. Borrowing from this interdisciplinary field of engineering, the designer is well served to define the goals up front, investigate all alternatives, create an energy model of the house as a system, integrate what was learned from the model back into the design, and reevaluate. Fortunately, there are many resources available to aid in each step of that process.

Architecture 2030 was founded in 2002 by Edward Mazria to address the impact of the built environment on global warming and to transform the U.S. and global building sector from a major contributor of greenhouse gas emissions to a part of the solution. The goals of the 2030 Challenge, issued in January 2006, are ambitious, but are achievable if the systems engineering approach is followed by building professionals. For instance, the first near-term goal of the 2030 Challenge is 50 percent reduction in fossil-fuel-emitting consumption of new construction and major renovation relative to existing building stock by 2010.

To address solutions, Building America is a private/public partnership sponsored by the U.S. Department of Energy (DOE) that conducts research to find energy-efficient solutions for new and existing housing that can be implemented on a production basis. Research teams in every climate zone have built homes of every style, size, and price point to determine the most cost-effective methods for designers and builders to meet ambitious energy efficiency goals. Building America has produced downloadable, climate-specific

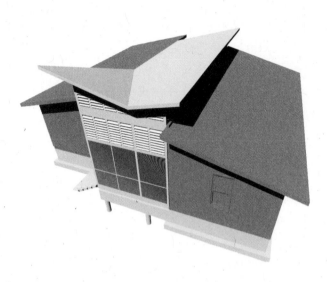

Above: Birdseye of the Auburn's Design Habitat recent project.

Right: The modules are put into place on the concrete foundation that the students poured themselves. (Studio 804)

best practice guides for architects, designers, builders, and building scientists that translate this real-world experience into practical how-to steps for optimizing building performance.[3] Applying the systems engineering approach, energy consumption of new homes can be reduced by as much as 50 percent relative to a new construction benchmark with little or no increased cost of ownership. Future research will focus on meeting 70 percent and net zero energy (NZE) goals. Combining the goal-setting of the 2030 Challenge with the practical solutions of Building America and others provides building professionals with a toolkit to transform our interaction with and impact on the world around us.

Green building programs that provide a framework for implementing these strategies, third-party verification of proper installation, and market recognition for exceptional design and craftsmanship benefit the designer, builder, and homeowner. There are now more than 85 local, regional, and national green building or energy efficiency programs in the United States with varying requirements. ENERGY STAR for New Homes, launched in 1995, serves as the cornerstone for most successful programs, and includes testing and verification requirements. By 2010, ENERGY STAR estimates that there will be 2 million ENERGY STAR qualified homes in the United States, saving 20 to 30 percent compared to standard construction, or 50 to 60 percent compared to current building stock.[4] Familiar to many architects because of the commercial crossover, the U.S. Green Building Council's (USGBC) LEED for Homes rating system emerged from pilot in 2007. It is based on the continued success of local and regional programs such as EarthCraft House in the Southeast, Built Green in Washington, and Austin Energy Green Building, to name a few.

House as a System

The earliest human shelters exhibited many of the traits that we now attribute to green building: These homes were site-specific, locally sourced, used the most advanced technologies to maximum benefit, and were energy efficient (for their time). One might even call them modern in that they lacked structural adornment. These were truly functional dwellings. That is not to say that the inhabitants did not decorate, but as befitting a subsistence lifestyle, they were pioneers in the form-follows-function design philosophy.

With affluence came ornamentation and, eventually, wastefulness. Today, American homes are being built at a record pace and to an ever-increasing scale. While the average American family has shrunk from 3.1 people in 1974 to 2.6 in 2004, the average American home has ballooned from 1,695 square feet to 2,349 square feet.[5]

It is incumbent upon design and building professionals to use the most advanced techniques and technologies, not as mere ornament, but to provide their clients with the most livable and sustainable homes possible.

A house, or any building for that matter, is a complex system, the performance of which must be designed, built, and evaluated holistically. When all participants in the design and construction process understand the interactions between various components and systems, significant synergies can be achieved. The ultimate goal of a sustainably built home is to optimize the comfort, energy efficiency, and indoor environmental quality of the home while minimizing the negative impacts and maximizing the positive impacts on the natural environment. While specific solutions will be client, climate, and site specific, all high-performance homes will have energy efficiency in common as the cornerstone.

Essential to the success of any high-performance residential design and building project is the requirement to treat the house as a system. Each component of the house affects the performance of other components in potentially positive and negative ways. For instance, very tight construction necessitates controlled ventilation for improved indoor air quality. It also typically allows for a smaller heating and cooling system, which translates into savings on both first cost and lifetime utility bills. Improper foundation drainage can raise relative humidity levels inside the home, which can lead to mold growth, which may damage building materials and endanger health. Every decision in the design, construction, and operation of a home can influence the house system. For green building to be successfully and economically incorporated into the design, it must be integrated from the start by all stakeholders, rather than viewed as an add-on.

Energy efficiency is a key element of the systems approach critical to achieving successful green homes. The minimum requirements for ENERGY STAR–qualified new homes are that they be: (1) 15 percent more energy efficient than the 2004 International Residential Code (IRC) and (2) that they pass third-party verification testing. The DOE Building America Builders Challenge goal is at least 30 percent more efficient than 2004 IRC, with additional verified quality criteria. In a sample of EarthCraft House single-family homes in Metro Atlanta in 2007–2008, the average efficiency was 28 percent better than IRC, with over 37 percent of all homes exceeding the 30 percent Builders Challenge threshold. In fact, 48 percent of these homes qualified for the 2005 Energy Policy Act $2000 federal tax credit for builders for saving 50 percent or more on heating and cooling. These efficiencies are achieved not only with efficient heating and cool-

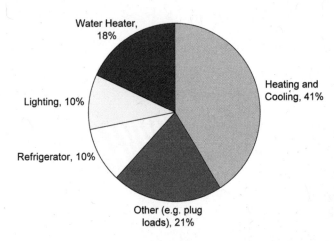

Water Heater, 18%

Heating and Cooling, 41%

Lighting, 10%

Refrigerator, 10%

Other (e.g. plug loads), 21%

Typical residential energy use in the southeastern United States.

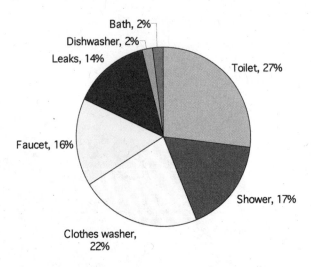

Bath, 2%

Dishwasher, 2%

Leaks, 14%

Toilet, 27%

Faucet, 16%

Shower, 17%

Clothes washer, 22%

Typical interior residential water use in the United States.

ing equipment, but with superior air-sealing details, proper insulation installation, careful choice of window location, high-quality fenestration, and ENERGY STAR lighting and appliances. It requires a house as a system approach and a whole team effort, from the designer to the builder to the subcontractors, to achieve efficiencies of 30 percent or better.

In designing efficiency strategies, it is critical to first understand where energy and water are used in most homes. While there are some climatic differences, the majority of the energy use in a home is for space conditioning: heating, cooling, ventilation, and humidity control. The single largest use after HVAC is typically water heating. So, as an architect or designer, the biggest opportunities for improvement are in reducing energy demands for space heating and cooling and water heating.

Water efficiency is increasingly important to achieving a high-performance green home. The EPA WaterSense program features guidelines for a variety of water-using appliances and for new homes.[6] The WaterSense program is still in development at this writing, but the intent is to establish an easily recognizable brand, similar to ENERGY STAR, for consumer products that are water efficient and function well. The first Wa-

terSense product to launch is toilets, which must meet a maximum threshold of 1.28 gallons per flush and a stringent flushing capacity test. Standards for lavatory faucets, showerheads, new homes, and other fixtures will be available shortly.

For water consumption, if there is an irrigation system that is used, on average 50 percent of potable water is used on the landscaping. Exterior water use can be decreased substantially by following the WaterSense for New Homes guidelines, including having the landscaping and irrigation system designed, installed, and audited by a WaterSense professional. Inside the home, the toilets are the largest users of water, accounting for approximately one-quarter of all the water use. The clothes washer uses nearly as much. Both showers and faucets account for over 15 percent of the total interior water usage. Importantly, plumbing leaks also account for a similar amount.

Because high-performance homes are also airtight, increased attention must be paid to indoor environmental quality. Tight homes must have controlled ventilation specified as a component of the heating, cooling, and ventilation systems. It is critical that during all times of the year outside air be brought into the building in a controlled manner and mixed with the air in the

living space. The solution for controlled ventilation will depend on the climate and the size of the home. Possible choices are dehumidifiers, heat recovery ventilators (HRVs), energy recovery ventilators (ERVs), which exchange moisture as well as heat, and timers attached to dampered fresh-air intakes on an HVAC system.

Care must be taken to separate any pollutants from the occupants, with special attention paid to combustion safety. If the home is being designed for an EPA Radon Zone I or II, radon-resistant construction techniques should be designed in from the start (www.epa.gov/radon/zonemap.html).[7] Not only will these techniques guard against this cancer-causing gas from entering the home, they will also prevent other soil gases like methane and water vapor from intruding as well. The installed cost of a passive radon venting system is $100 to $300. As will be discussed in greater detail in a subsequent chapter on materials selection, it is best to avoid using construction materials that off-gas volatile organic compounds (VOCs) because of the impact of indoor air quality.

Importantly, modern high-performance homes often function differently from the homes that most of us grew up in. Therefore, homeowner education is also an important component in ensuring that the homeowners enjoy the max-

The modern kitchen shown here supports the design ideas for the home, to use clean lines and a colorful materials palette.

imum benefits of the sustainable features that have been designed into the building and landscape. It can also be helpful to use automated controls that do not require maintenance or upkeep from homeowners. Examples include automatic lighting controls that turn off when no occupants are in the room, irrigation systems that link to weather satellites and do not water the landscape if a storm is coming, and HVAC systems that will turn on to dehumidify even if the temperature is not over the set point.

Many designers, builders, and owners of high-performance homes choose to participate in local, regional, or national energy efficiency or green building programs. Green building programs provide a blueprint for energy- and resource-efficient homes as well as market recognition for building a superior product. Third-party verification with quantitative testing ensures that the home was built to the standards to which it was designed and to which both the builder and owner expect. ENERGY STAR for New Homes is a national energy efficiency program sponsored by the U.S. Environmental Protection Agency (EPA) and DOE that serves as a building block for most green building programs. Taking the "trust but verify" approach, green building programs typically include multiple additional categories such as site, water efficiency, indoor air quality, resource-efficient design, waste management, and so on.

Designed to Earn the ENERGY STAR is a new partnership opportunity for architects and plan designers whose home plans incorporate energy-efficient specifications and details meeting rigorous guidelines. This program provides guidance on energy efficiency measures as well as market differentiation and tools for architects who are designing high-performance homes.

Although the examples given in this chapter will focus on new construction, the concepts are directly applicable to renovations as well. In fact, several green building programs have renovation products, such as EarthCraft Renovation; and the USGBC and the American Society of Interior Designers (ASID) have developed REGREEN for designers as well as homeowners. It is important to remember when designing a renovation or an addition that, while you may only be drawing lines on the paper for one part of the house, the house is a system and it all must work together. Often, tremendous efficiencies can be gained by looking for opportunities to upgrade mechanical systems, reroute ductwork, or seal a vented crawl space during the course of the project. There have been many stories of homeowners who have increased the size of their homes, yet their energy bills have stayed the same or decreased.

Using the whole-house approach during the design phase will result in more holistic and creative problem solving and in significant time and cost savings for the client. Integrative strategies where energy, resource, and water efficiency are a goal rather than an add-on or option will require fewer changes and workarounds as the project progresses. Energy modeling and heating and cooling load calculation tools can be used early on to play what-if scenarios to weigh the impact of various design decisions on the heating and cooling requirements in the home. Software can also be used to model daylighting, passive solar design, and exposure for photovoltaics or solar thermal water heating.

BUILDING ENVELOPE

The *building envelope* is defined as the thermal shell of the building where the insulation and *air barrier* are continuous and contiguous. It is critical that both of these conditions are met in a high-performance home. In fact, it is a requirement for ENERGY STAR, LEED for Homes, EarthCraft House, and other certifications.[8] The building envelope will include the walls (insulated walls and fenestration); roof, ceiling, skylights, or some combination; and floor and/or foundation walls. Typical places where there can be "building envelope confusion" with the insulation and air barrier include chases and dropped ceilings in attics, unblocked joist cavities under bonus rooms, and cantilever floors that are either unblocked or the insulation does not completely fill the joist cavity. It is critical that these and all areas of the building envelope be detailed properly to resist heat, air, and moisture flow.

The location and components of the insulation and air barrier of the building envelope should be specified on the elevations and floor plans. Particular attention must be paid to detailing how the materials are joined at breaks in the floor, wall, and ceiling planes. Resources are available to provide details of key air-sealing points that can be added to drawing sets.[9]

Heat flows through the building envelope via *conduction*, *convection*, and *radiation*. The formula for heat flow due to conduction is:

$$q = uA\Delta T$$

Equation 1

where q = heat flow, u =conductance, A = area, and ΔT = temperature difference. Heat flow via conduction is measured in U-factor. Using this equation, it is easy to see that as the conductance of a material increases more heat flows. Concrete, which has a higher conductance value of 6.7, compared to wood at 0.8, allows more heat to flow. Likewise, a wall of 100 square feet area allows twice as much heat to flow than a comparably built wall of only 50 square feet. The often overlooked variable of this equation is the temperature difference, or ΔT. Heat flows from hot to cold at a faster rate than from warm to cool. This means that a small interior wall adjacent to a hot attic can gain more heat than a comparably insulated exterior wall.

The heat flow equation is valuable to determine the influence of various design choices on the effective R-value of the building envelope. It can be rearranged to determine the average U-factor for a wall assembly made up of various components, like insulated walls, windows, and doors (equation 2). In a high-performance home, we would want to minimize heat flow so as to reduce the demand for heating and cooling.

$$u_{avg} = \frac{u_1 A_1 + u_2 A_2 + L}{A_{Total}}$$

Equation 2

The most energy-efficient home would be designed like a picnic cooler with thick insulation on all sides, no windows, and no air or water leakage. It would minimize heat loss in the winter and minimize heat gain in the summer. This design, obviously, would not be a very pleasant home in which to live, and the neighbors would not be very happy. The architect's job in designing a high-performance home, then, is to judiciously cut holes in the insulation with the goal of maximizing views, daylighting, and cross-ventilation. Because the house is a system, each hole that is cut can add to the heating and cooling load on the house that will be met by the HVAC system. Properly designed fenestration can also reduce the need for additional artificial lighting.

Well-placed and well-chosen windows and doors are essential to a well-designed home. In terms of their influence on heat conduction across the building envelope, fenestration is rated with a U-factor. The National Fenestration Rating Council (NFRC) is an independent, nonprofit organization that sets testing and labeling standards for windows, doors, and skylights. Importantly, it is the entire assembly that is tested, not just the glass. At a minimum, the NFRC label will show U-factor and solar heat gain coefficient (SHGC), discussed shortly. Most often, it will also include visible transmittance, air leakage, and condensation resistance. Maximizing visible transmittance while minimizing U-factor is often the optimum solution. The choice of SHGC will depend on climate zone and whether or not the home is being designed for passive solar heating.

Unlike fenestration products, the effectiveness of insulation products is typically measured by the R-value or resistance to heat flow. The R-value is simply the inverse (1/u) of the U-factor. Insulation products are typically sold based on their R-value, and R-value is often used to describe the efficiency of a particular building assembly such as a wall.

The actual R-value achieved by insulation is significantly affected by installation practices. For example, loose-fill insulation products, often used to insulate attic floors, provide an R-value of approximately 3 per inch thickness of material. However, to achieve this rated R-value, the material must be installed at the correct density and loft, and air cannot filter through the product. The ENERGY STAR program, through the implementation organization Residential Energy Services Network (RESNET), provides guidelines for the proper installation of insulation materials and rates the quality of installation. The U.S. DOE has issued climate-zone-specific recommended insulation levels, which exceed local codes in most instances.[10]

Let's use equation 2 to examine the effect of window area and U-factor on average U-factor for a wall assembly. Given R-15 insulation, a 10 x 50-foot wall, four double-paned wood windows with rough opening dimensions of 5 x 5 feet and U-factor of 0.39, the average U-factor for the wall would be u = 0.13. The average R-value of the wall is R-7.6 (1/U, or 1/0.13).

$$u_{avg} = \frac{(1/15)(400) + (0.39)(100)}{.500}$$

In this example, with a 20 percent window-to-wall ratio (conservative for many modern homes), the resistance to heat flow was cut in half. And those were good, ENERGY STAR–qualified windows; less efficient windows would have caused an even greater energy penalty. Given the enormous impact that fenestration has on wall assembly heat conduction, it is critical that designers make discriminating decisions regarding window placement and area, considering climate zone, house orientation, and site conditions.

ENERGY STAR qualifies windows, doors, and skylights depending on climate zone. All ENERGY STAR qualified fenestration must be tested and labeled using the NFRC standards. When choosing glazing, if the window is NFRC labeled, the entire window was tested. Otherwise, be sure to inquire as to whether the U-factor is for the entire window or just the glass. The material used for the frame can have a significant impact on the thermal performance of the window.

Designers of modern homes are often drawn to fenestration designed for the commercial market, which is not typically tested using NFRC

Table 4.1 Representative Window U-Factors (Btu/hr x ft^2 x °F)[11]

Frame Material	Operable Double	Operable Triple	Fixed Double	Fixed Triple	Curtain Wall Double	Curtain Wall Triple
Aluminum without thermal break	0.79	0.69	0.61	0.47	0.7	0.55
Aluminum with thermal break	0.58	0.47	0.54	0.4	0.59	0.45
Aluminum-clad wood/reinforced vinyl	0.51	0.41	0.48	0.34		
Wood/vinyl	0.49	0.4	0.48	0.34		
Insulated fiberglass/vinyl	0.43	0.35	0.45	0.32		
Structural glazing					0.55	0.39

*glazing e = 0.20

standards. Not only are commercial storefront windows and curtain wall systems often not tested to these standards, but metal frame windows, both with and without thermal breaks, have much higher U-factors than the ENERGY STAR-qualified fenestration that one would expect in a high-performance home (Table 4.1). In fact, manufacturers are often reluctant to sell to residential customers because of inferior performance in this application. If specifying non-NFRC-rated fenestration, the frame and glazing will have separate U-factors. Computer models, considering the window size and shape, can estimate the combined U-factor. High U-factor windows not only increase heat flow and heating and cooling costs, but also create cold surfaces that frequently cause condensation.

Heat also flows through windows via radiation. Solar heat gain coefficient (SHGC) is a measure of the amount of heat that is transmitted through the window via radiation, the flow of heat through a space. This heat transmission is resisted with a low-emittance (low-e) coating applied to the interior surface of the glass that both reflects heat back and, once hot, does not emit heat. Spectrally selective glazings, many of which are invisible to the human eye, are available that are climate specific. In colder climates, the glazing is designed to reduce radiative heat loss from the warm interior to the cold exterior, but will allow the sun to warm the home. In warmer climates, the glazing has both low emittance and high reflectance. In addition, glazing

with low-emissivity coatings help block ultraviolet radiation, which reduces light degradation of interior materials.

The preceding discussion and formulas for R-value and U-factor assume perfect product installation. Certain products are more conducive to proper installation than others, and it is essential that the builder and all trades are on board with the goals set by the team at the beginning. In general, spray-applied insulation is easier to install in a way that completely fills every cavity, although all insulation can be installed to RESNET Grade I standards with careful attention to detail. Energy models can be used to determine not only the effects of varying R-values, but also different installation grades.

The ceiling, roofline, or a combination, can be insulated and act as the building envelope. Approximately 20 percent of the total heating and cooling load in a typical home is transmitted through the roof. The roofing also plays a role in energy efficiency and can be used as a design feature. Highly reflective roofs (e.g., bare metal) reflect more of the sun's heat back toward the sky and can be as much as 100°F cooler in the summer.[12] This is especially important in cooling climates, where using ENERGY STAR-qualified roofing products can reduce peak cooling loads by 10 to 15 percent.

Advanced framing, also called *optimum value engineering*, refers to a variety of wood-framing techniques designed to reduce the amount of lumber used and waste generated in the con-

struction of a house, which also results in a higher effective R-value for the building envelope. A structurally sound home is constructed with lower material and labor costs than a conventionally framed home by employing techniques such as spacing wall studs, floor joists, and roof rafters up to 24 inches on center; using two stud corners and drywall clips or scrap wood as drywall backer; and eliminating structural headers in nonload-bearing walls. Examples of advanced framing details that can be incorporated into plan sets are available online.[13] Estimates of cost savings are $1000 on materials for a 2400-square-foot home, 3 to 5 percent for labor, and up to 5 percent on heating and cooling.

Chases carrying plumbing, electrical, or duct systems between floors should be designed to be part of or be contained within the building envelope. Imagine an attic with an insulated floor on a cold winter morning when it is 20°F. If that cold air can travel down a chase to an uninsulated wall, then that wall becomes a cold, condensing surface. Not only will this be a comfort issue for the homeowners, but it will likely lead to condensation and cause durability problems as well. It is much easier and less expensive for the framing crew to cover these chases with sheet goods and have the tradesman cut holes of the appropriate sizes than it is to go back after the fact and try to fit a jigsaw puzzle patch around a chase with wiring, plumbing, and so on running through it. Plans should be drawn with these chases capped to ensure this best construction practice.

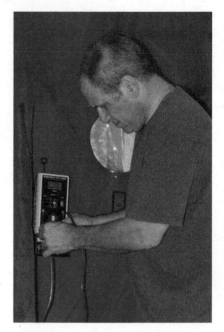

Green Building consultant Carl Seville.

Equipment set up for a blower door test, used to test the airtightness of the building envelope.

HEATING, COOLING, VENTILATION, AND MOISTURE CONTROL

Space conditioning (heating, cooling, filtration, ventilation, and humidity control) equipment in a high-performance home is designed to efficiently meet the demands on the home and provide quiet and durable performance. These various tasks can be performed by one or multiple systems. As with other design choices, the optimum will depend on the climate, whole-house design, budget, and ability of homeowners to properly operate and maintain equipment.

Heating and cooling equipment is designed to meet the peak winter heating and summer cooling loads according to industry standards prescribed in ACCA Manual J. Computer software accounting for the entire building envelope, infiltration, duct system, and internal loads is used to calculate the loads. Rules of thumb for sizing equipment no longer apply to high-performance homes. If a larger than necessary system is installed, it will lose efficiency, will suffer premature failure due to constant on-and-off cycles (short cycling), and will not sufficiently dehumidify the home.

One of the functions of an air conditioner is to remove moisture from the air. This is called *latent cooling*. Because this occurs after the system has been running for 15 minutes or more, longer run times are an advantage for effective dehumidification and overall system efficiency. It is important to properly size the air conditioner to the specific needs for a home. Units that are too large cost more to buy and short-cycle, which cuts efficiency, degrades equipment life, and lessens dehumidification.

A critical design decision for the optimal performance of an HVAC system is in choosing the location of the system itself and the location of the ductwork or other distribution system. For forced-air systems, both the air handler and ductwork should be located inside the building envelope. This will protect the system from extremes of hot and cold such as can be experienced in an attic or crawl space and ensures that any air leaking from the system stays within the living space. Further, it is ideal to centrally locate the air handler so that the duct runs are short and straight. An attic with an insulated roofline, or a basement

High-performance homes are tight homes with little uncontrolled air infiltration. The air barrier stops air infiltration and allows the insulation to do its job of stopping heat conduction. High-performance homes dispel the common myth that tight homes are unhealthy and that leaky homes are desirable. With uncontrolled air leaks, the interior of a home is often too dry in winter and too humid in summer. Air leaks in standard homes often bring inside pollutants such as pesticides to treat termites, radon, and excess moisture, as well as allow a pathway for entry of insects and rodents.

Air infiltration is measured with a blower door test, where the house is depressurized using a calibrated fan and pressure gauge. A high-performance home would experience approximately 0.25 air changes per hour or less under natural conditions (ACH$_{nat}$) compared to typical standard construction of 0.50 ACH$_{nat}$ or greater. It is not uncommon for older, existing homes to experience more than one air change per hour. Fewer air changes mean less pollen, moisture, and pollutants are drawn in from outside. It also means less air that has been heated or cooled is being pushed out through cracks and gaps in the building envelope. The home is thus more energy efficient, has better indoor air quality, and is quieter.

Designers can either employ advanced products to achieve a tight building envelope or pay careful attention to detail with conventional products. Advanced products that consistently produce low blower door results when properly installed include spray-applied foam insulation, structural insulated panels (SIPs), and insulating concrete forms (ICFs). Using conventional stick framing and nonfoam cavity insulation, the builder must pay special attention to detail at each penetration, joint, and change in the plane of the framing and finish materials. Most homes certified in green building programs to date are stick-built, underscoring the importance of third-party verification for both the builder and homebuyer, to ensure that the home was built as specified.

or crawl space with insulated walls, can be an ideal space in which to locate an HVAC system.

Proper installation of the system is essential to proper function and occupant comfort. The air handler and ductwork must be permanently sealed so that conditioned air does not leak out. Even if the ductwork is inside conditioned space, the goal is to deliver conditioned air to a specific room, not to a space between floors or an attic. The best way to achieve a permanent seal is with duct mastic applied at the pressure boundary of each connection and with caulk between the HVAC boot and subfloor or drywall. These details can be specified in construction drawings. A duct pressure test (e.g., Duct Blaster) is used to measure duct leakage in green building programs to ensure that the systems were properly installed.

Duct design and installation is also critical to a comfortable and efficient home, and the home's design can facilitate an efficient duct layout. A home should be designed to minimize compression and turns in the ductwork. Open web trusses or other engineered floor systems with cutouts for ducts can greatly simplify installation. HVAC contractors should be encouraged to investigate high-performance duct systems such as those using high inside wall supplies and commercial grills, which are superior at mixing air within a room. An ACCA Manual D duct design, which incorporates all components of the duct system, including fittings and grills, will help ensure proper air delivery and occupant comfort. The DOE Building America program actively researches best practices for space conditioning, and the Web sites of the program technical teams are excellent resources for up-to-date information on the latest techniques and technologies.

HVAC efficiency plays a large role in the overall building efficiency and also has important implications for combustion safety. Furnace efficiency is rated by the Annualized Fuel Utilization Efficiency (AFUE). The lowest efficiency available today is 78 percent for a naturally drafted gas furnace. Choosing a unit with 90 percent or higher efficiency has the obvious benefit of reducing energy costs; it also has the important advantage that most higher-efficiency units are also sealed combustion. With a sealed com-

bustion furnace, outdoor air for combustion is brought in through a solid plastic pipe directly to the furnace, and flue gases are expelled directly out through a separate pipe. Flue gases do not mix with house air, and the vent pipes can be run horizontally out of the home rather than needing to go vertically up through a chase. This gives the designer and builder increased flexibility on equipment location and eliminates the potential need to build a combustion closet to separate a natural draft furnace from the living space.

Air conditioner efficiency is rated by the seasonal energy efficiency ratio (SEER), with a higher number being more efficient. There are many additional options available that also add to the efficiency of the systems. Higher-end air conditioners include dual-stage compressors, which contain a smaller compressor for the moderate load and a larger compressor for peak load. This type of system will run on the more efficient, smaller compressor most of the time and will dehumidify better. Electronically commutated motors (ECM) and variable-speed blowers can also contribute to increased efficiency in a properly designed and installed system.

The cooling efficiency for an air-source heat pump is the same as for an air conditioner. The heating efficiency for a heat pump is measured as the heating season performance factor (HSPF). Heat pumps manufactured after 2005 are required to have an HSPF of at least 7.7. The most efficient air-source heat pumps have an HSPF of 10.

A geothermal heat pump relies on pipe buried belowground where the temperatures are more stable. (Large bodies of water may be used instead of the ground to run the piping but are often not considered due to the ecological and environmental impacts of heating or cooling the water.) Water or another environment-friendly fluid circulates in the pipe. In winter, the earth temperature is warmer than the air temperature and the fluid collects heat. In summer, conversely, the temperature is lower and the fluid is cooled. The piping is connected to a special type of electric heat pump. On the inside of your home, a geothermal heat pump delivers heated and cooled air much like a standard heat pump or furnace and air conditioner. Most geothermal heat pumps

Green Building consultant doing a duct blaster test to check for leakage in the HVAC duct system.

Staff members of provider organizations, like the one from Southface Energy Institute shown here, perform services such as the predrywall inspection, helping builders make sure they haven't missed a detail such as caulking windows and doors.

also have a desuperheater, which can help provide hot water. Geothermal heat pumps have a higher installation cost than air source heat pumps but are more efficient and offer additional benefits.

Ductless minisplit systems are similar to heat pumps and air conditioners but the minisplits are commonly designed to handle smaller loads, making them ideal for bonus rooms and additions. They can also be very practical options on renovation projects. They consist of the outdoor compressor, with the indoor compressor being mounted on the wall in the room needing conditioning. There are no ducts to seal, so efficiency is often greater than with a ducted system. Today's models come in all shapes and sizes, making them very fashionable and functional.

Because high-performance homes are built tight, controlled ventilation should be used to mix indoor and outdoor air. Supply only, exhaust only, or balanced systems can be used, depending on climate zone and budget. In most cases, it is best to ventilate the home in a controlled manner such that fresh air is tempered and filtered before reaching the occupants. This follows the "seal it tight and ventilate it right" approach. The American Society of Heating, Refrigerating, and Air-Conditioning Engineers (ASHRAE) has issued guidelines for recommended ventilation rates depending on the size of the home and number of occupants. Common methods for achieving these goals are to use an energy recovery ventilator (ERV), in which both heat and humidity are exchanged, a heat recovery ventilator, in which heat is exchanged, or a controlled fresh-air intake into the forced-air HVAC system.

Spot ventilation is also critical in all homes, especially high-performance homes. Any area in which moisture is produced, such as showers, baths, laundry rooms, and kitchens, must have an exhaust fan ducted to the exterior of the home—not into crawl spaces or attics. Many fans are available with the ENERGY STAR designation, which will run efficiently and quietly. Fan noise is rated on *sones*, with a low rating being more quiet. Advanced controls can be added that will delay turning off the fan for a specified length of time, allowing for the bathroom to be completely dehumidified, or that will automatically turn on the fan when the humidity in a room reaches a certain level.[14] These and other such control strategies help to ensure that the spot ventilation effectively removes moisture and other contaminants from the home. Spot ventilation can also be used in attached garages to remove pollutants and prevent them from entering the home.

In humid areas, it may be wise to use additional dehumidifiers, which can be especially effective during the spring and fall when humidity is high but temperatures are moderate. On the other hand, activities of daily living, such as showering, cooking, and simply breathing, produce enough moisture that humidifiers should not be necessary in tight homes.

Filtration is a critical component of any forced-air system. The primary purpose of a standard 1-inch-thick filter is to protect the mechanical equipment from particulate contamination that could damage it or degrade efficiency. The secondary purpose is to clean the air for occupants to breathe. Filtration systems should be viewed as the last line of defense against pollutants, after attempting to eliminate, separate, and ventilate sources of poor indoor air quality. The most common measure of filter efficiency is the minimum efficiency reporting value (MERV). A MERV 8 filter or higher is considered high efficiency. Thicker, pleated filters (at least 3 inches) provide more surface area for air to pass through and generally result in lower pressure losses than 1-inch pleated filters, resulting in greater system efficiency. It is important that the filter be considered when performing the Manual D duct design because of the pressure drop across the filter.

WATER HEATING

Water heating is the second largest single use of energy after space conditioning in most homes. Most water-heating technologies can be described as either storage or on-demand. Efficiency is quantified by energy factor (EF), with a larger number being better. Traditional storage tank systems keep water warm all the time whether there is a need or not. On-demand systems do not store water, but heat it only when hot water is called for at a faucet or appliance. Homeowner education is critical for clients using on-demand systems that allow for endless use of hot water, as many report initial spikes in energy and water consumption due to unfamiliarity with the technology.

Domestic hot water can also be provided by highly efficient solar thermal systems used in conjunction with a storage tank. They are discussed in greater detail in the "Active Solar" section later in the chapter.

With any system, plumbing design plays an important role in energy and water efficiency and occupant satisfaction. Homeowners do not like to wait at the tap for hot water to arrive, and letting water run down the drain is a waste of both water and power. Plumbing systems should be designed such that the amount of water in the pipes between the water heat and fixture is minimized. The EPA WaterSense for Homes program requires this to be 0.38 gallons for manifold and core plumbing systems and 0.13 gallons for demand-initiated recirculating systems.[15] One type of system that should be avoided is a hotel-style recirculating system that recirculates hot water constantly, which can double the energy bill for heating water.

LIGHTS, APPLIANCES, AND MISCELLANEOUS ELECTRICAL LOADS

The remaining 40 percent of energy consumption in a typical home is composed of lighting, appliances, and miscellaneous electrical loads. As the building envelopes and mechanical systems of homes become more and more efficient and the home electronics market increases, this percentage is actually growing. It is important for designers and architects to specify systems that encourage homeowners to live high-performance lifestyles and to educate homeowners about the effects of their buying and living decisions on energy consumption.

ENERGY STAR appliances must meet energy and, if applicable, water efficiency standards in order to earn the mark. Specifying such appliances that will save 10 to 50 percent compared to standard models is a good first step. The EnergyGuide label provides more detailed test results, including estimated annual energy consumption and operating cost, which allow consumers to compare directly one appliance to another. ENERGY STAR–qualified appliances include clothes washers, refrigerators and freezers, dehumidifiers, dishwashers, and room air conditioners.

Lighting has a large effect on both an occupant's experience of a space and on energy consumption. Lighting design should take maximum advantage of natural light without overheating the building or causing glare, and also provide artificial light for specific tasks or when the sun is not shining. ENERGY STAR qualifies both light fixtures and lightbulbs, providing a familiar resource for energy-efficient products.

There are excellent choices for both tubular and compact fluorescent fixtures suitable for residential applications. Quality fluorescent bulbs, or lamps, have extended lives and provide excellent color rendition. Because they are used the most often, good choices for specifying energy-efficient lighting are the family and living rooms, kitchens, dining rooms, bedrooms, baths, and outdoors.

Energy-efficient T5 tubular fluorescents are often used in kitchens and baths and in light coves for area lighting. Compact fluorescents (CLFs) use approximately 75 percent less electricity than standard bulbs, generate 75 percent less heat, and last up to 10 times longer. Compact fluorescents are available with screw-in bases as well as pin-type bases for dedicated fixtures. The advantage of the dedicated CFL fixture is that the lamp can often be replaced without having to replace the ballast, and the fixture must be used with an efficient bulb.

Light-emitting diodes (LEDs) are an emerging efficiency option. In today's market, they are typically used for undercounter and other task lighting needs. LEDs are even used for ENERGY STAR-qualified decorative light strings, such as Christmas lights. LEDs are available in colors spanning the visible spectrum and can be hidden behind translucent building materials to create functional and artistic lighting displays.

In addition to the choice of lighting type, lighting controls play an important role in energy consumption. For instance, specifying motion-activated exterior lights will greatly decrease the amount of time that exterior lights are on while still ensuring security of the home. Inside the home, a variety of lighting controls can be used. Many rooms would benefit from vacancy sensor controls that require an occupant to turn on the light, but will turn off automatically if there is no occupant in the room for a specified period of time. Using dimmers is another way to decrease energy consumption. If dimmers are used, realize that special dimmable CFLs must be used in these fixtures.

Miscellaneous electrical loads are a growing portion of the energy consumption pie as homeowners add to the number of electronics and chargers within homes. These devices consume energy even when most people consider them to be turned off because they power clocks, monitor satellite or online broadcasts, or draw current into chargers even with no device attached. There are ENERGY STAR-qualified products available in nearly every category of home and office electronics to make choosing more efficient models easier. Newer technologies and controls are being developed that can completely shut off power to certain circuits when not in use to obviate these "vampire loads." It is wise to design entertainment centers so that individual components, such as televisions, DVD players, and stereo equipment, can plug into a single power strip that is easy to flip off when equipment is not in use.

INDOOR ENVIRONMENTAL QUALITY

In the past several years, the U.S. Environmental Protection Agency (EPA) has detailed a growing body of scientific evidence indicating that the air within homes and other buildings can be two to five times more polluted than outdoor air in even the most industrialized cities. Additional research indicates that people spend approximately 90 percent of their time indoors. Thus, for many people, there can be an increased health risk from exposure to air pollution indoors versus outdoors.

Because the house is a system, nearly every design and construction decision has an impact on indoor environmental quality, many of which have been discussed already, such as air sealing, space conditioning, and spot ventilation. There are several additional areas in which architects and designers can significantly impact indoor air quality.

Moisture Management

Excess moisture can pose significant health risks by contributing to mold growth, dust mites, and other problems. Mold needs relative humidity (RH) levels—a measure of the amount of moisture in the air relative to temperature—above 70 percent to become established, and dust mites require RH greater than 50 percent. Relative humidity ranges from 30 to 50 percent are ideal for human health and deter most biological pollutants from becoming established.

The most effective strategy for maintaining healthy interior RH is to prevent outside moisture, in the form of groundwater, precipitation, and humidity, from entering the home; to vent sources of interior moisture such as baths and kitchens to the exterior of the home; to provide controlled, whole-house ventilation; and to install dehumidification equipment in humid climates.

Moisture management of the building envelope to keep groundwater and precipitation from entering the home is critical. Most interior moisture problems result from poor moisture management outside the home. A comprehensive moisture management system, designed for the local climate, soil type, and building materials used, should be specified on the construction documents. From the roof to the foundation, all components of the building envelope should be designed to drain water out and away from the home.

Moisture management begins at the site planning stage of construction. Soils should be tested and amended to ensure proper drainage, and all grading should slope soil away from the foundation. Most sites will require a foundation drainage system. For below-grade walls, a drainage board and waterproof coatings should be installed that connect with the foundation drain. Typical dampproofing coatings are not sufficient to prevent moisture from penetrating below-grade walls. Do not connect gutters to foundation drainage systems. Direct water collected by gutters away from the home, or collect the water in a properly designed rainwater cistern for reuse.

To prevent soil moisture from being wicked by capillarity into a concrete slab, it is important to use a sub-slab gravel bed. To further increase moisture protection, plastic sheathing can be installed on top of the gravel. The gravel and plastic also help prevent radon and other soil gases from entering the home. Capillary breaks should also be installed between the footer and foundation and between the foundation wall and sill plate.

Protecting exterior walls and fenestrations (doors and windows) from moisture has challenged design professionals for centuries. Time-tested basics such as wide roof overhangs and head flashing above windows and doors are critical first steps. There are also a variety of new sheathings, sealants, and other products that are effective at preventing moisture penetration into the building envelope.

Weather-resistive barriers can protect exterior wall systems from water penetration. These barriers perform like a shell for buildings—liquid water that has penetrated the exterior finish does not pass through, yet water vapor inside the wall can escape. By keeping building materials dry, a weather-resistive barrier improves building durability, decreases maintenance costs, and reduces the risk of moisture-related decay from insects and mold.

Building paper is a traditional barrier, typically made from a paper or felt material that is asphalt coated to increase its strength and resistance to water penetration. It is primarily employed to protect against moisture as a drainage layer. House-wrap refers to spun-plastic sheet materials that cover exterior walls to protect against moisture penetration. In some wall systems, sealed insulating sheathing such as rigid foam board can serve as the weather-resistive barrier, eliminating any need for building paper or housewrap.

As part of a whole-wall design, weather-resistive barriers need to be integrated with other wall system components, including framing structure, insulation, vapor retarder (if used), air retarder (if separate), and flashing systems. For added protection, consider a vented rain screen to provide an airspace between the exterior finish material and the wall framing. The airspace prevents water from being wicked from the backside of the exterior finish to the framing. Standard brick veneer provides a vented rain screen. Advanced products are available that combine the functionality of the weather-resistive barrier and vented rain screen, or the rain screen can be created with furring strips.

Choosing quality windows and doors that are weather-resistant is an important element of healthy building design. The units must also be properly installed. Flashing rough openings prior to installing windows and doors is critical. Ensure that the flashing aligns with the weather-resistance barrier for the exterior walls so that water is shed away from the structure. Improper flashing and treatment of rough openings is a frequent cause of moisture damage to building envelopes.

Flashing at the roof edge and for penetrations is also critical to moisture management. Best practices such as drip edge, flashing boots for penetrations, and step flashing can prevent moisture problems. While it is important to ensure a watertight seal from the exterior, the roof assembly should be able to dry from the inside out in the event that moisture condenses on the underside of the roof decking.

Radon-Resistant Construction

Radon is an odorless, tasteless, invisible radioactive gas that occurs naturally in some soils and groundwater. Radon is produced by the breakdown (radioactive decay) of uranium in soil, rock, and water. The Surgeon General has warned that radon is the second leading cause of lung cancer in the United States today. As radon seeps from soils or groundwater it mixes with outdoor air and its health risk is greatly reduced. However, air pressure inside the home is usually lower than pressure in the soil around the home's foundation, which tends to draw radon and other soil gases into the home, where it is concentrated and can pose a serious health risk.[16] The EPA estimates that as many as 1 in 15 homes has elevated annual radon levels. Radon problems have been identified in every state. The EPA has determined the risk of exposure to radon for every county in the U.S. and ranks that risk by Zone 1 through 3, with Zone 1 posing the greatest risk.[17]

At the same time radon can pose a serious health risk, it also is easy to minimize exposure to building occupants through inexpensive radon-resistant construction practices. Several of the moisture management measures discussed in the previous section offer protection against radon and other harmful soil gases. In addition, an inexpensive insurance policy against radon is to install a passive below-grade venting system at the time of construction. Using plastic piping, a vent is run from the sub-slab gravel drainage bed through the plastic vapor barrier and vertically up through the roof of the home. The penetrations in the slab, as well as all connections in the pipe, are made airtight. The natural stack effect of warm air rising will tend to depressurize the area under the vapor barrier and draw soil gases up. The home can be tested for radon gas once occupied. If radon levels are found to be high, a low-wattage fan can be added to the soil gas vent to actively draw the gas out of the soil and vent it from the home. The passive system can be installed during construction for as little as $100, compared to up to $2,500 to mitigate an existing home.

Volatile Organic Compounds

Some chemicals commonly found inside homes can be hazardous to human health at high concentrations. Volatile organic compounds (VOCs) are a category of chemicals that vaporize under normal conditions and can enter the lungs. VOCs are emitted by a wide variety of construction products, including paints, sealants, adhesives, finishes, wood preservatives, cleaning supplies, pesticides, interior furnishings, and even some building materials. Perhaps the greatest risk from VOCs is to the installer. It is important to be in a well-ventilated area while using products known to contain VOCs and to ventilate areas where products containing the compounds are being stored. Today, there are many low- or no-VOC products available.

Passive Solar Design

Passive solar design is one strategy for taking maximum advantage of the free energy provided to the home year-round by the sun, while providing beautiful connections to the outdoors and plenty of natural light. The home is designed and constructed to run energy efficiently, to be warmed by the sun during the heating season, and to be moderated by high thermal mass and proper ventilation during the cooling season. Passive solar homes are designed with the local climate, landscape, and topography in mind—using seasonal temperatures, humidity, wind, and solar radiation to determine the site, orientation, vegetation, floor plan, and overall building layout and materials.

The primary features of passive solar design are:

- *Energy-efficient design*: Like all sustainably designed homes, energy-efficient building envelope and systems are critical to the proper functioning of a passive solar home. Energy efficiency should always be the first step in passive solar design.

- *Orientation and site selection*: The major window area must face within 30 degrees of due south to maximize solar gain in the winter and minimize overheating in summer. Deciduous trees can provide shade and help reduce summer cooling loads, but should not shade south-facing windows in winter.

- *Increased south-facing glass area*: Solar radiation entering the home through south-facing glazing provides a significant portion of winter space heating. South-facing windows receive about three times as much sunlight as east and west windows in the winter and one-third less sunlight in the summer.

- *Reduced east and west glass area*: East and west glazing contributes significantly to summer cooling loads. North glazing allows for natural light year-round without posing a significant penalty in the cooling season. A combination of north- and south-facing glazing offers the best strategy for daylighting and cross ventilation.

- *Thermal storage mass*: Materials such as concrete floors, interior concrete or masonry walls, and tile are used to store heat and modulate interior temperatures in both winter and summer.

- *Effective window shading and ventilation*: Latitude-appropriate window shading and ventilation reduce summer cooling loads while allowing winter heat gain.

- *Moisture control systems*: In most climates, a moisture control strategy is used to increase durability, indoor environmental quality, and occupant comfort throughout the year.

- *Heat distribution*: Because passive heating occurs on the south side of the home, a heat distribution system can be used to deliver comfort to the rest of the rooms. Simple designs provide for an open floor plan that allows solar heated room air to flow by natural convection from the south to the rest of the home. Low-speed fans and blowers can augment convection. Locating day-use rooms on the south side of the home takes maximum advantage of the solar heat when it is generated.

These components can be combined as a system in various configurations. It is critical to understand how the system works in order to ensure that the goals of year-round comfort and energy efficiency are being met when making design choices.

During the winter months heating season, three primary elements interact to provide a significant portion of the home's heating needs:

- Energy-efficient design and installation reduces the overall heating needs on the home.

- Increased vertical south-facing glazing allows additional solar radiation into the home, which can be captured as heat energy.

- Thermal storage mass can provide a means to store heat inside the home and moderate the temperature once the sun has set.

During the summer months cooling season, a passive solar home must compensate for the hot, sometimes humid, outside climate and large amount of heat that can come into the home through windows throughout the day. The true challenge of passive solar design is to ensure low summer cooling bills compared to a similar standard home by incorporating.

- Energy-efficient design and installation reduces the overall cooling needs on the home.

- Few, if any, east- and west-facing windows reduce cooling loads.

- Latitude-specific shading for south-facing windows minimizes solar gain.

- Large thermal mass reduces midday temperatures.

- Operable windows and fans ventilate the home during mild weather.

There are four basic types of passive solar designs. The most common is the Direct Gain System in which the living area collects solar energy and stores it in floors or walls made of concrete of other masonry materials.

Understanding the following basic principles can drive design decisions for room layout within the home:

- *Day-use rooms*: Breakfast rooms, sunrooms, and playrooms work well on the south side of the house. They should adjoin rooms that are used frequently to take full advantage of solar heating.

- *Frequently used rooms (morning to bedtime)*: Family rooms, kitchens, dens, and dining rooms work well on the south side. Be conscious of potential problems with glare from sunlight through large expanses of windows.

- *Sunspaces*: These rooms can be isolated from the house if unconditioned. In winter, the doors can be opened to let solar heat move into the home. At night, the doors can be closed, and the sunspace buffers the home against the cold night air. In summer, sunspaces protect the home from outside heat gain; for best performance, they should not be air conditioned.

- *Privacy rooms*: Bathrooms and dressing rooms can be connected to the solar-heated areas, but are not usually located on the south side since large windows are not desirable on most sites.

- *Night-use rooms*: Bedrooms are usually best on the north side, unless used often during the day (such as a child's bedroom). It is often difficult to fit thermal storage mass into bedrooms, and privacy needs may limit opportunities for installing large glass areas. However, some household members may prefer bedrooms filled with natural light, which can use passive solar features effectively.

- *Seldom-used rooms*: Formal living rooms, dining rooms, and extra bedrooms are best on the north side, out of the traffic pattern and airflow.

- *Buffer rooms*: Unheated spaces such as closets, laundries, workshops, pantries, and garages work best against the north, east, or west exterior walls to protect the conditioned space from outside temperature extremes.

- *Exterior covered areas*: Porches and carports on the east and west provide summer shading. However, west-facing porches may be uncomfortable in the afternoon. Avoid porches on the south side, as they shade winter sunlight. In addition, second-floor decks over south-facing windows will usually shade first-floor passive solar windows in winter.

Successful passive solar designs apply the whole-house approach to strike a balance between seemingly competing demands. Additional features can be incorporated into the home that serve both functional and aesthetic roles. Internal and external louvers can be used to shade glazing, diffuse light as it enters the space, and create a design statement. Light shelves, which bounce daylight upward toward the ceiling and deeper into a living space, increase the effectiveness of daylighting strategies.

Active Solar

Active solar systems include solar thermal (hot water and air) and photovoltaics (solar electric). Technological improvements and government and utility incentives[18] are driving down the costs of these systems, but they are both more expensive than designing and building an energy-efficient home in the first place.

Solar thermal systems circulate water, air, or another environmentally friendly fluid through a heat collector that is exposed to the sun. The most common solar thermal systems provide domestic water heating where the solar-heated fluid is either used directly or the heat is exchanged with potable water. Solar thermal systems generally use a storage tank and require freeze protection in most parts of the United States. These systems tend to be the more cost-effective of the two solar technologies. Solar thermal can also be used to heat water for a pool or hot tub.

Photovoltaic (PV) cells turn solar radiant energy into electricity. PV cells are combined into solar panels, which are typically 1 to 2 feet wide by 2 to 4 feet long. Panels are then assembled into arrays. Systems are sized by the number of kilowatts (kW) produced and typically quantified in terms of kW per square foot of panel. A modest-sized PV array, producing 2 kW of electricity at peak sun, would measure about 200 square feet. An array to power a typical new home would need to produce approximately 10 kW and would measure about 1000 square feet. A PV array should be oriented to within 15 degrees of due south with at least six hours of unobstructed daylight per day.

The solar-generated electricity can be used directly in the home, stored in a battery, or fed back into the electrical grid. Electric utilities will often buy back power from rate payers, sometimes at an even higher rate than they sell it. Many states and local governments and utilities offer incentives for both solar thermal and solar electric systems. In addition, there are currently federal incentives for solar technologies. Current information on energy efficiency tax credits is available from the Database of State Incentives for Renewables and Efficiency (www.dsireusa.org).

PV arrays are available in various forms, from solar shingles, which can be integrated with asphalt shingles, to thin films, which can be adhered, to metal roofs to traditional panels. Building-integrated PV in which a building component such as glazing actually generates electricity is also available and presents interesting design options.

More information on solar technologies and renewable energy can be found through the American Solar Energy Society (ASES), a national nonprofit dedicated to increasing the use of solar energy, energy efficiency, and other sustainable technologies in the United States.

Wind

Wind energy is a source of renewable power that comes from air current flowing across the earth's surface. Wind turbines harvest this kinetic energy and convert it into usable power, which can provide electricity for home, farm, school, or business applications on small (residential) or large (utility) scales.

Wind energy is one of the fastest-growing sources of electricity and one of the fastest-growing markets in the world today. These growth trends can be linked to the multidimensional benefits associated with wind energy.

Like other renewable energy resources, wind power should be applied once all consideration has been made to reducing the energy loads of a home. While wind is currently the cheapest source of renewable electricity for large-scale power generation, few individual homes install wind turbines. Optimum wind turbine sites have an average wind speed of 12 miles per hour or greater, at a minimum height of 30 feet. Because the power produced by a turbine is exponentially related to the speed of the wind, higher wind speeds can have dramatic effects on power production. For example, increasing the wind from 12 mph to 20 mph increases the power available by a factor of 4.6. ($12 \times 12 \times 12 = 1{,}728$, $20 \times 20 \times 20 = 4{,}913$). Likewise, turbulence created by objects around the turbine can have a large impact on power production. Ideal sites have no obstructions within a 500-foot radius of the turbine. Additional information on wind technologies can be found through the American Wind Energy Association (AWEA).

Summary

Architects and designers of green, modern homes use the whole-house approach to create energy-efficient, comfortable, and beautiful living spaces for their clients. By incorporating sustainable design principles at every stage of the design and build process and winning buy-in from all team members, significant synergies can be achieved. Understanding how the house functions as a system, where energy and water are used in a home, and the effects of various design decisions on overall home function are the first steps toward meeting the critical and ambitious goals laid out by the 2030 Challenge, DOE Building America, and others. Resources and technologies are available, including high-performance green building programs with stringent testing and verification requirements, to aid designers, builders, and homeowners toward a more sustainable future.

MATERIALS FOR THE MODERN HOME

5

■ James Burton, AIA, and William Carpenter, FAIA, PhD

Introduction to Modern and Sustainable

Within the context of the modern house, materials form an integral part of the architect's vision. Materials reinforce the architect's ideas by expressing them through thoughtful assembly. Since the start of the modern movement in the early twentieth century, architects have used materials in expressive and experimental ways. Frank Lloyd Wright advanced the production of concrete textile blocks by inventing an entirely new wall system. He also created a new roofing membrane using horsehair and tar, which failed. Mies van der Rohe was an expert in materials selection; for the Barcelona Pavilion, he carefully chose and book-matched the stone panels. Charles and Ray Eames experimented with steam-bending plywood for the Herman Miller Company and then used the material in their furniture designs. This tradition of expression and experimentation continues today with architects such as Herzog & de Meuron, Pugh + Scarpa, and Office dA, Inc.

The modern design elite did not deliberately develop a sustainable understanding of materials. Although they were aware of regional and indigenous material practices, they also experimented with the new. They built on the basics of dealing with gravity, wind, sun, and water, using strategies that have been around for centuries,

even millennia. With the introduction of new materials such as modern steel and insulated glass, architects began to examine the proportion of solid and void relationships. The first glass box house would not, by today's standards, be considered sustainable. This is the paradox of the modern choice: to use time-tested materials in new and effective ways, use new materials in rational ways, or to blend the best of both. These three general categories will always be available and all can nurture sustainable design to some degree.

MEANING OF THE MATERIAL

Appearing on the political TV show *Meet the Press* late in his life, the renowned poet Robert Frost was asked if he had one message for the world and, if so, what would it be? He responded, "Mankind needs to deal more with the material." With this simple statement, Mr. Frost pointed out the obvious: You cannot talk about "the material" without talking about materials. It suggests that the manmade and the natural must coexist in harmony. Any discussion about sustainable and modern design also requires an exhaustive study of how raw materials are chosen, shaped, installed, and appreciated over time. They form our protective shells, spend or save energy, and represent our place on earth at any given time.

Humans perceive materials in so many ways. Is the material light or dark? Does it feel like warmth or coolness, softness or permanence? These ways of defining materials add to our personalization of the places we inhabit; more, such

We are seeing the beginnings of a movement away from synthetic materials—those that rely on human manipulation—to naturally manufactured materials—those that utilize organic systems for their production. Biopolymers are a successful foray into this field. Let us hope that this trend continues and that we can again work with nature rather than against it in our quest for innovation.

ANDREW H. DENT, PhD,
Vice President, Library and Materials
Research, Material ConneXion, Inc.

human connections with materials tell a story about the people of a place and their beliefs. They may choose a universal logic that can be used anywhere in a unsentimental way, or they may want a custom-fit for themselves and their context—the region and site-specific conditions. It is rare for a client to allow an architect to choose materials for their structure without his or her input. Materials serve a very personal role in shaping the places we inhabit and in expressing who we are to the outside world. It is best for the client and the architect to have similar tastes when it comes to choosing the materials for a project.

During the postmodern movement in the early 1980s, meaning was brought back to the forefront of architecture, but somehow materiality was not. The movement could not bring integrity to material details. Materials such as the exterior insulation finish system (EIFS) provided a superficial representation of the architect's ideas. But material thoughts are complex. A noted professor and architect from Jackson, Mississippi, Christopher Risher, once said, "One reason to use natural materials is that they require maintenance, and how neighbors repair or maintain the surfaces creates a contagious pride that defines place as others are motivated to do the same." Then, ten years later, he said, "The modern condition requires thought about promoting maintenance-free materials that give a homeowner time to live a life away from the drudgery and expense of maintaining exterior surfaces." This apparent contradiction was probably related to industry trends and economic developments. Both statements and the change in material trends have validity by showing how the decisions concerning materials are important, but difficult to make and so require patient thought. Clearly, the selection of materials is affected by time, trends, and outside opinion. Adding sustainability as a factor to the mix makes it even more complicated. Refreshingly, Stephan Kieran and James Timberlake, in their book *Refabricating Architecture: How Manufacturing Methodologies Are Poised to Transform Building Construction* (New York: McGraw-Hill Professional, 2003), encourage designers to use meaningful and complex materials and assemblies, which are grounded in sustainable thinking.

Modernizing the choice of materials allows for greater flexibility by offering more choices. At the same time, making buildings sustainable adds a rigor and restraint more complicated than any factor ever before faced by the design process. This generates an essentialism based on environmental and functional efficiency while also opening the door to whimsical beauty. Consider a façade made of recycled road signs or license plates that is both environmentally conscientious and "fun." Humans will always require diversity and change in their surroundings, and this can be expressed to the greatest extent in materials. Thus, a mantra for the new modern and sustainable aesthetic might be: Reduce, reuse (renew), and recycle.

THE MOMENTUM BEHIND SUSTAINABLE MATERIALS

Advances in sustainable materials and construction practices are being made every day, driven by economic motivators to improve the places we inhabit. Sustainable is taking on a momentum; and hopefully, it will become an everyday part of practice accepted simply as good construction practices, versus bad. In some cases "green" has already become defined as legal versus illegal, evidenced for example by the required elimination of lead paint and arsenic-treated wood throughout the building community. Will fiberglass blanket insulation be next? Some of these decisions guiding change have to be made from the top down. Pressure has to come from the design community in order to overcome the big-money lobbies. Thanks to the need for these innovations in the design community, green products and materials continue to evolve.

The ultimate goal of sustainable design, lofty but possible, is twofold: first, to build carbon-neutral structures with low-maintenance, sustainable, long-lasting materials that are both affordable and ensure healthy air quality; second, to create an aesthetic appeal lenders are comfortable with, to ensure needed financing will be provided. As architects succeed in building houses that attain these goals, society will come to appreciate a new aesthetic driven by material and technological advances—one that finds a harmony of function with beauty, representing an evolving zeitgeist. Modern use of materials, driven by necessity, will ultimately be accepted.

The purpose of this chapter is not to tell designers how to invoke change in a client or, indeed, an entire community, because each region is different and faces individual conditions that must be considered. Rather, the purpose is to encourage both architects and clients to become well informed before making difficult yet inspired decisions on materials.

General Categories of Sustainability

Designers will need to address myriad issues in determining which materials are sustainable. In fact, in determining whether a material is sustainable or not, they should investigate every aspect of the material. To begin, what is the material made of? Good, healthy choices are those that do not offgas in the building after construction, and usually contain no volatile organic compounds (VOCs) or added formaldehydes. Materials made from recycled or recyclable materials are obvious choices.

The next factor to consider is the performance of the material. How does it transmit or reflect light, heat, water, or energy? Does it generate energy? Next is the functionality and aesthetics of the material, which contributes directly to its longevity and cultural significance. A material that requires little or no maintenance is important in our busy, modern world; but employing a toxic finish to achieve this end would not mean anyone's definition of sustainable.

Finally, it is wise to ask questions that extend beyond the material itself. For example: Does the company that produces the material follow sustainable practices? What is the manufacturing standard for the material? Is the material easily fabricated or installed by local trades, thereby reducing shipping emissions?

The most comprehensive definition of sustainable materials will combine the best of these attributes without adding major negative aspects to the building, its inhabitants, the site, or the overall environment.

MATERIAL ENERGY
AND LONGEVITY

Determining the amount of energy a material saves or expends in its creation or life cycle is one criterion for evaluating its sustainability. *Embedded energy* (a.k.a. embodied energy) is the amount of energy required to allocate the raw material, fabricate the usable product, ship it from its point of manufacture to its final location, and installation. In general, low embedded energy for a material usually represents a good, sustainable material.

Another way to consider embedded energy of a material is to examine its longevity. For example, a brick may have a high level of embedded energy, but it is low maintenance, has a long life cycle, and can be easily reused in other projects if a building is taken down.

At this time, it still takes considerable research to discover the true embedded energy of a material, but this should become easier over time as sustainable practices become more widespread.

CULTURAL SIGNIFICANCE
OF MATERIALS

One of the most important yet least discussed aspects of sustainability is the cultural implications that materials and their details have in defining "place." It is indisputable, for example, that the colored plasters and stuccos of Venice produce a special quality when enhanced by the reflected light from the surrounding waters there. Or consider how brick comes to mind at the mention of Thomas Jefferson's Monticello. Similarly, the bright colors on the "painted ladies" in San Francisco, and the coastal structures in Key West, evoke the quality of light inherent in those places—a quality that would be impossible to achieve in, say, Buffalo, New York, or Milwaukee, Wisconsin.

Unfortunately, there is no magic bullet when it comes to identifying the ideal sustainable material for a given purpose; and the process is never ending, for the technology of materials will continue to evolve, meaning that architects will always have to synthesize new material inventions with existing norms. Using regional materials in a new way, or blending universal materials and

details, has always indicated the direction modern design is heading. The shift between regional expressions and a universal truth is a cultural debate that need not be settled; rather, it should be ongoing, as it is human nature to want both—stone, brick, stucco, and wood-lap siding, as well as glass, concrete, steel, and metal panels. The drive for a universal perfection, coupled with the restraint necessary when working with time-tested tactics, can produce ways of incorporating materials in order to express what the architect is hoping to achieve, even at these polar extremes. Materials can aid the architect in finding a successful hybrid of these two attitudes.

Highly regarded architect Louis Kahn once asked, "What does the brick want to be?" This inductive way of approaching design implies materials selection is the driver of form and style. Materials have intrinsic qualities to the occupants of a place. For example, it is generally understood that wood is "warm" and that glass, steel, and concrete are "cool." New materials, such as panels made from recycled polyethylene, have a quality that has yet to be determined, by the context they are placed in and a culture's judgment of it. Architects and designers will be instrumental in helping define the values of new materials as they become available and are tested in real-world applications. How we shape and use these new materials will determine whether they are modern or sustainable, or both; but without question it is a modern concept to allow materials to inspire new directions in design. Every time a new material or product becomes available, modern designers will contribute to the design implications of that material as they find new performance characteristics for it in their buildings. New materials gain resonance as they inspire designers around the world, who then share their experiences and the lessons they learn.

THE IMPORTANCE OF EDUCATION
IN MATERIALS EXECUTION

Teaching materials execution in a modern and sustainable way may be the first movement where a trend toward "all things new" can actually help significantly improve the human condition. The

process of choosing, detailing, and installing materials has followed a continuum of academic and field-based logic. Integrating a new layer of physical analysis to this process to reach a modern sustainable classification can only improve the condition in which the material is placed. Many movements in design after the early- and mid-nineteenth-century modern ignored the importance of materials and construction, particularly in postmodern and deconstruction design. This failure inspired what came to be called design/build educational programs to help students understand the connections among gravity, sun, weather, and the built environment.

Now, sustainability has come to the forefront of education, combined with teaching technology in architecture. The education process can still blend a grassroots understanding of materials with the canons of design analysis. The discussion of sustainable and modern design will only be enhanced and become richer by combining the analysis of materials with the philosophies of modern design practice. This new movement—modern sustainable—will be founded on how materials are made and put in place. In this way, student education, in conjunction with continuing education for professionals, will expand the knowledge base, to, ultimately, integrate sustainability into design discussions at all levels.

We must understand our place in nature. This is ever more difficult today when most of us are so plugged into our electronic devices we are losing touch with the natural world. Materials can help us achieve that all-important balance with nature. One of the original sustainable traditions was to use local, handmade products that incorporated natural materials. There is still room today for craft in modern design, but affordability and quality control lead most designers to choose mass-produced materials and products.

MASS PRODUCTION
VERSUS HANDCRAFTING

Many proponents of modern design have embraced the Japanese sensibility of honesty, integrity, and a connection with nature. In her book *Nature, Form & Spirit: The Life and Legacy of George Nakashima* (Harry N. Abrams, 2003),

Mira Nakashima eloquently expresses the struggle of her father, George, to create art from natural materials. Mr. Nakashima was an architect and furniture maker who, in his early years, worked for Antonin Raymond, the representative of Frank Lloyd Wright in Japan. Raymond's influence on Wright can be seen in his wood construction and spartan functionalism that stems from the Japanese aesthetic. During the Mingei movement, Nakashima exemplified the handmade of the Soetsu Yanagis Mingei movement, the creation of art for life. In response to the computer era of design, which he believed led to overproduction and "mountains of garbage," Nakashima was an early promoter of a sustainable approach to design, which dictated that machinery be used only for rough work and that hand tools be used for finish work.

The book also describes the efforts of Soetsu Yanagis's son, Sori, to understand and come to terms with the need for product and material affordability. Currently, Sori makes models by hand, which are then mass produced. Mira Nakashima makes the connection to a more Corbusian and Bauhaus approach to design and craft—that is, the efficient machine versus the original handcrafted piece. Perhaps, in the future,

Opposite page: In the Carter residence, built for Amy Carter, daughter of former president Jimmy Carter by Lightroom Studio, the new studio was the final phase in the design process and was developed largely by using digital fabrication techniques and three-dimensional modeling created by Tim Nichols, AIA.

Left: Rear view of the Carter residence from the garden.

Below: Roof terrace view from the Carter home, showing the stair volume and partial green roof and bocce court.

we may see a successful hybrid of the hand-crafted and the mass produced, one that allows for affordability and quality control yet maintains the beauty of the original.

In the book mentioned earlier in the chapter, *Refabricating Architecture: How Manufacturing Methodologies Are Poised to Transform Building Construction*, Kieran and Timberlake take the controversy down to its essence, saying, "Hand-craft was once the tool of commodity, but today it is the machine that is the tool of commodity." Using the construction of cars and airplanes as an example, they go on to suggest that prefabricating modules and components in controlled environments may be the answer now, or in the near future, to a durable and superefficient universal aesthetic that reaches beyond a local "feel." This would be as revolutionary as the modern movement in the transformation of our factories.

Currently, we reap the benefits of mass-produced paneling, cabinets, and other items like hardware, enabling us to increase efficiency in the construction industry. More specifically, taking the cabinet industry as an example, it uses a very effective method to build, which utilizes 3-inch increments for stock cabinets. This eliminates the need for filler pieces to fit individual kitchen sizes, thereby reducing overall waste and cutting down time in the field for installation. However, these sizes don't work for everyone, so semicustom cabinets are produced as a way to address the increment problem while offering more options for components. Moreover, high-level cabinetry makes it possible for homeowners to take their cabinets with them as they move from home to home.

When examining this manufacturing issue from a broader view, we see a shift toward mass production of prefab houses. From a limited catalogue of options, featuring fixed-price products with few extras, usually based on upgrades or difficult site conditions, clients can order an entire house from a factory. So we can already begin to see the construction industry being transformed by mass production. There are many possibilities for this efficient system.

THE IMPLICATIONS OF "DOING THE RIGHT THING"

More and more businesses today seek to incorporate environmental conscientiousness in the production of their sustainable materials. Like many aspects in surrounding the issue of sustainability, this is a new and complicated concept. Take the SJ Morse Company, for one, providers of plywood paneling for many LEED-certified projects. Steven Morse, the son of a Colorado architect, has been touting the benefits of promoting a diverse use of sustainably harvested wood veneers from South America. (Wood remains the primary renewable resource used to build with on the planet.) He explains that in the past only a few types of woods were desirable, resulting in the clear-cutting of forests to obtain those species; thereafter, the land was used for farming. But by adding more trees to the list of "desirables," Morse points out, the locals in South America are better able to make a living because of the increase in quantity based on diversity. Morse's company also specializes in veneers that utilize the most parts of the tree, which are then applied to a variety of surfaces, including wheatboard cores, medite, marine-grade plywood, and lightweight geo core, that help to ensure healthy indoor air quality. Distributing the raw veneers in

this process requires more energy but sustainable harvesting of these other types of trees adds value to the land and encourages the farmers to fight the pressures to clear-cut the land. Yes, the cost is high but the rewards come in the natural beauty of the products, a high level of quality control, and socially correct practices.

Another way to incorporate sustainable policies and to drive real change in the green products business is to consider the makeup of the workforce of a company—for example, by specifying healthy and sustainable materials made by a company owned by minorities or women. One such company, Yolocolorhouse (www.yolocolorhouse.com), owned entirely by women, produces paints in a modern color palette that help to warm or soften a modern style, or to provide a minimalist "punch" when color is needed.

Standards and Certification Organizations

In offering a guide to standards organizations, it is important to understand the value of each certifying group, considering both its positives and negatives. Some of these agencies are funded by certain technologies, others are supported by industry, and still others are completely independent. It is also important to keep in mind the interests of these groups and to stay abreast of changes in their positions. Breakthroughs in research and economic pressures affect everyone's decision-making process, and all groups will experience growing pains, which ideally will improve their grading systems over time. But no matter how comprehensive the standards become, there should always be enough flexibility to allow for the freedom that good design requires.

Of course, designers should also rely on their own judgment in choosing materials. But what the certification process offers is the ability to assure clients that their project has been analyzed by an outside source that declared it to be sustainable. This avoids the problem of "greenwashing," where a person declares a product to

be sustainable but cannot or will not provide proof for this declaration. In short, certification aids both the consumer and the designer to reassure that the product is, in fact, sustainable.

All architects, designers, and contractors should familiarize themselves with the following five organizations:

- *Leadership in Energy and Environmental Design (LEED)*: LEED is a green building rating system developed by the U.S. Green Building Council (USGBC; www.usgbc.org). LEED certification started as a public building rating system and is now offered for a collection of building types, including residential projects. The comprehensive rating system is voluntary and focuses on strategies for site development, water savings, energy efficiency, materials selection, and indoor environmental air quality. The downside of this system is that it is costly, sometimes adding $4000 to $10,000 for documentation, testing, and validation of strategies. The design strategies alone usually, but not always, add to the cost of a project. One failure of LEED is that, to date, it does not focus on the cultural significance of materials and details. It does raise interesting questions, however, for example, when it penalizes a project for using wood as an aesthetic, nonstructural adornment. LEED might also be criticized for a lack of attention to the overall energy usage of the finished building. In sum, LEED is a friendly process open to all, even to those new to the sustainable movement, which helps popularize the green movement without setting the bar too high too quickly. Over time, LEED will need some adjustments and updating if it is to continue to be effective.

- *Cradle to Cradle*: This certification system, administered by the McDonough Braungart Design Chemistry (www.mbdc.com), reviews materials for the overall life-cycle impact. Its goal is to encourage the use of closed-loop materials or those easily composted or may provide fuel for other systems when a material's original use is over. Founders William McDonough and Dr. Michael Braungart have set higher-level goals for material energy cycles, which has come to be known as cradle-to-cradle analysis. The idea that materials could have almost endless usefulness, even in the decomposition phases, is radical and noteworthy. For it to be implemented on a widespread basis would, however, necessitate a complete overhaul of the construction industry, which, needless to say, would be a slow process as very few businesses today produce materials that meet this standard.

- *Energy Star*: Energy Star (www.energystar.gov) is a rating system regulated by the Environmental Protection Agency and the Department of Energy. This system has become widely recognized by consumers as validating the energy efficiency of appliances and other products. Now the program is being expanded to include homes—testing airtightness, energy efficiency, and insulation values of the entire home. This has real possibilities in the builder's market: to be able to offer inexpensively built homes that also offer value to the owner after move-in.

- *Forest Stewardship Council (FSC)*: The FSC (www.fsc.org/en) is an independent nonprofit group that promotes third-party certification of sustainably managed forests. Its certification rating system is based on management practices in three areas: harvesting practices, ecosystem health, and community benefits.

- *Architecture 2030*: Architecture 2030 (www.architecture2030.org), a program spearheaded by architect Edward Mazria, is part educational and part certification tool, based primarily on the energy efficiency of a building. Its stated goal is to have carbon-neutral designs for all new buildings by 2030. It does not focus as much on healthy materials, lighting qualities, ventilation, or cultural significance of systems and materials. The 2030 Challenge does try to lay out a rational formula based on energy performance, which cannot be altered by exhaustive systems of trade-offs and parts analysis.

Other ratings and certification groups to be aware of are:

- *U.S. Life-Cycle Inventory National Data Base (LCI)* is a work in progress by the National Renewable Energy Laboratory (NREL) and its partners to evaluate the embedded energy and longevity of materials. Go to www.nrel.gov/lci for more on this organization.

- *Greenguard* certifies performance of the healthy aspects of a material. It is regulated by the nonprofit group Greenguard Environmental Institute. Its Web site is www.greenguard.org.

- *Building Green, Inc.,* is the publisher of *Green-Spec*, a directory of green building products organized by the Construction Specifications Institute (CSI) and the *Environmental Building News* (http://www.buildinggreen.com).

- *Rainforest Alliance*: Certification www.rainforest-alliance.org/certification/index.html

- *EarthCraft Homes*: http://southface.org/web/earthcraft_house/ech_main/ech_index.htm

Where to Find Sustainable Materials

Currently, it still requires research and some tenacity to find comprehensive and accurate information about sustainable materials and how and where to find them; fortunately, however, this is changing, and at a steady pace now. This section offers some guidelines for finding reliable sources for this information.

ON-SITE OR LOCAL SOURCES

Locally, two good sources are always word-of-mouth and area trade papers. Listen to what others are talking about within the industry in your community. For larger distribution areas, it is possible to research materials through the CSI's format collections—although this system does require more effort to find the proper products. A more effective approach may be to search relevant Web sites, such as those given in the previous section.

Sometimes, the solutions you are looking for may be closer than you might think—for example, from the construction site itself or near the site. The timber frame industry, for one, is going back to the historical practice of using a portable mill on-site to shape trees into timbers or boards. This allows the wood to stay in its own microclimate so that when it is used on the site, twisting and checking is unnecessary. Additional benefits are that it can be more affordable than purchasing boards or timbers outright; and less energy is consumed by eliminating transport of trees by large trucks to a mill, then to a supplier, and finally to the site.

Site gathering can work with other materials; all it takes is imagination to think of the possibilities for appropriate use.

RECLAMATION SOURCES

Salvage yards are becoming more common sources for such essential items as windows, doors, lumber, hardware, and fixtures. Recycled windows, doors, and floor joists were used, for example, at Studio Loggerheads, a low-cost construction experiment in the Blue Ridge Mountains of Virginia or the Cypress Cube in Atlanta, Georgia.

Old buildings that are being demolished are likewise valuable sources of materials. An old house that is being torn down may offer an excellent supply of stone or brick, even floorboards and mantelpieces, for reuse. In a tear-down situation, be creative to think of many ways to reuse as many materials as possible.

The term "dumpster diving" has gained cachet in recent years, and in that time its definition has expanded from the literal meaning—looking in garbage dumpsters or landfill sites to claim items that have been discarded—to include "digging" around for insider information to learn about defective or excess quantities of items that are scheduled for disposal from factories or manufacturing plants. In the case of the latter, with planning, this allows for pickup before the materials are hauled off to the landfill or smelted, thus also saving a high expenditure of energy. This technique gained attention as a result of the Rural Studio project, launched by Samuel Mockbee of Auburn University's College of Architecture, Design & Construction. Steve Badanes, one of the founding principals of the Jersey Devil, a design/build firm based in Stockton, New Jersey, referred to Yancey Chapel, built by Auburn students from recycled tires in 1994–1995, as one of the top 10 most important works of architecture in the history of the country. The point is, with a little imagination, and sometimes more than a little effort, found objects can become architecture, while diverting valuable resources from landfills and incinerators.

SPECIAL ORDERS AND SPECIALTY ITEMS

Although lumberyards are starting to provide better products, today high-quality green products still need to be special ordered, as they are more expensive and space is limited. As with information sources and resources, this will no doubt change for the better over time. To speed this changeover, whenever possible, request FSC-certified lumber so that lumberyards will begin to realize the demand for this sustainable product. Also seek out cabinet lines that are providing healthy materials and finishes, such as wood composite boards, recycled agricultural products (wheatboard), and formaldehyde-free plywood and medium-density fiberboard.

In order to blend the benefits of universal materials and systems it is usually necessary to work with products that are not made locally. Thus, people use windows from Wisconsin, cabinets from Canada or Italy, and zinc roofing from Germany. In such cases, the benefits of quality, durability, and/or affordability are considered to outweigh the negative aspect of energy consumption caused by transporting the items. Tested materials, systems, or prefabricated components can attain high levels of quality control, as well as provide products that are innovative and energy efficient. At this time, materials with these features typically are not readily available at the local lumberyard or supply store. Examples are specialty glazing systems, foundation and wall systems, roofing products, high-end or "healthy" cabinetry, dense low-maintenance exotic woods, efficient lighting systems, and solar panels.

Entire prefabricated houses also are usually designed and built without regional materials or techniques, but with high-performance, low-maintenance, and affordable packaging. Availability and familiarity by local trade groups are issues to consider with this approach. More specifically, the specialty systems sometimes require extra subcontractors to install, which takes away work from the local contractor's crew, which requires them to find more projects per year. This is not a sustainable practice. Companies that provide products like SIPS and ICFs ultimately want the framing crew to learn how to use their products so that this eventually ceases to be an issue. This, of course, imposes a learning curve that adds cost for the clients who are early adopters of these new products. Obviously, product prices will not come down until there is widespread use. It is also unwise to ask local craftsmen to try and re-create a version of some universal product from scratch. This will be a slow, costly, and difficult-to-warranty product, versus a proven system that will be readily available, cost less, and offer a warranty.

The stainless steel doors offered by Neoporte are an example of a universal (high embodied energy) product line endorsed by the USGBC because of their durability and lack of maintenance; this helps eliminate toxic stains or sealants. Their quality and beauty would almost certainly guarantee future reuse if a project were demolished or renovated. In contrast, an example of a universal material that doesn't always work is the living roof system. In some rural areas, local residential roofers may have insurance rates based on cold-flashing techniques, but the living roof typically uses hot-flash techniques, which require subs from out of the area, which ultimately adds cost.

Finding the right balance of universal products is all important to ensure longevity of, and pride in, a project while adding the specific qualities needed that are not typically available locally.

RECYCLED AND UPCYCLED MATERIALS

Recycled and upcycled materials are not yet consistently identified in the industry. There is no standard labeling, which means doing research to pinpoint recycled products or materials that are easy to recycle. By using recycled materials the energy benefits can be reaped almost immediately in the reduction of greenhouse gases; so in order to reach goals for curbing greenhouse gases in the next 10 years, it is important to specify more materials with these attributes. Examples of common recycled or recyclable materials follow.

- *Recaptured gypsum wallboard*: Gypsum is one of the most abundant minerals on the planet. If supplied near a site, this material can produce a 16 percent energy savings. Gypsum wallboard systems can also be made from recycled paper with renewable corn or wheat starch binders. Its low embodied energy is amplified by its low waste process: Gypsum panel waste can be recycled.

- *Plastics and resins*: 3Form (www.3form.com) is a company that produces plastics and resins and whose image revolves around environmental issues. Many of its products incorporate natural themes. Its "100 percent" product line is made from old detergent and milk bottles, is UV stable, and is resistant to most chemicals. 3Form is a company with forward thinking plastic and renewable technologies.

- *Recycled paper brick*: This can be used as countertop material. It is a high-strength surface

---

Making a Material Connection

Material ConneXion is a global platform for material solutions and innovations, offering consulting services, a materials library, and material manufacturer solutions. Based in New York City, Material ConneXion has an international network of materials specialists located in offices in Bangkok, Cologne, Daegu, and Milan. These experts serve as advisors to Fortune 500s and small, forward-looking companies alike, as well as government agencies. The firm's motto is "Every Idea Has a Material Solution."

For more information, send e-mail to info@materialconnexion.com.

produced from 100 percent recycled waste glossy paper. A proprietary process that uses high pressure to remove the air and water from the recycled material creates this beautifully finished material.

- *Recycled ash-glass porous construction filler:* This material, composed of two residue products, fly ash and granules from recycled glass, is used for soundproofing; it is lightweight, strong, fire-retardant, and recyclable.

- *Visible postconsumer waste polymer sheeting:* This is made from scrap and waste materials such as coffee cups, CDs, production scrap, old banknotes, and toothbrushes, to create the distinct designs on this colored sheeting.

- *Concrete pavers and tiles made from larger concrete cutouts:* Use of this material incorporates both recycling and landfill diversion practices. For example, during construction at Boxhead, a custom-built home in the Shenandoah Valley, 8-by-8 terrazzo ground concrete cutouts at a nearby waterjet countertop service became available from leftover floor outlet cutouts used for a large government building in nearby Washington, DC. After confirming the quantity, a concrete tile concept was conceived and implemented. As new batches came in, the design evolved to include the wall for the shower and the bathtub platform.

- *Tires:* These can be recycled in many creative ways. Recall the Rural Studio project at Auburn University mentioned earlier. The Earthship houses pack old tires with dirt to form retaining walls for the homes bermed into the earth. One concern is, however, offgassing after construction is finished. Some believe, if adequately sealed, this should not be a problem.

Also, a number of companies are producing so-called supermaterials that are starting to get attention.

- Nanosys has invented a paint that generates electricity. Still in the development phase, the process uses nanotechnology.

- The Essroc Italcementi Group has invented an unsealed cement product that pulls pollution out of the air, using a photocatalytic process to decompose certain organic and inorganic substances present in the atmosphere. This same process also enables the cement to function as a self-cleaning surface. The first pour of this product in the United States showed that stains from fallen acorns lasted as long as the leaves were on the oak trees, preventing direct sun from reaching the concrete. But in winter, after the leaves fell and the sun and rain could reach the surface, it cleaned up naturally. The downside to this product is the cost, which currently stands at almost six times that of standard concrete, thus requiring thought about where to use this product in a cost-effective way. Precast panels, where the product would be needed only for a thin layer on the outside facing is one idea. Roof tiles may also be considered as an efficient use of this product.

- Konarka offers solar films and power plastic, representing the future of carbon-neutral design. The solar panels are designed to work in any climate, no matter how little sun breaks through the clouds. In the past, photovoltaic panels were large and cumbersome, but as the technology improves, this will be less of an issue. Moreover, solar panels no longer have to face a specific angle, anymore. This flexibility allows for transparent solar film to be applied to windows, between standing seams on a roof or as a siding.

- SmartWrap, by Tyvek, Inc., is a mass-produced, mass-customizable composite building membrane made from a flexible substrate and printed on laminated sheets, which are rolled together in a film and embedded with organic light-emitting diode (OLED) technology. This system provides lighting and information display. There is also a solar cell component, which can generate power, change color, and supply lighting.

- A new cementicious insulating concrete form, (ICF) system, uses an insulative concrete form. Company engineers place the concrete in the wall according to the thermal needs of the building, based on its climate. This radical yet logical design takes into account that every region has different requirements for the shift from a static R-value performance to a dynamic R-value, which relates to thermal shifts during the day and into the night. The company determines how thick the insulative layers should be for the project and where in the cross-section of the wall to locate the thermal mass to help release energy at the right point in time. For example, to accommodate the large swing from 115-degree daytime temperatures to 40 degrees at night in the deserts of the Southwest, you would need both cooling and heating. Heat, which can be transferred through the walls and stored in the thermal mass, can be seen as "free," effective heat, if it is not released to soon. This passive solar energy system serves as an attractive, maintenance-free alternative to other masonry systems with two coats of stucco on the outside and drywall or plaster covering the inside; it is an integral system that can cut standard energy costs by 150 percent.

Choosing Wall and Component Systems

Historically, choosing a wall or component system has been one of the most critical decisions in creating a building envelope. There are many points to consider when selecting the material, including: separation from inside and outside, revealing to both, hiding and protecting, and code requirements, which have become stricter based on increased strength-of-nature forces.

STRUCTURAL INSULATION PANEL SYSTEM (SIPS)

One system that can serve as both the envelope wrap and the structural system for the building is structural insulation panel (SIP), invented by Alden Dow, one of Frank Lloyd Wright's apprentices, in the 1950s. After the earthquake of 1995 in Kobe, Japan, only six houses were left standing; all were constructed using SIPs. The sandwich of two layers of oriented strand board (OSB) and a core of expanded polystyrene bead foam combine to offer structural capabilities unmatched by most framing systems. The panels are fire resistant and treated for pests with natural boraid solutions; and new developments in insulated building systems (IBS) provide a mold and mildew prevention system integrated in the surface material. These panels are now being used for mass production by Pultie Homes, one of the largest homebuilders in the country, taking advantage of the strength and the high R-value. The zero air infiltration does require an upgrade in the mechanical system to introduce fresh air. A heat recovery ventilator is ideal for this, which also adds energy efficiency.

SIP roof panels can span 15 feet without rafters, using structural splines at 4 feet on center. This is a modern approach to creating a roof that does not require venting, which allows for low profiles along with overhangs that control the sun, protect the siding, and bring the outside in with high windows. Using SIPs as a finished surface is a modern expression of the product, one that also saves money and energy. At the aforementioned Boxhead, the design concept was to cover the OSB with beeswax; but to save money, a water-based urethane was used. This was used for wall and ceiling surfaces, which required extra care of the panels. In contrast, SIPs go up quickly and provide a sheathed product with insulation all in one.

The downsides of working with SIPs are (1) the cost of the crane used during installation and (2) the need for experienced subcontractors who are familiar with the system. Other issues to address are that plumbing should not be on an outside wall, and that acoustic battens may be necessary on copper roofs due to noise caused by expansion and contraction.

THERMOMASS BUILDING INSULATION SYSTEM

The THERMOMASS Building Insulation System is a product that most modern designers probably have been waiting for. Whereas in the insulating concrete form (IFC) system the concrete is hidden behind the foam insulation, requiring siding and drywall to be applied after it is installed, the THERMOMASS system buries

the foam inside of the concrete so that the durable, maintenance-free material can be seen, while saving money on sheathings or siding and reaping the benefits of insulated concrete.

STEEL

Steel is being considered by the American Institute of Architects (AIA) as a sustainable material to work with. Its dimensional stability, strength, and typical high recycled content outweigh the high embedded energy of manufacturing. Cantilevers are a modern capability that steel has afforded. This will continue to be the case for main structural members and for such designs as open stairs that form sculptural elements and allow light to pass through a space.

ENGINEERED WOOD

The obvious benefit to building with engineered wood, which has been in use for over 100 years, is that it is a natural renewable resource. Incorporating smaller sections of wood increases efficiency, and adding glue improves stability and strength. The early *Environmental Resource Guide* (ERG), published by the AIA, shows paralams, a beam made out of wood strands and glue bindings, as the preferred product.

Downsides to working with engineered wood are that builders must breathe in glue during installation, and sawdust settles in the soil. Ultimately a design that does not require many beams would be more affordable and possibly more sustainable.

STRUCTURAL COMPOSITE LUMBER

Structural composite lumber flooring and decorative surfaces are made of shrink-resistant, formaldehyde-free engineered wood surface made from variable width strands of up to 12 inches in length. Isostatic compressed wood yields timber of extreme hardness, density, and durability. The wood cells are compressed and the wood's structure is maintained.

Other Envelope and Construction Systems

- Straw bale construction, which depends on the humidity of the region

- Bendable concrete—engineered cement composites (ECC)

- ICF systems, which require siding to cover the insulation

- Translucent concrete

- Board-formed concrete for recycling forms as paneling and flooring

- Concrete flooring for heat sinks and radiant floors

- Concrete counters for a minimal or subtractive aesthetic, which can be precast with overpours on walls or floors

- Recycled concrete as pavers outside or as tiles inside

- Concrete roofs as thermal bunker

- Air-entrained concrete

- Carbon-fiber-reinforced concrete, a commercial technique good for earthquake zones

- Fly-ash concrete, a wastestream product from power plant emissions cleansing

- Stucco, a natural, low-maintenance surface for exterior or even interior use

- Bamboo-strand beams and plastic beams, which may have a strong future as renewable or recyclable products

Other Masonry Systems

- Habel blocks are lightweight, strong, and easy to work, but because they are susceptible to scrapes and denting, they need a protective coat or layering of another material inside or out. This covering can still produce a modern effect, with some effort.

- Air-entrained concrete blocks have a similar characteristic to Habel blocks.

- Brick has been largely ignored by modern designers perhaps due to the cost or its strong roots in traditional work. But brick is reused more than most materials and can be expressed in a modern way. Its durability and maintenance-free aspect make it a worthy material, considering its high embedded energy.

Roofing Systems and Roof Pitch

Roofing systems and roof pitch are the clearest indicators of a modern design. The move toward low and sleek proportion was a move away from the more standard gable and mansard-shaped roofs. Low-pitched or flattish roofs have their roots in agrarian tradition, still visible today in prerailroad huts and other outbuildings. These types of roofs are easy to build and require fewer materials to effectively cover the footprint. Translating this design for homes, whether inspired by the shapes of airplanes, boats, and trains, or agrarian outbuildings, allows for cozy spaces; and sloped ceilings serve a practical purpose, too—they are low enough for easy cleaning or changing lightbulbs.

LOW-PITCHED AND LIVING ROOFS

Today it is possible to cover low-pitched roofs with living materials, such as succulent plants. Building Logics, for example, offers a system (patented in Germany) that comes with a 40-year warranty. The energy savings generated by the insulative qualities of the plant material and latent cooling in summer have been recorded as up to 40 percent. "Living roofs" also retain up to 70 percent of runoff, an important benefit for areas with stormwater problems. And by helping to cool roofs, the system also combats the heat island effect seen in urban/suburban zones.

Many types of plants can be installed on the living roof, depending on the system you choose. Succulents offer the advantage of low maintenance, in that they do not require mowing necessary with sod roofs. (They are installed on an extensive roof on about 3 inches of soil). The roots do not penetrate the waterproofing; when they come in contact with the internal copper layer, they disperse. The copper is the main disadvantage, in the form of pricing. Because it is part of the commodities market, the price fluctuates with market shifts; 2006 was an expensive year for copper, for example.

Low-pitched roofs usually require a membrane or metal roofing. Copper and zinc roofs are considered sustainable because of the longevity of the material and the maintenance-free aspects. These materials are also being used as siding. They do have high embedded energy content, but the 100-year payback is a decided benefit. Architectural copper made in the United States is 90 to 95 percent recycled content. These materials also have a natural beauty. Zinc is the predominant roofing material used in Paris. Water that runs off a zinc roof is nontoxic to plants. The high metal content of both materials means they are almost 100 percent recyclable.

Insulation

Insulation is one of the most important elements in creating an energy-efficient home. It may seem surprising then that this has been a category of homebuilding that has been inadequately addressed for some 30 years. One reason may be the batt insulation lobby, which misled the public in regard to the performance of its product, and this has delayed a shift away from fiberglass. In testing the product, the outdoor temperature is set at approximately 70 degrees, to establish the R-value. When it is either 100 degrees or 32 degrees outside, the R-value drops dramatically. This, as well as the now-known carcinogenic qualities of fiberglass, may spell the end for batt insulation.

Most builders, plumbers, and electricians prefer building with studs instead of panel systems, because of the inherent flexibility with systems, there are some new alternatives to consider.

SPRAY FOAMS

The spray foam industry has shifted away from the use of ozone-depleting chlorofluorocarbons as blowing agents, preferring instead spray foams, such as soy-based products, for thermal performance and to eliminate air leaks. Two-pound spray polyurethane foam uses a closed-cell structure that provides one of the highest levels of insulation, at R–6.5 to 7.0 per inch. This structure has a water retention reading of less than 1 perm at 3 inches, which allows buildings to breathe while also keeping moisture out. You can solid-fill a wall with foam insulation for this reason; and because there is no cavity space, molds can't grow. Also, foam will add shear strength to a stud wall, whereas batt insulation will not.

There are a couple of downsides to spray foams:

• First is offgassing, which takes approximately six months to complete. And though there are no formaldehydes, the chemical makeup would not be considered healthy when compared to other insulators, but which do not perform quite as well.

• Second, spray foams require insulated recessed lightboxes, an added cost. If you don't use an insulated box, you have to maintain a 3-inch airspace between the box and the light housing to meet the fire code.

COZA, part of Cottonwood Manufacturing, Inc., utilizes recycled paper products, borate pest control, and a natural plant-based adhesive to create a fire-retardant insulation with a high R-value and excellent acoustic properties. This product has no phenol formaldehyde or ammonium sulfate, and the presorting of the recyclables before manufacturing precludes plastic contaminants. Overall, this system combats molds and produces little dust during installation, so it is "friendly" to users and installers.

Other healthy-material systems make use of recycled shredded denim or sheep's wool batt. However, any system that leaves air pockets in the material and between studs is a potential breeding spot for mold. As the temperature drops in the wall from outside to inside (or vice versa in warmer climates), water will condense and become trapped in a wall, where mold will begin growing.

Insulated drainage panels made by R-Control Building Systems feature two panels composed of molded blocks of expanded polystyrene beads bound with a waterproof binder on a laminated filter backing. This design protects basements against hydrostatic pressure, a constant pressure of water on the exterior surface of the wall. This "outsulation" system also protects against backfill damage, which prevents water penetration.

GLAZING SYSTEMS

Makers of both new and proven glazing systems are still struggling with the threefold issue of bringing in light, allowing for the preferred views, while achieving an R-value for insulation that is anything close to standard walls. Glazing on southern walls in homes utilizing passive solar strategies should use standard insulated glass to maximize the heat gained, while on northern walls it makes more sense to have low-e and argon-filled insulated glass to provide extra insulation on a cold wall. The problem with mixing the types of glass is that there is a difference in appearance.

There are some new systems available, which hopefully is the beginning of a trend of improvements in this category:

• Kalwall, for one, is an insulated panel system made of a UV-stable plastic glazing "sandwich," filled with fiberglass batting in a metal frame. The result is a frosted-grid look. The system can also integrate clear, operable windows for ventilation. The diffused light, which provides privacy, has an R-value of 5. If you use the new nanogel, a super insulator made of silicon, for the fill of the panel, Kalwall can achieve an R-10 insulation rating for the system.

• Solera, by Advanced Glazings, is a frosted insulated panel similar to Kalwall, but the surface is glass and the panels fit into a standard storefront window frame. This allows for greater flexibility of dimensions than Kalwall. Solera–T provides a better distribution of natural light into any space than most systems. This natural lighting has been proven to boost appetites in restaurants and enhance learning in schools by as much as 10 percent or more. The only downside to this system is the R-5 thermal rating. The company is researching a version to infill the core with nanogel, which should raise the insulative value—but also the cost.

• Triple-glazed glass is the only window system that might be considered a superinsulator because there are more layers for pockets of air. It is especially good to have this extra insulation in the winter when the sun can shine through the window; and at night, curtains can be used to capture heat.

Proper passive solar design requires that the square footage of south-facing glass be approximately 20 percent of the area of the floor space being warmed. Small amounts of glass on east, west, or north walls are necessary for ventilation, view, and a variation of light color. The south windows will perform best if they are clear glass instead of low-e, because the low-e reduces passive solar heat gain during the day.

If local sourcing is one of the main strategies for sustainability, then having a local craftsperson build your windows would be a logical choice. This can be an effective choice; however, if you are considering LEED certification, be sure the windows are built to meet the requirements. This might mean a tedious three- to six-month process, requiring review of shop drawings, computer modeling, and the shipment and testing of sample window types to the National Fenstration Rating Council (NFRC) for ratings. Custom windows by local craftsmen also require some faith in the small business with regard to warranties and timely delivery.

Finishes

Sustainable finishes comprise the most promising product category for performance and for creating a variety of textures and colors within a space. There are a couple of things to keep in mind when determining a material's sustainability. First, consider the life-cycle cost and durability of flooring materials. For example, according to the Tile Council of America, carpet lasts only six years on average. Other finishes, such as sheet vinyl, poured epoxy, and vinyl composition tile last only about 10 years. Resin terrazzo is good for 15 years; but all-natural materials such as ceramic tiles, stones, and hardwoods are all good for at least 50 years. Concrete without stain may also be good for 50, while stained concrete may look good only for 25 years. Portland cement terrazzo is good for 30 years.

Finishes to consider that have successfully limited or eliminated harmful agents are:

• Bamboo-strand flooring from Arch Systems (www.archsystems.com) uses bamboo har-

vested from mature Moso bamboo, a rapidly renewable material. This oriented strandboard (OSB) product is durable, with a hardness rating of 2600 psi. It also contributes to credits for LEED projects.

• Glass tile from Oceanside Glasstile (www.glasstile.com) is made from 86 percent silica sand and up to 86 percent recycled material.

• Mesquite wood tile made from small-scale wood by Ann Sacks (annsacks.com) adds natural beauty while adding warmth.

• UltraStock-MR by Temple-Inland (www.templeinland.com) is an interior medium-density fiberboard (MDF) rated for wet areas. This sheathing incorporates moisture-resistant resins and other additives, making it functional for bathrooms, laundry areas, and kitchens.

• Kirei board (www.kireiusa.com) is a contemporary interior panel that combines waste straw of the sorghum plant with formaldehyde-free binders.

• Maplex (maplex.com) by Weidman is made from renewable-resource softwood fibers from sustainably managed forests. No offgassing chemical additives are used, making it 100 percent nontoxic and biodegradable.

• Lotusan Exterior Paint has a self-cleaning attribute that can modernize sheathings such as concrete composite sidings or possibly marine grade plywood.

Many architects still resist using materials that try to look like other materials—such as "stone" walls made out of stamped concrete—believing it to be a form of dishonesty. But more and more, applied finishes are blurring the line of what is real, as new materials and production techniques begin to differentiate products. One product that is very appealing in this category is Mikado porcelain tile by Ergon. This very elegant and modern tile line is inspired by a stripwood or strip-stone look. It has qualities that cannot be found in real stone or wood—it is shock resistant, stain resistant, and doesn't absorb water. Two other products that blur the line between real and manufactured are Bambu and

Ebano, which have a long life cycle and are very reasonably priced for the quality.

Other materials to consider:

- Compressed paper product countertops

- Medite (a formaldehyde-free medium-density particleboard)

- Wheatboard bamboo and bamboo plywoods

- Cork flooring and coconut flooring from non-fruit-bearing trees

- Safecoat paints, primers, and adhesives

- Benjamin Moore premium latex paint

- Fiber cement panels

- Dakota burl composite board

- Woven seagrass

- Quilted banana fiber woven into antimicrobial textiles

- Tectom ceiling boards (you could eat them!)

Advances in chemistry also have led to many new high-tech synthetics, composites, and hybrid materials, which are stretching the modern aesthetic in new directions. Hybrid logic in the past combined the strengths and beauty of materials like wood and steel to create something that one material could not achieve on its own. Concrete and steel fused together in the curing process is an early example of the best of the attributes of two materials working together to achieve something that had never been done before. As chemical engineering breakthroughs occur, blending materials into composite materials or entirely new materials will continue to result in innovative products, such as:

- Natural-fiber-reinforced polymers and thermoplastic composites reinforced with coir, jute, kenaf, flax, agave, sisal, bagasse, wood, rice hulls, and sunhemp

- Aerogel, claimed to be the best insulator on the planet, is a loose bead space-age product that can provide a thermal insulation value of R-13 per inch. The system can integrate viewing panels of glass. One question concerning this

Separate, Ventilate, Filtrate, and Eliminate

The healthy house mantra is "separate, ventilate, and filtrate." Separation is the main strategy for healthy material logic. Separation involves sealing off toxic elements from the environment that the owner uses, through healthy sealants and covering systems.

Elimination means choosing not to order materials that contain, for example, petroleum coatings or formaldehydes that offgas. There are also steps builders must take to establish healthy construction site practice:

- Eliminate smoking on-site.

- Use natural oils for release agents (e.g., Wesson oil for concrete walls).

- Avoid burning kerosene heaters, which require the mechanical system to be up and running before any wood floors are installed to stabilize the humidity.

One sure way to know whether nontoxic strategies to homebuilding have been successful is to begin to see sensitive species found thriving near or in a house such as blue-tailed skinks, spiders, and others.

Here are some healthy-house products to consider:

- Use the Rub-R-Wall system (www.rpcinfo.com/rubrwall.htm) instead of bituminous mastic to keep all moisture out of a basement, which helps eliminate mold. A similar system, made from postindustrial recycled polypropylene by Colbond (www.colbond-usa.com) works as a drainage core that has padding for backfilling.

- A breathable air barrier by StoGuard (www.stocorp.com) is a seamless, fluid-applied system that provides protection against moisture intrusion. This is a vapor-permeable material applied to sheathing behind the cladding layer. It is used behind brick, wood, cement siding, cement stucco, and insulating finishing systems.

Other healthy materials include:

- Water-based urethanes, which have improved for floors, especially concrete or stone floors.

- Sodium silicate, used with concrete floors and masonry pavers, is a penetrating sealer that has passed the tests for the most reactive sensitivities.

- Beeswax applied to medite in place of drywall and paint.

- Eco-friendly paints, such as those available from Safecoat, Benjamin Moore, and others, that have low or no VOCs.

The struggle to set standards for healthy materials will continue, as it is a complex issue. Some clients with compromised immune systems may have adverse reactions to fly ash concrete, whereas typical concrete is not a problem. The point is, materials that are considered sustainable may not necessarily be healthy for all users. Thus, the question will be whether healthy construction will need to be a special subset of sustainability ratings (a higher level).

material is whether the dew points form condensation in the wall, fostering mold growth. According to the company's research, the gel beads actually force the moisture/air out with venting top and bottom of the wall cavity. The effect is a custom Kalwall-like system. There might, however, be problems with bugs getting into the cavity and dying.

- Eco resin by 3Form has a high-level recycled content. Recycled crushed glass is the most logical look, while many other added elements add personality and color to this line.

- Fossil Faux Studios (www.fossilfaux.com/ff_site/index_2.html) is known for creating functional art. The firm specializes in resin panels with items mixed into the pour, from grass to computer chips. A new line called Renewal uses 50 to 80 percent recycled postconsumer content. The company uses cast-off materials from its own wastestream to provide a product advertised to help gain LEED credits.

- Chalk-polymer composite is a film packaging material that mimics eggshell chemistry to reduce dramatically the amount of material needed to contain a liquid or solid substance. This product uses 50 to 70 percent less polymer than standard compositions.

- Composite polymers processed from corn and sugar beets ferments the plants' sugars, which yields the lactic acid needed to construct the product.

- Aluminum foam, produced from recycled aluminum cans, creates a textured panel with variable porosity, either left raw or coated with acrylic. These panels can form wall or ceiling panels and have even been used for custom tabletops.

- Insulated metal composite panels, such as those provided by Centria Architectural systems and others, are composite products that have a high rating for LEED points. They have been popular for commercial use and show promise for prefab construction, as well as for maintenance-free custom work. The panels have high insulation value, high recycled content, and low emittance of toxins; they reduce waste scrap and are durable and energy efficient, and offer the quality control of a unified system that can also be a regional material.

Conclusion

The future of modern sustainable design aesthetics and material choices driven by zero-carbon envelopes is limited only by our imagination. New smart house systems could one day offer such features as art or music that change as visitors walk through, based on their personal data tags. Digital ink has not evolved to mainstream use, but walls that act as information displays or mood shifters will become more common, allowing for changes that affect us daily. For example, a color could be displayed on the walls of the house to improve the appetite of a child with anemia. More natural light could curb the appetite of a housewife or husband to help with a weight problem. For those who live further north, there may be a need for light therapy to ward off seasonal affect disorder (SAD).

The downside to future design logic is that there is already at least 2 to 3 degrees of global climate change in the pipeline, so even if we made radical changes in the way we live starting today we have to consider that the materials we choose now may be wrong for a future that is 3 to 8 degrees on average hotter than it used to be. States that formerly needed more heating than cooling may shift to needing more cooling. This is where high ceilings, combined with radiant floor heating, make sense, because the heating does not stratify at high elevations, and the high ceilings would help in the future for natural cooling strategies.

A general strategy for choosing materials for our changing environment is to use heavy thermal mass as well as superinsulators, which coordinate with proper overhangs, sun controls, and ventilation strategies. Boxhead implemented some of these ideas in Winchester, Virginia, a zone that may see this shift in climate. The use of SIPs on the roof and northern walls integrate insulative qualities with the thermal mass of 16-inch-thick insulated concrete block walls to the southeast and concrete radiant flooring. Solar panels, if affordable, will work in any climate and so would be a good choice.

Effective design requires balancing problem-solving techniques with an aesthetic sensibility. The search for the right materials that will enable both is half the battle; synthesizing and perfecting the final design is the other half. During a transitional period of learning to implement more sustainable modern materials, we must also remember not to lose track of the cultural aspects they affect. Ultimately, there are many degrees of economic and regional diversity that can be represented by making the appropriate choice of materials and details. The rich can afford those products that are more Miesian, while the less affluent may need more of a nonstructural aesthetic, as seen in some of Le Corbusier's work. Energy efficiency, healthy materials, affordability, craft, and functionality—these are the characteristics that sustainable materials must foster in establishing a meaningful modern and sustainable aesthetic, whether urban, suburban, exurban, or rural.

Landscape Architecture and the Sustainable Modern Home

■ Lynn Saussy, ASLA, and William Carpenter, FAIA, PhD

SUSTAINABLE LANDSCAPE ARCHItecture has its roots in the traditional practice of the early nineteenth and twentieth centuries, pioneered by leaders such as Frederick Law Olmsted, Jens Jensen, and Ian McHarg.

Olmsted, considered the father of landscape architecture in the United States, understood that human health is directly tied to contact with nature and the environment and this attitude became the "touchstone of his art."[1] Olmsted felt strongly that his landscapes should provide relief from the "rigidity, confinement, and protrusion of ordinary conditions of the city."[2] His goal was to "refresh and delight the eye, and through the eye, the mind and spirit."[3] To achieve this ideal, he masterfully manipulated existing site conditions, moving expansive amounts of earth and stone to create berms, plateaus, outcroppings, and lakes; and he cleared the land of existing plant material to replant according his own design.

Jens Jensen, a native of Denmark who immigrated to the United States in 1884 and practiced landscape architecture in the early twentieth century, "advocated grouping native plants as they grow in nature, creating landscape that evokes particular local origins. Rather than tying a house to its site with an orderly formal garden, which he thought of as undemocratic, he wanted his flowing landscape to suggest natural settings that might have predated the house."[4]

Ian McHarg, a prominent landscape architect in the 1960s, wrote *Design with Nature* (John Wiley & Sons, Inc.), which further propelled the call to professionals to take a more sustainable approach to design. His idea of layering data collected for a site created a way to identify the best use of the site for a particular use. He wrote: "Restore the earth, heal the earth and thyself."[5]

Today, the health, welfare, and safety of the public are the cornerstones of the landscape architecture profession, and the landscape architect's charge is to serve the public by creating environments that uphold these principles. To date, all ecological processes, such as the treatment of water runoff, were "hidden" in the garden design; and all evidence of human influence was absent from the final product.

In the twentieth century, global warming and its effects on our planet can no longer be ignored. If we are to become sustainable stewards of the land, the first step is to take a new focus, one squarely set on the health of the environment.

Above: View from the street showing the roof terrace.

Right: View at the entrance of the compressive space down the main "street" in the residence.

Sustainable Landscape Architecture Defined

What does a sustainable landscape look like? A comprehensive answer to that important question can be found in *Sustainable Landscape Construction: A Guide to Green Building Outdoors* (2000, Island Press), by William Thompson and Kim Sorvig, extracted here.[6]

The sustainable landscape does not *exclude* human presence or even human engineering; however, it does not blindly *glorify* human intervention nor equate gentle human influence with massive human domination. The sustainable landscape does not waste energy or resources on trying to disguise human influence. Rather, it eliminates (functionally, not just visually) influences that are destructive or disruptive. Other influences it reveals and even celebrates. In revelation and celebration, it becomes an artistic expression.

The sustainable landscape follows natural and regional form whenever this can improve the ecological functioning of a built or restored landscape. It builds nature-mimicking forms primarily because these harbor rich diversity of life and ecological function, and secondarily because many people prefer the visual effect.

The sustainable landscape integrates and balances the human geometries with natural ones. It is not enough to allow natural form to take the leftover spaces; spatial and visual integration between nature's fractal forms and humanity's Euclidean ones is essential. The means to this integration are those of the arts as well as of the sciences.

The sustainable landscape is unlikely to be dominated by the visually simple and near-sterile extremes of urban or engineered space. It is likely to incorporate elements of urban space as people transform cities and industries to a more sustainable model.

The appearance of a naturalistic landscape often contributes to ecological function, but does not guarantee it. For this reason, neither naturalistic nor sustainable landscapes should ever be viewed as substitutes for "wild" places, which will remain critically important no matter how "ecological" built landscapes become—or appear.

An Approach to Sustainable Landscape Architecture

There are three components to the following suggested approach to sustainable landscape architecture: the site, the team, and education.

SITE

It is common knowledge but not yet common practice to start the design process by understanding the site, for without that knowledge, you cannot adequately serve the client, the architecture, or the budget. The site—whether it be a forest, a desert, a prairie, a rainforest, or a grassland environment—is, essentially, the "menu" from which we "order" our garden design. It is only by carefully examining the possibilities, as well as the limitations, of a site that all interested parties can come to terms with the available space for the client's program and how to maintain its integrity.

The first step in this process is to conduct a topographical survey of the site. This should be a mandatory requirement for any project, one that in the long run will save the client money. By analyzing the existing topography, structures (if any), drainage patterns, soil toxicity, existing trees, and plantings, solar orientation, and prevailing winds, you will learn two important pieces of information: where to situate the home on the site and what the sustainable footprint—the size—of the home should be, to ensure the continued health, or to improve the health, of that environment. This information will alert the team and the clients to any problems early in the design process.

The site analysis should include these elements:

- Calculate the effect of the planned home on neighboring properties; for example, avoid shading out nearby gardens or significant views.

- Evaluate the site to determine whether it is indeed suitable for the client's needs.

- Maintain a focus on preserving ecosystems and diversity of the site.

- Consider program options for lawnscaping. Encourage the clients to use whatever the site "brings to the table," and encourage them to see other ways of developing the site, if necessary.[7]

- Minimize the impact of the site on its environment; maximize the natural benefits of the site.[8]

By raising their clients' environmental consciousness, landscape architects are in a powerful position to spread the sustainable earth philosophy; and in this way both they and their clients can become leaders in restoring the natural beauty and health of their communities.

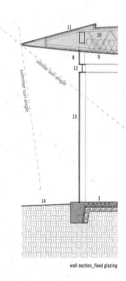
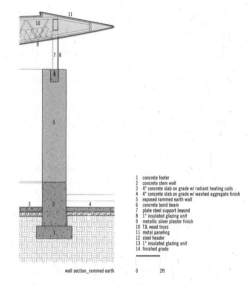

1 concrete footer
2 concrete stem wall
3 4" concrete slab on grade w/ radiant heating coils
4 4" concrete slab on grade w/ washed aggregate finish
5 exposed rammed earth wall
6 concrete bond beam
7 plate steel support beyond
8 1" insulated glazing unit
9 metallic silver plaster finish
10 TJL wood truss
11 metal paneling
12 steel header
13 1" insulated glazing unit
14 finished grade

0   2ft

wall section_fixed glazing   wall section_rammed earth

Wall section detail.

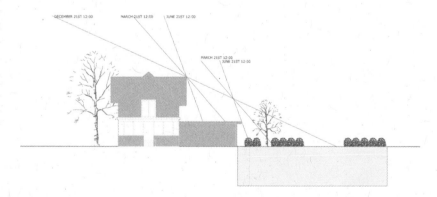

Building section.

Collaboration: A Design Conversation

Edward L. Daugherty, FASLA, describes his experience working with architects for more than 50 years in the Southeast United States. He emphasizes the importance of collaboration—having a "design conversation"—among all the disciplines, and particularly between the landscape architect and architect.

As a child I always thought I'd be an architect—I drew buildings, entered competitions based on my drawings, and won many of them. I wanted to go to Georgia Tech to study architecture, and so I did. This was during World War II. What I learned there was the philosophy: Put any building on any site—the site didn't matter. This did not make sense to me. I saw it as destructive. I thought, "Well, that is a nice building but how does it relate to the land? How does it relate to its neighbor? What is the context in the city?" This troubled me.

Following the one year of study at Georgia Tech, I served in the Army for two years and I decided when I got out that I would study landscape architecture for a year to become a better architect. I studied landscape architecture at the University of Georgia for a year [and] found out the field was much more important than just placing a building on a site.

I continued my studies in landscape architecture at Harvard for three more years. My professor at Harvard, Norman T. Newton, taught me something that is quite simple but true: "Good design is good if it does good." Not only does it solve the problem but it does good! To build on this, like the medical creed doctors promise to uphold, "to do no harm," the landscape architect and architect need to collaborate to do no harm.

I learned in school that the only satisfaction in practice was in collaboration. I had the good fortune for three years to collaborate under the same roof with architects, planners, and landscape architects. I observed that collaborating on two or three big projects a year, you "fed" each other, you questioned each other, and in the end, 80 percent of the students realized the other guy had something to contribute.

So it seems to me that that is the art—knowing when to let go and let the other guy make the decision. When you both have something to contribute, it is like a conversation, a design conversation. At the same time, you are courteous with each other and respect each other's opinions, even though you may not agree; but you respect each other's opinion. Maybe you season it a little bit, let it stew, think about it, and out of it comes something that is probably better than what one person alone would do.

On the other hand, you've got Frank Lloyd Wright saying each man should practice the craft he knows. He didn't want any help or comments from anybody else. We are caught between the dilemma of the one view of cooperation among the artists and the other view—leave me alone, I am going to do my thing.

Today, [in 2007] I still believe the dominant architectural theme is I can put any damn building on any damn site I want. This hasn't changed much. Someone once said, "The land will tell you what to do or what it wants to be." So if you do start out with that point of view, that what the nature of the site is as it exists is important, then you design a building that relates to it. If you lived beside a sea, you would not support a scheme that dried up the sea. If you live in a forest, you are not going to endorse a design approach or legislation that neglects the forest.

To this day, buildings are designed come hell or high water. The only thing that restrains the disturbance of a site to any degree is the governmental regulations (the height of walls, extent of clearing, degree of slopes). There is nothing appropriate about city or municipal government regulations judging aesthetics. But on the other hand, we have devices like the Historic Preservation and the Urban Design Commission that do concern themselves with aesthetics.

The essence of the message I would have is this: Good design is good if it does good; and that if all things are considered, then you work with the land to achieve something unique. Every architect wants his or her building to be unique, but it is only going to be unique if he or she starts from a different point of view each time. If [the architect] starts with the idea that a building has to sit on a plateau, then the building is always going to be the same.

TEAM

The sustainable home design team comprises the professionals hired to carry out the project—the landscape architect, architect, engineer, arborist, soils engineer, ecologist, builder, and landscape contractor—working in concert with the client. All the members of the team must be committed to the sustainable philosophy, as this will drive the design process. It's also important that all members of the team trust and respect one another—leave the egos at the door. Collaboration should be the order of the day.

EDUCATION

Probably the most essential tool that will enable us to create sustainable landscapes is education—educating ourselves, the other design professionals, and the clients. One of the keys to Earth's wisdom is that everything in nature is recycled. Everything. Everything serves more than one purpose and is interconnected, interdependent. This is what we need to learn from nature. This means we will have to make decisions "in favor of maintaining habitat and biodiversity, living within our ecological means, and making choices of scale and appropriateness of proposed landscape program."[9]

Our calling as landscape architects requires us, in part, to inspire all disciplines involved in the design process and our clients with our knowledge and understanding of nature. So much the better if we can ease their way, to help

everyone involved to feel successful, that they are good "parents" of the earth.

Note: A list of resources can be found in the appendix to this chapter, to help you help your clients to understand the positive outcome of sustainability.

Educating the clients/homeowners represents our greatest challenge but also our greatest opportunity to create and preserve healthy home sites. Doing so will require extra effort on the part of the team of professionals. One good way to accomplish this goal is to use examples of successful sustainable projects. Three examples are given here to use as educational tools for clients, present and future.

Case Study: Personal Home of James van Sweden, FASLA

This case study describes the design process for James van Sweden's personal home. Van Sweden is a partner in the firm Oehme, van Sweden and Associates (OVSLA), a landscape architecture firm based in Washington, DC. The firm is committed to the sustainable approach to landscape design—"to lay lightly on the land." Another partner in the firm, Eric Groft, describes their approach this way: "All sustainability starts with conscious common sense."

Step One: Assess the Health of the Site

The site for van Sweden's home was a soybean field that for decades had been pummeled, ditched, and sprayed with herbicides. Soil tests revealed extremely high levels of toxicity. The biggest challenge was to return the land to its natural, stable, and nontoxic state. To that end, University of Maryland's Dr. Frank Gouin and University of Georgia's Darrell Morrison were consulted to restore the soil. They recommended that alfalfa be planted over the entire site. After two growing seasons, this succeeded in completely wicking out the toxins from the soil. Once healed, the land was overseeded with switchgrass (*Panicum virgatum*), the final stage in restoring the health of the site.

The new subdivision where the site was located consisted of a main entry road and a cul-de-sac. The van Sweden property was adjacent to an old road that went to the original ferry dock. He chose to utilize the existing ferry road, rather than connect his driveway to the subdivision road, thereby limiting the amount of paving that had to be done. The driveway was constructed of locally crushed gravel, which is more pervious than asphalt.

Step Two: Collaborate with an Architect

Suman Sorg, AIA, was chosen to design the house. The sustainable measures he implemented are as follows:

- Construct a 60-foot-long masonry trombe wall on the east façade of both the house and the guest house to act as a major heat sink, using a double width of concrete block (20 inches), with a cavity. The wall absorbs heat in the morning, which keeps the house cool all day.

- Install large overhangs, especially along the west side of the house, over the expanses of glass, to shade the house and prevent excessive heat gain.

- Place doors and windows to allow cross-ventilation.

- Design the roof like a trough to hold water, which drains directly into the pond in front of the house, which in turn serves as a cooling element.

- Install water-saver toilets, energy-efficient heating systems, and zoned control systems to reduce water and energy consumption.

Sustainable directives for the exterior were to:

- Limit the number of cars onto the property and prohibit them from coming any further than necessary.

- Direct guests into the site and to the front door.

- Separate pedestrian flow from vehicular traffic.

Van Sweden also wanted a low-maintenance, sustainable landscape—"No lawns for the twenty-first century," he said. "I did not want a garden like the typical evergreen azalea gardens in Georgetown, but a designed meadow. This is a different kind of beauty, and very dramatic. It is interesting each season."

Groft explained further: "We didn't want there to be an overly designed area at the house that would not blend with the switchgrass meadow, so we planted some switchgrass and a little blue stem around the house, as well."

And it turns out to be very sustainable.

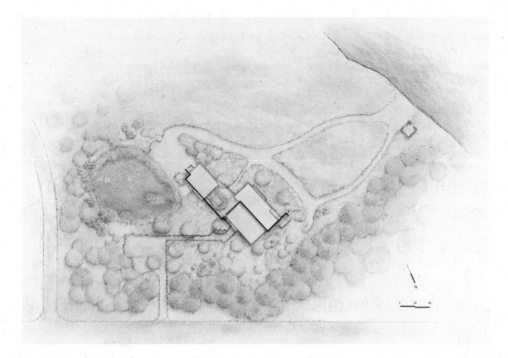

Right: Ferry Cove site plan showing relation to marsh and orientation.

Below: Garden view showing native plantings and large overhangs.

Left: Exterior view from marsh.

Below: Exterior marsh view.

Step Three: Restore the Area after Construction

"After construction," says Groft, "the initial task is to heal the wounds caused by construction of a house site. So it was first subsoiled, a method where you dig 2 feet down, refluff the topsoil, and then add organic matter. Those areas around the house were planted like a garden, using container-grown perennials and grasses from a local nursery."

Adds van Sweden, "The garden was watered for the first couple of years, to get it established, and now does not need any supplemental watering."

Features of a Designed Meadow

Perennials and grasses grow to the same height each year so there is no pruning, as is necessary with shrubs. Less energy input is key to a sustainable landscape.

The meadow is mowed only once a year in late winter and early spring. This generates a large volume of material to compost, so an area on-site was allocated in the design for the shredding and composting of the mowed materials.

It's also important to point out that the firm does not use only native plants, as some sustainable proponents advocate, but they use only noninvasive varieties. "If a plant gives us a lot in the garden and is maintainable, with no labor or water needs, then we think it is a good plant," Groft explains.

A designed meadow also becomes a filter for stormwater before it returns to the bay and/or back into the water table.

Van Sweden also reforested the area along the road using native evergreens and hardwoods, to create both a completely private human sanctuary, as well as a sanctuary for wildlife. "This area is a flyway for birds. There are also wild turkeys, snakes, fox, owls, and even an osprey nesting on the shoreline, and a peregrine falcon fishing here. My contractor saw a rare grasshopper sparrow hopping in the meadow, too," van Sweden boasts.

In summarizing the guiding principles behind OVSLA's design philosophy, Groft says: "Man has to live on the earth but we have to quickly transition back to nature so that you get a good blend, and everyone is in harmony with nature."

Terrace view showing horizon view and driftwood chairs.

Above Left: Exterior detail of façade showing the simple palette of materials and elegant site relationship.

Above Right: Detail of the terrace showing native grasses and juxtaposition of textures.

Left: Interior view of dining room.

Case Study: Addition to the Hojnacki Residence

An addition to the Hojnacki residence, Roswell, GA, was designed through the collaboration of the architect Katherine Hojnacki, ASID; and landscape architect, Lynn F. Saussy, ASLA.

The team on the Hojnacki project worked together for a year designing the new addition. Ex-

isting elements off the new structure included gardens, a pool, and retaining walls. The landscape architect was called in once the outside frame of the addition had been completed.

The program called for connecting an outdoor eating area off the new kitchen to the middle yard and lower yard with the swimming pool. One of the important goals was to preserve as many of the trees on the site as possible, so that stormwater could be dealt with in an environmentally sound way. All decisions were made based on ensuring minimal maintenance.

The following sustainable measures were implemented on the project:

• Protect existing trees on site with fencing; transplant and heal in a mature-specimen Japanese maple, and several crape myrtles.

• Reroute exhaust piping for darkroom to avoid roots of a young red maple tree.

• Used blanket drains under plantings or walkways (eliminate soil) to drain stormwater down

into earth and the excess out into rain garden. In this system, a perforated pipe in a V-trench is covered with a layer of #57 gravel, then with a filter fabric and a 6-inch layer of sandy topsoil mix.

• Reuse all excess step treads for steps to pool equipment.

• Minimize garden maintenance by choosing appropriate, noninvasive plantings and establishing minimal lawn areas. This included plantings that would not require irrigation once established. Many natives and drought-tolerate species were chosen for each location.

• Use stone and pebbles used for mulch under most plantings, to eliminate the need to replenish after decomposing.

• Choose hardscape materials requiring no maintenance, in this case, concrete and natural stone.

• Patronize local nurseries for plant sources.

Opposite page top: View from the rear garden showing the outdoor dining room and its glass rail allowing the owners to see an unobstructed view to the pool terrace and garden space.

Opposite page bottom left: View from the entry platform to the garden and pool terrace. The permeable stone surface allows rainwater to flow off the terrace pavers into the drainage system.

Opposite page bottom right: View from the pool terrace up to the garden space showing the large one-ton slabs of limestone which are 9" thick and form a strong sculptural anchor in the garden space. The stand of black bamboo is lit from below and has a delicate lighting effect at night.

Above: View from the pool showing the new tower which contains the master bathroom at the top, the living room in the center, and the exercise room at the base. Bathers can enter the pool shower room directly off the pool terrace. The two horizontal band openings are the kitchen space (with an operable sash) and the photography gallery off the pool terrace.

Case Study: An Addition to the Dominey Residence

The addition to the Dominey residence, Decatur, GA, was designed through the collaboration between architect William Carpenter, FAIA; landscape architect Lynn F. Saussy, ASLA; and the owners: creative director/accountant.

On this site, the owners and architect designed and built the carport and hearth area shown here.

The architect was instructed to take precautions around a water oak tree, which was the central element of the outdoor garden rooms. The tree roots were spanned with gravel before the concrete flooring was poured. At this point, the landscape architect was called in.

The landscape architect's design reflected the owners' love of modern design and minimalism. Their objective was to create a low-maintenance, private garden for the whole family and to preserve the large, centrally located water oak.

The outdoor rooms for entertainment were in place.

The following sustainability measures were undertaken:

• Choose mostly native plants. For example, native ferns with a stone mulch cover between the two structures can tolerate the deluge of rainwater.

• Make a food source—in this case, native blueberries—easily accessible from the deck for family to feed the birds.

• Use stone mulch that doesn't need replacing, as do conventional mulches like native pine straw or pine bark.

• Use no-maintenance concrete for stepping-stones and landings.

• Install fencing made of pressure-treated pine panels and stained with nontoxic bleaching oil.

• For plantings, select noninvasive species for function and textural beauty, fragrance and screening qualities.

• To accommodate a growing family (a baby was on the way), incorporate a path system to make all areas of the garden accessible.

• Plan a sunken area for a future play structure.

• Plant a slow-growing, drought-tolerant grass (Zoysia) for the lawn for the family play area.

• Use local hardscape materials for major pathways.

• Use irrigation-soaker hoses to minimize evaporation and eliminate trenching, which destroys tree roots and, ultimately, the trees.

Following completion of the garden, it was included on a fundraiser tour for the Decatur Preservation Alliance, Decatur, GA. The landscape architect was on hand for the event and was pleased on several occasions to hear visiting children say such things as: "This is the best garden; I don't want to leave it," a clear indicator that the design captured the essential aspects of a successful sustainable garden. Not only was it emotionally and spiritually uplifting, it was environmentally sound as well.

The sensitive site planning and porous surfaces allowed Lightroom to preserve the existing pin oak tree on the site.

Permaculture Design:
Another Way to Evaluate Sustainability

The article reprinted here, from the February 11, 2008 edition of Ecospace, a "green" online newsletter, highlights another way to look at creating sustainable landscapes and lives.

Creating the Conditions
for Sustainability to Happen

In the constantly expanding field of green, how do we find a place to start? What do we do if we want to live sustainably, but don't know where to begin?

One answer, or perhaps, *the* answer, lies in using the discipline that looks to natural models for arriving at the solution: the art and science of permanent culture—Permaculture Design.

This now-flourishing discipline, first codified and promoted in the early '70s by Australian ecologist Bill Mollison, is based on an ethic of earth and people care. As a methodology of design, Permaculture reveals that in all intact natural ecosystems, certain characteristics of design and function allow the system and its members to flourish over time; and by filling the needs of each member with the resources of the others, they then become sustainable.

Leading designer and permaculture teacher, Larry Santoyo, calls these characteristics "the indicators of sustainability." "If we use these indicators as a checklist in our own lives, we, too can start to become sustainable," he says. (http://www.earthflow.com, "EarthFlow Design Works: A Permaculture Design Company")

By examining the systems in which we participate (home, school, work, play, community, etc.) and seeing where improvements can be made, we can create the conditions for sustainability to happen.

Santoyo adds that if we use the indicators (along with an overlay of the earth- and people-care ethic) as filters to guide us in solving our needs, we will arrive at what is sustainable—and what is not! If our current solutions don't fit through the filters, they cannot be considered sustainable.

To start with, "fill fundamental functions first," he advises us. Look at the most basic needs of food, water, shelter, and clothing, and see how you are currently solving those needs. Are the indicators present? Are the conditions created for sustainability to happen?

One such indicator is "multifunctionality of single elements." A tree, for example, provides habitat and food, moderates climate, stores and releases water, and offers many more services to its ecosystem. Other elements of its network then flourish (birds, animals, soil biota) and return the favor by cycling nutrients to the tree and dispersing its seeds to enrich a new ecosystem.

Life works the same in a human system.

As illustration, Santoyo goes on to say that buildings could be multifunctional, not only providing shelter; but, through Permaculture Design, it's completely possible for them to provide for their heating and cooling needs as well.

Conclusion

In closing, the following poem by Ian McHarg (*Design With Nature*), sums up the expressed goal of sustainability for the modern landscape—that the first priority is the health of environment, which in turn benefits all living things, humans, animals, and plants.

Matter, of this is the cosmos, sun, earth and life made
Sun, shine that we may live.
Earth—home
Oceans—ancient home
Atmosphere, protect and sustain us
Clouds, rain, rivers and streams, replenish us from the sea
Plants—live and breathe that we may breathe, eat and live
Animals, kin.
Decomposers, reconstitute the wastes of life and death so that life may endure.
Man, see the path of benign planetary enzyme, aspire to be the world's physician.
Heal the earth and thyself.

Sources

Here you will find sources for information on sustainability from the Web, books, newspapers, and magazines.

Web Sites

www.asla.org: Official Web site of the American Society of Landscape Architects. www.ci.austin.tx.us/sustainable. Austin, Texas, is one of America's top 10 green cities.

www.coopamerica.org: Co-op America publishes the National Green Pages, a directory of thousands of socially and environmentally responsible businesses, products, and services.

www.newdream.org: The Center for a New American Dream offers the "Guide to Environmentally Preferable Purchasing."

www.responsibleshopper.org: Responsible Shopper is designed to help you learn more about the companies whose products you may use.

www.sustainlane.us: SustainLane advances cross-sector sustainable development for state and local government. According to its home page, its open-source knowledge base speeds discovery, research, and networking with more than 105 best-practice documents and a secure directory of participating government officials from more than 400 cities, counties, and states.

www.sustainablesites.org: The American Society of Landscape Architects (ASLA) and the Lady Bird Johnson Wildflower Center (the Wildflower Center) are leading an effort called Sustainable Sites. The Sustainable Sites Initiative (SSI) will consolidate, analyze, and advance research to establish sound metrics for factors most critical to site sustainability.

A sustainable site would be one that links natural and built systems to achieve balanced environmental, social, and economic outcomes to improve quality of life and the long-term health of communities and the environment.

www.epa.gov/waters/enviromapper: EnviroMapper for Water is a Web-based geographic information system (GIS) application that dynamically displays information about bodies of water in the United States. This interactive tool allows you to create customized maps that portray the nation's surface waters along with a collection of environmental data.

www.epa.gov/greenspaces: Site for U.S. areas with specifics for each area to reduce, reuse, recycle, rebuy.

www.compostingcouncil.org: The U.S. Composting Council (USCC) is dedicated to the development, expansion, and promotion of the composting industry based on science, principles of sustainability, and economic viability. The organization will achieve this mission by encouraging and guiding research promoting best composting practices, establishing standards, educating professionals and the public, and enhancing product quality and markets.

Construction Documents for Homes

■ Robert Cain, AIA

Incorporating LEED for Homes

Construction documents (CDs) are the group of documents used to describe the construction of a building project. In the home construction industry, preparation of CDs is often considered the least prestigious aspect of the building process, viewed by some as similar to dental work—necessary, but a real pain. In fact, well-planned and crafted CDs can be the essential foundation for achieving quality results in building construction. Yet, owners seeking quality in their homes often don't understand the CD and construction process well enough to recognize how crucial CDs are to achieving superior final results or goals and, therefore, unintentionally allow others to discount their importance. Some builders, for example, believe their track record and experience eliminate the need for producing anything beyond basic documents. As for design professionals, they may tend to focus heavily on the importance of the design concept and downplay the construction document process. Moreover, to reduce the cost of CDs, engineers frequently are not consulted in the design process; or when they are asked to participate, often are expected to perform in perfunctory, narrowly focused, or limited ways.

For many homes (speculative homes, in particular) CDs are often regarded by the industry as a mere sketch around which all the critical decisions for the project will be made, and not, as they should be, honed documents that define and describe every aspect of the project. For builders in some jurisdictions of the United States, a set of CDs for a house may consist of a stock floor plan and primitive elevations, or even less. When professionals are employed to create them, CDs command the largest portion of the fees for design services. CDs should require the most intense involvement and interaction of people participating in the design process; when they are not properly considered and executed, CDs can present the greatest risks for project delays, high construction costs, alienation of project team members, building performance issues, failure, and liability.

If your LEED for Homes project requires CDs, you should give serious consideration to the various CD components to be utilized and focus all efforts on making and coordinating as many decisions during the CD process as possible. LEED for Homes imposes an entirely different decision-making, documentation, construction, verification, and inspection processes from standard residential construction and practices, making proper planning essential. It's remarkably easy to forfeit credit for critical and easily achieved LEED points simply through poor planning. Thorough and comprehensive CDs are one of the major tools to employ in ensuring success in the LEED for Homes program.

LEED for Homes Pilot Program

The LEED for Homes pilot program targets single-family and low-rise multifamily projects because of the widely varied and often questionable approaches to construction of these types of projects in this country and the resulting poor performance with regard to energy use and air and water quality issues. Since single-family and low-rise multifamily housing use 22 percent of the energy consumed in this country and 74 percent of the water (excluding construction and manufacturing expenditures), LEED for Homes is a logical extension of the USGBC LEED Program.

Interestingly, and for quantifiable reasons, household energy use varies dramatically across the United States, making application of LEED for Homes more complex. For example, the Pacific region consumes 35 percent less energy than the South Central region and 32 percent less than the Northeast region. The Pacific states have a generally mild climate, reducing energy needs, whereas demand for space conditioning in the warm, humid South Central and South Atlantic regions leads to higher electricity usage, and the cold winters in the Northeast and North Central regions result in high consumption of natural gas and heating oil. The LEED process will assist in curbing implementation of stock plans and preconceived notions. Well-crafted CDs are critical to achieving LEED for Homes goals.

It is well known that strict building codes and environmental regulations can directly affect energy consumption. California's laws and codes, for example, contribute to low per-household energy consumption. Building type also influences energy consumption. Multifamily buildings use less energy per person than single-family homes. Thus, New York City, the densest city in the country, also has the lowest consumption rate for residential electricity usage. If this country is to reduce energy consumption and improve air and water quality, it will require the home construction industry to adopt a new paradigm for the construction process. The LEED for Homes Pilot Program

Construction Documents Terminology

The definitions given here are of terms often employed in construction documents for the design and construction of a home. Some may not be part of current builder practice but are included here because of their critical contribution to custom-designed homes or low-rise multifamily projects using a broadly based team. The relationship of typical contract and construction documents is shown here.

Contract documents: The package of documents that describe the legal contract for services between two or more parties for the construction of a project (for most homes, between the builder and the owner or buyer) and may consist of the following components: an owner-contractor agreement, conditions of the contract (including general, supplementary, and other conditions), working drawings, specifications, addenda, modifications, changes, and any other items stipulated as being specifically included.

Project manual: A manual, often prepared by the architect or designer, that can include the specifications, bidding, or negotiation instructions, the form of construction agreement, the general conditions of the contract for construction and any other description, terms, detailed instructions, or condition of construction and/or demolition work.

Construction documents: The working drawings and specifications components of the contract documents.

Working drawings: Include detailed scale drawings intended for use by the builder, subcontractor, or fabricator, and contain the graphic and notational information necessary to manufacture components of the project and to construct the project. Working drawings often are composed of civil, landscape, architectural, mechanical, electrical, and plumbing drawings. For some projects, specifications may be included on the working drawings.

Specifications: Written descriptions of a technical nature that cover materials, equipment, construction systems, referenced standards, and standards of workmanship. Specifications may be issued as part of the project manual or included on the working drawings.

Agreement for Homebuilders: The agreement between the U.S. Green Building Council (USGBC) and a homebuilder or the party responsible for the design and construction of a LEED home(s). A sample agreement can be found at: www.contects.com/pdf/leedsteps/2007 Builder Agreement.pdf.

Owner-contractor agreement: The legal form of agreement between the owner and contractor or builder defining the terms of the construction process. The construction agreement is often included in the project manual. For custom-designed homes commissioned by the owner, the American Institute of Architects (AIA) publishes documents frequently used in the industry. Some of the documents often employed: A101-1997 Standard Form of Agreement between Owner and Contractor–Stipulated Sum; Standard Form of Agreement Between Owner and Contractor for a Small Project; A205-1993 General Conditions of the Contract for Construction of a Small Project; A107-1997 Abbreviated Standard Form of Agreement between Owner and Contractor for Construction Projects of Limited Scope-Stipulated Sum; A141-2004 Standard Form of Agreement between Owner and Design-Builder. A summary of AIA documents can be found at www.aia.org/SiteObjects/files/docs_paperpricelist.pdf.

Conditions of the contract: The portions of the contract documents that define, set forth, or relate to: contract terminology; the rights and responsibilities of the contracting parties and of others involved in the work, requirements for the safety and for compliance with laws and regulations; general procedures for the orderly prosecution and management of the work; payments to the builder; and similar provisions of a general, non-technical nature. Conditions of the contract are typically in standard forms of the industry and are often modified for a particular project and may be further described or modified by supplementary conditions. Also published by the AIA: A201–1997 General Conditions of the Contract for Construction.

Supplementary conditions: A custom-written part of the contract documents that supplement or modify the provisions of the general conditions and apply to specific requirements of the contract not covered by other documents. See AIA document: A511-2001 Guide for Supplementary Conditions (free download at www.aia.org/docs_free_paperdocuments).

Bidding requirements: Documents providing information and establishing procedures and conditions for the submission of bids or pricing. For a project being bid, they may consist of a notice to bidders or advertisement for bids, instructions to bidders, invitation to bid and sample forms, and other instructions required to clarify the intent of the bidding process.

Owner-architect agreement: A contract between the architect and client for professional services. Services described in the agreement include the architect's design services and may include civil, structural, mechanical, electrical, plumbing, and other engineering or specialty services. The AIA references: B141-1997 Standard Form of Agreement between Owner and Architect with Standard Form of Architect's Services; B151-1997 Abbreviated Standard form of Agreement between Owner and Architect.

Addendum: A written or graphic instrument prepared for issue to the builder or contractor during the bidding or negotiation period, defining changes, modifications, clarifications, or interpretations of the construction documents.

Change order: A written order to the builder issued after the execution of the construction agreement authorizing a change in the work or an adjustment in the contract sum or the contract time.

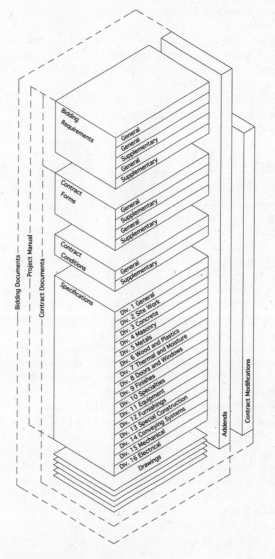

Construction documents diagram.
Courtesy McGraw-Hill.

proposes to influence the paradigm by providing a national consistency in defining the features of a green home and to enable builders everywhere in the country to obtain a green rating on their home. LEED for Homes represents a consensus standard for green home building developed and refined by a diverse cadre of national experts and experienced green builders. We should all view construction documents in a new light for, if well conceived, planned, coordinated, and documented, they are an effective way to communicate LEED goals in the construction process.

Integrating LEED into the Process

Of the more than 2 million new homes built in this country every year, the majority are constructed speculatively. In recognition of this fact, LEED for Homes has organized the program as a third-party verification system through LEED for Homes Providers to partner with builders recruited and registered for the LEED for Homes program. LEED for Homes, as a verification process and a vehicle to reach as many new homes as possible, primarily addresses the relationship between the provider and the builder. Other parties often involved in the process are identified in the LEED for Homes process as the "project team." Project team members may include an owner and should include professionals with both knowledge and experience in each of the LEED for Homes resource categories. LEED for Homes thus interjects new requirements into the typical homebuilding process.

By requiring the involvement of knowledgeable professionals, the process will often expand to include a variety of project delivery types. For example, the builder of a new home may add an architect, landscape designer, and mechanical engineer to assist in achieving LEED sustainability goals. Another example could assume an owner with sustainable goals who contracts an architect and builder to design and build a "green" house. For this reason, a careful study of how LEED for Homes integrates itself into the broader spectrum of project delivery is neces-

sary. Therefore, for the purpose of this chapter, the LEED program influence on the full scope of construction documents is important.

ENUMERATING THE PROCESS

Assuming a speculative home is the candidate, LEED for Homes identifies five basic steps for a builder to follow in participating in the program:

1. Contact the LEED for Homes Provider and join the program.

2. Identify the project team, identify goals, and design the home.

3. Build the home to the stated goals.

4. Certify the project as a LEED home.

5. Market and sell the LEED home.

Note that step 5 does not disappear if the home is custom-designed for an owner. An owner is required to fulfill certain public information requirements that take the place of requirements placed on the builder to incorporate LEED-related information in marketing, sales, and buyer education efforts. LEED for Homes does recognize custom homes in certain ways. Potential homeowners who wish to build or buy a LEED home should contact a LEED for Homes Provider for a complete explanation of the process; go to www.usgbc.org.

Planning for CDs begins in step 2 after establishing goals, during the conceptual design of the home and before conducting the required design charrette. Many LEED homes will be adaptations of existing home designs. However, points are potentially available to those seeking to reach the higher levels of certification, and they will benefit the most from creating a new design targeted to LEED requirements and a specific site. Project teams that decide to use CDs as a tool to direct LEED decisions should digest and dissect the LEED for Homes Checklist (www.aibd.org/for_professionals/LEED for Homes.pdf) and manual (www.aibd.org/for_professionals/LEED for Homes.pdf). A useful exercise once team members have been determined is to assign each LEED point to a particular team member or discipline, define how each point will

be incorporated into the CD drawings or specifications, and maintain a CD checklist to ensure incorporation.

PREPARING CONSTRUCTION DOCUMENTS

Step 2 preparations by the design team could proceed as follows:

1. Based on the home site and anticipated particulars and features desired for the home, carefully consider the potential members of the project team. Once the team members have been selected, educate and instruct them in regard to the goals to be accomplished for their discipline or related disciplines. Some potential design team members:

Surveyor: A complete topographic survey will prove invaluable for many projects. Document all constructed conditions, topography at 2-foot-maximum contour intervals (preferably 1 foot); utilities; paved areas; trees (with caliper size), shrubs, and relevant vegetation (especially specimen or indigenous); streams, rivers, or lakes; floodplain, setback requirements, and so on. The more information commissioned, the better able the team will be to address the Sustainable Sites and Water Efficiency categories. AIA Document G601-1994 Request for Proposal—Land Survey provides a solid checklist of survey requirements.

Soils engineer: Soils engineers are almost never consulted on a residential project. Certain sites, however, can present difficulties necessitating consulting a soils engineer. If, for example, an existing or nearby structure exhibits signs of differential settlement or other issues, a minimal soils investigation should be considered. Case in point: Discovery of lenses of poor soil through quickly executed hand auger tests in a recent home design made it possible to *plan* a basement, as opposed to learning it was necessary once excavation had started.

Arborist: Why plan your project around those still impressive-looking 80-year water oaks when they'll start dropping major limbs within 5 years and be gone in less than 10? A good arborist can assist you in planning around existing plant material.

Environmental consultant: Most jurisdictions will require an environmental survey and possibly a remediation plan if there are existing structures or conditions on-site requiring demolition.

Civil engineer: For many jurisdictions, water quality and land disturbance are of particular concern. A civil engineer familiar with the jurisdiction can provide insight and guidance, as well as documents required to get the project through jurisdictional review and permitting.

Landscape designer: A considerable number of points are available in the Sustainable Sites and Water Efficiency categories that can be addressed by a landscape designer. Just having one create a plan, no matter how minimal, is worth 2 points.

Structural engineer: Efficient use of materials involves accurately calculating sizes. Rules-of-thumb and oversizing are sustainably inefficient shortcuts. Structural engineers can provide insight into the material efficiencies of engineered framing materials.

Mechanical, electrical, and plumbing engineers: Manual D and Manual J calculations are required in the LEED process, as well as compliance with ASHRAE exhaust and ventilation requirements. Specialized high-efficiency and geothermal heat pumps are not unusual in LEED homes. Someone on the team should be very familiar with the type of conditioned air these systems deliver and the amount and method of delivery required to maintain occupant comfort.

Local jurisdictional officials: Though not official team members, officials should be familiarized with a project before they see the CDs on their desk, as some of the LEED points will require their approval. For example, a meadow of native drought-tolerant grasses and flowers (SS2.4; 2 points) could be interpreted as violating yard ordinances. Another example: Exactly how far will the jurisdiction allow you to go with a graywater reclamation system? Or, under exactly what conditions will they allow you to use rain-harvest water for potable water?

2. Download and read the LEED Project Checklist from www.aibd.org/for_professionals/ LEED for Homes.pdf. It identifies points available for certification in the eight different credit categories.

3. Download and read the LEED for Homes Program Manual, including appendices, from www.aibd.org/for_professionals/LEED for Homes.pdf.

4. Prepare a three-ring binder with headers for each of the credit categories and breakdown into subcategories. Include the checklist and description of credits from the manual for each category. Use this binder to track decisions affecting LEED points. Insert (or remove) product literature and other materials as the project progresses.

5. Prepare a similar three-ring binder organized according to a standard specification division format. Much of the industry still uses the 1995 Construction Specifications Institute's (CSI) MasterFormat, although in 2004, MasterFormat was updated and expanded to 50 divisions. The 50 divisions may suit commercial projects well, but many believe the expanded format is unwieldy for homes. The binder will become your reference during the design and construction documents process. Document each decision regarding products by inserting critical information about them into the binder. Specifications will become an essential method of transferring LEED requirements to subcontractors. To the front of this binder add categories to cover documentation of the design, construction document, and construction process, such as:

   • Correspondence

   • Meeting notes

   • Shop drawings log

   • Field reports

6. Preliminarily identify the LEED Checklist items that can be easily achieved and assess the potential level of certification. If more are required to reach minimal certification or higher, identify and note these.

7. Create and develop the design of the home; keep records religiously as the design evolves and decisions are made.

8. Conduct the charrette and document the decisions.

9. Create a LEED task checklist, with assignments for all team members.

CRAFTING THE PROJECT MANUAL DOCUMENTS

Contract Documents

Follow this process:

1. *Define all contracts*: Contractual agreements are an integral component of the contract documents as they define performance expectations and payment criteria for all members of the project team, from owner to builder, architect, engineers, and consultants. Contracts should define relationships between all parties providing services for the project, including owner and architect, owner and builder, owner and design builder, or architect and consultants/engineers. Contracts are executed prior to incurring reimbursable services. For LEED projects, services related to LEED tasks should be clearly defined through the contracts, and method and amount of compensation specifically addressed. As contracts are typically designed to integrate all agreements between parties and supersede prior negotiations, representations or agreements, contracts should be crafted with care.

2. *Agree upon the general conditions*: The General Conditions of the Contract for Construction is a complementary document incorporated by reference into a variety of other

documents, including the owner-contractor agreement and contractor-subcontractor agreements, in order to establish a common basis for these primary and secondary relationships on the typical construction project. It is considered a keystone document in that it coordinates all parties involved in the process and allocates legal responsibilities; therefore, its form and any modifications should be agreed upon prior to executing the contract for construction.

3. *Make contract modifications*: Because of variations in the nature of individual owners and builders and legal and jurisdictional requirements, standardized contract documents cannot cover all aspects of basic project requirements. Project-specific information must be included in the project manual in one of four ways:

- By providing information in negotiation or bidding requirements.

- By providing additional information in the owner-contact agreement

- By modifying the general conditions by drafting supplementary conditions of the contract

- By providing information in the specifications text, particularly in the General Requirements (Division 1 of the Specifications)

4. *Draft responsibilities for LEED tasks, which were defined during preparation for CDs, into the appropriate project manual document.*

Note the LEED Agreement for Home Builders interjects another level of contract into the list of possible project contracts and should be referenced in all other agreements to which the signer is party.

Working Drawings

A well-crafted set of working drawings constitute a major component of the construction documents and should be coordinated with project manual documents, particularly the specifications. Language used in the specifications to describe products should match language used in the notes, schedules, and descriptions used in the working drawings. For example, concrete masonry units described in the specifications should be labeled as such on the drawings, not as "concrete block."

Organize the materials you will use for the working drawings. Determine and understand the application of codes, ordinances, and jurisdictional requirements for the project.

Plan the organization and layout of the drawings required for the project. Working drawings should be designed to describe the building from the general to the specific.

General drawing (site plans, building plans, elevations, and building sections) precede more specific drawings (wall sections, details, schedules, mechanical, electrical, plumbing, and structural drawings).

Working drawings can provide a clear and useful LEED for Homes tool. Drawings can be specifically referenced to indicate the LEED category of the product or work described. An Environmentally Preferable Product (see MR2.1 in the LEED for Homes Manual), for example, can be referenced to the project MR2.1 spreadsheet (see Specifications) and the LEED for Homes manual. The drawing notation for EPP "concrete" containing appropriate amounts of fly ash or slag as "concrete MR2.1" in working drawing sections and details succinctly identifies the material as an EPP for those executing the work.

Following is a very brief description of typical elements comprising a set of working drawings, as well as the typical organizational hierarchy of general to specific:

1. *Cover sheet*: The first sheet of the set of working drawings should introduce the project to the people who will be using them: the builder and the builder's personnel, code officials, subcontractors, and so on. The following are typical to the cover drawing:

- An index (shown here) listing every sheet of the drawings and its contents

- A location plan showing a map of the general area with the site location and the appropriate jurisdiction noted

DRAWING INDEX	
S-i	SITE PLAN
C1	EXISTING DEMO PLAN
C2	GRADING- E&S PLAN
C3	TREE PROTECTION
L1	LANDSCAPE PLAN
L2	LANDSCAPE DETAILS
A-1	BASEMENT FLOOR PLAN
A-2	FIRST FLOOR PLAN
A-3	SECOND FLOOR PLAN
A-4	CLERESTORY PLAN/MASTER BEDROOM ROOF PLAN
A-5	ROOF PLAN AND FINISH SCHEDULE
A-6	NORTH AND SOUTH ELEVATIONS
A-7	EAST AND WEST ELEVATIONS
A-8	BUILDING SECTIONS
A-9	BUILDING SECTIONS
A-10	BUILDING SECTIONS
A-11	BUILDING SECTIONS
A-12	BUILDING SECTIONS
A-13	BUILDING SECTIONS
A-14	WALL SECTIONS
A-15	WALL SECTIONS
A-16	WALL SECTIONS AND DETAILS
A-17	DOOR AND WINDOW SCHEDULES AND DETAILS
A-18	DETAILS
A-19	DETAILS
A-20	DETAILS
A-21	DETAILS
A-22	DETAILS
S-1	FOUNDATION PLAN
S-2	FIRST FLOOR FRAMING PLAN
S-3	SECOND FLOOR FRAMING PLAN
A-4	ROOF FRAMING PLAN

Sample drawing index

- The street address of the project

- A list of the building codes (including the year) under which the house was designed

- The zoning for the property and brief summary of zoning requirements, such as front, side, and rear yard setbacks; height limitations; and so on

Other information, depending on the project:

- A stunning rendering of the designer's vision of the house

- Outline specifications or references to the specifications, if included in the project manual

- Site survey

- Legends of graphic symbols (shown here) employed for materials and drafting

2. *Site survey*: A topographic survey signed and sealed by a registered land surveyor. A common scale for residential surveys is 1 inch to 20 feet, expressed as $1~IN = 20~FT–0~IN$. Surveys for small projects may be included on the cover sheet.

Drawing legend

Basement plan

3. *Site plan*: A plan of the site generated by the designer or civil engineer showing the outline of the house placed on the site, exterior elements such as decks, walks, drives, lighting, trees and natural features to remain, and other, as well grading contours establishing the final grades to be accomplished by the builder. Site plans are often the same scale as the survey, but may be larger if the plan is complex. Site plans may also be included on the cover sheet.

4. *Landscape plan*: A plan of the entire site or area appropriate for the proposed project. If the project is located on a portion of a larger site, a key plan should indicate the portion to be addressed. The plan should show the developed landscape, plantings and gardens, planting lists, sizes, tree calipers, spacing, and the details and particulars of the landscape installation. LEED for Homes category Sustainable Site (SS) applicable points should be clearly identified. Landscaped plans often include complete specifications on the drawing(s) and are typically the same scale as the site plan.

5. *Foundation plan*: The foundation plan is the first plan in the sequence of plans of the building. The sequence (foundation plan, first-floor plan, second-floor plan, etc., roof plan) describes the building from bottom to top. The foundation plan should show the locations of all foundation walls, retaining walls, columns and their associated footings, as well as crawlspaces and basements. Details and wall sections regarding the foundations are often located on these drawings. Since the builder will use this plan to lay out the house, dimensional data regarding wall thicknesses, column centerlines, and other plan features are critical.

Foundations provide a potentially bountiful harvest for LEED points. Concrete, form release agents, concrete block, mortar, waterproofing/dampproofing, vertical drainage systems, protection board, foundation insulation, filter fabric, foundation drainage pipe, radon protection, nontoxic pest control, reinforcing, capillary breaks, sill seal products, and more are all easily found and documented Indoor Environmental Quality (IEQ), Environmentally Preferable Products (EPPs),

and Sustainable Site (SS) components for LEED points.

An example is shown here of a residential basement plan and foundation plan illustrating an insulated basement with photovoltaic, solar thermal, rain-harvest, graywater, and geothermal equipment layouts.

6. *Floor plan(s)*: A floor plan is typically generated for each level, floor, or partial floor of the house, as shown here. The plan views the floor as if cut horizontally through the house at the windowsill level (although the location can vary depending on the height of desirable information to be shown) and should specify the locations of walls, partitions, doors, stairs, cabinetry, appliances, and plumbing fixtures, as well as dimensional data referencing the items. Electrical outlets, fixtures, circuitry, and switching are often shown as well. The rooms of floor plans are named and numbered and the room size is referenced. Floor plans almost always include references to building or wall sections and exterior and interior elevations. A common floor plan scale for homes is 1/4~IN = 1~FT–0~IN.

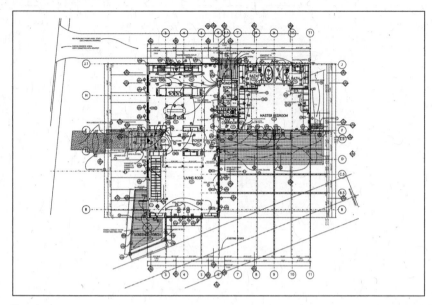

Floor plan

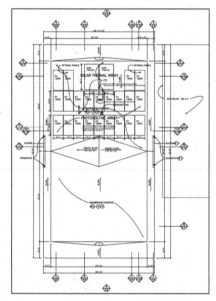

Roof plan

drawn at the same scale as the floor plan, but may be a smaller scale, or not drawn at all for simple, straightforward roofs.

Consider integration of highly reflective and environmentally preferable products such as roofing systems and rain-harvest systems. Describe EPPs, IEQ terminal components such as exhaust systems, and EA components such as photovoltaics. An example is shown here of a residential roof plan with photovoltaic and solar thermal array layouts.

9. *Exterior elevations*: A drawing showing the vertical elements of the building, both interior and exterior, as a direct projection to a vertical plane as if the viewer were standing back looking at the element with no three-dimensional distortion. Such a view shows items that cannot be clearly illustrated on the floor plan or ceiling plan. Every exterior wall should be shown in elevation. Interior elevations should be given where control of the various elements to be shown is desired. Elevations are frequently drawn on the same scale as the floor plan, often up to 1/2~IN = 1~FT–0~IN for complex interior elevations or cabinetry.

Describe MR2.1 EPPs, Energy and Atmosphere (EA) Windows, exterior aspects of EA Lighting (if applicable) on elevations. An example is shown here.

10. *Building sections*: A building section is often a general reference section through the entire building or a substantial part of the building and is used to show floor elevations, roof profiles, overall vertical dimensions, materials in general, and as a location to reference more specifically noted wall sections and details. Wall sections are cut-through areas of the building providing the best illustration of the various wall conditions to be encountered in the house. Since building sections often don't reveal a great deal of detail, they are often drawn at the same scale as the floor plan and are referenced to the foundation plans, floor plans, and elevations.

Describe MR2.1 EPPs, EA2.1 insulation on building sections, as shown here.

However, a complicated area of the plan, such as a bath, may be referenced and shown elsewhere with more detail and at a larger scale, say 1/2~IN = 1~FT–0~IN.

LEED for Homes requires documentation of the area of all conditioned space according to ANSI 2765. Floor plans are ideal for space summaries.

7. *Reflected ceiling plan*: If the ceiling plan is complicated, a separate drawing of it as if reflected in a mirrored floor can be useful in coordinating architectural features, light fixtures, electrical circuitry, mechanical devices, sprinklers, fire and security alarm components, and so on.

The LEED ENERGY STAR light fixtures, exhaust fans, ceiling fans, and other Energy and Atmosphere (EA) items can be effectively coordinated on the reflected ceiling plan.

8. *Roof plan*: Show roof slopes, roof drains, leaders, scuppers, collection boxes, photovoltaics and thermal solar systems, equipment anchorage devices, all roof penetrations including vents through the roof, fans, skylights, and so on, on roof plans. The roof plan is generally

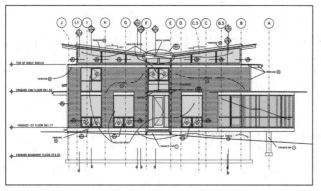

Elevation

Building section

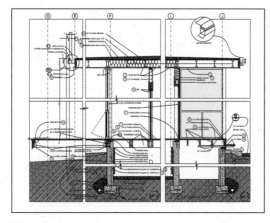

Wall section

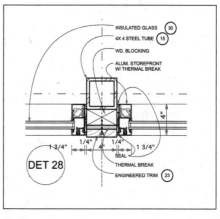

Window detail

11. *Wall sections*: This is a detailed drawing of a major exterior or interior wall condition illustrating all its various components, which are often larger-scaled (3/4~IN=1~FT–0~IN) portions of the building section warranting full explanation of the wall's assembly. In the wall section, all building methods and materials are graphically represented and described with notes or text. The nomenclature used in the text description should complement but not duplicate description of products and materials described more accurately in the specifications. For example, wood siding in a wall section should be labeled "wood siding," not "beveled southern yellow pine, grade C, 5~IN exposure." The specification should list "wood siding" in an index and elaborate on the particulars.

Describe MR2.1 EPPs, EA Insulation, as shown here.

12. *Details*: A minor section or drawing of a larger-scaled portion of another drawing indicating in detail the design, location, and composition of the elements and materials shown. Commonly scaled anywhere from 1–1/2~IN = 1~FT–0~IN to full size, the detail is used to clearly show aspects of the design that could be misinterpreted at a smaller scale, and is often referenced from an elevation or wall section.

Details will often contain many LEED components and are an excellent opportu-nity to detail ENERGY STAR requirements, EA Insulation, EPPs, and Materials and Resources (MR) techniques for advanced framing. Refer to the example shown here.

13. *Door schedule*: A list of all doors in the house shown in tabular form indicating sizes, thicknesses, type and construction, and special conditions. Each door is referenced by symbol or number to locations on the plans; specifications for door hardware specified to each door type; and details of jamb, head, and sill conditions.

Include R-values of exterior doors in the door schedule for use in Manual J and HERS calculations. Opportunities exist for recycled content complying with EPP requirements for interior doors.

14. *Window schedule*: A list of all windows shown in tabular form indicating sizes, number of lights, type of glazing, method of operation, and any special requirements. Like doors, windows are identified by number or symbol to their locations on the plan, along with details of jamb, head, and sill conditions. Window schedule notations of thermal breaks, R-value for Manual J and HERS calculations, as well as ENERGY STAR requirements are critical.

15. *Finish schedule*: A list of all rooms or spaces in the house in tabular form indicating the finished substrate and applied finish for each wall surface, floor, and ceiling condition. Most finish schedules also include a commentary column for situations requiring verbal explanation or reference to specific details.

   Note EPP finishes such as low-VOC paint, as shown here.

16. *Electrical drawings*: Often combined with architectural drawing on residential projects. Electrical drawings should provide a complete description of the power requirements, including a power plan showing all required outlets, circuitry, and any special systems. as well as a reflected ceiling plan indicating the location of all light fixtures, their circuitry and switching, speakers, special lighting, ceiling outlets, junction boxes, smoke alarms, and so on. Electrical plans show the location of the power entrance into the house, the location and size of panels, a load summary, and on complicated houses a circuit breaker layout. The following are typical to electrical drawings:

- Outlets, type, and location (duplex, dedicated, isolated ground, GFI, etc.)
- Conduit, size, and type (data, communication, phone)
- Switches, wiring, circuiting, volts
- Light fixtures (model number and lamps)

Other information, depending on the project:

- Direct connections (junction boxes, etc.)
- Emergency lighting, exit signs
- Alarm and security system
- Fire alarm system
- Sound systems, speakers, monitors, cameras
- Special equipment (kitchen, entertainment)

- Special technical devices (computers, gauges, medical, etc.)
- Special wiring (signs, heating, saws)

Electrical components interface with a broad-range section in LEED for Homes categories: EA, MR, IEQ, ENERGY STAR. Scheduling of components in the electrical drawings may make sense if sufficiently detailed drawings are planned for the project and an experienced professional familiar with the LEED for Homes program is involved.

17. *Plumbing drawings*: These, too, are often combined with architectural drawings on residential projects, or not shown at all. They may be submitted separately and directly, depending on the jurisdiction, by a licensed plumber for permitting. The following are typical to a set of plumbing drawings:

- A floor plan with lines and symbols representing all piping
- Symbol legend, general notes, and specific key notes
- Fixture schedule, specifying the manufacturer and model for each item
- The sizes for all piping, cold/hot water, sanitary, vent lines, and so on
- Diagrams, such as water riser, sanitary stack
- Information regarding the water heater

Other information, depending on the project:

- Details drawings, such as water heater, water meter connection, floor drains
- Diagrams or details referencing special equipment requirements
- Fire protection notes
- Fire sprinkler notes and symbols (e.g., sprinkler lines and heads)
- Special air lines
- Natural gas lines

FINISH SCHEDULE

		NORTH WALL		SOUTH WALL		EAST WALL		WEST WALL		FLOOR		BASE		WOOD CEILING		REMARKS
		MATERIAL	FINISH	MATERIAL	FINISH	MATERIAL	FINISH	MATERIAL	FINISH	MATERIAL	FINISH	MATERIAL	FINISH	MATERIAL	FINISH	
01	UTILITY ROOM	*	NO FINISH	*	NO FINISH	*	NO FINISH	*	NO FINISH	CONCRETE	PAINT (EPOXY)			WOOD DECK		*WALLS RECEIVE RIGID INSULATION
101	FOYER	CABINETRY	*	CABINETRY	*	GLASS		GLASS		WOOD	CLEAR FINISH	MDF	CLEAR FINISH	WOOD	CLEAR FINISH	*PARTIALLY OPEN TO CEILING OF ROOM 105 ABOVE *NATURAL FINISH (VERIFY)
102	LIVING ROOM	GYP MDF	PAINT	GYP/MDF GLASS	PAINT	GYP GLASS	PAINT	GYP GLASS	PAINT	WOOD	CLEAR FINISH	MDF	CLEAR FINISH	WOOD	CLEAR FINISH	*VERIFY MDF FINISHES
103	DINING ROOM	CABINETRY	*	GYP	PAINT	GYP	PAINT	GYP GLASS	PAINT	WOOD	CLEAR FINISH	MDF	CLEAR FINISH	WOOD	CLEAR FINISH	*NATURAL FINISH (VERIFY)
104	KITCHEN	CABINETRY TILE	* **	CABINETRY	*	GYP GLASS	PAINT	GYP	PAINT	WOOD	CLEAR FINISH	MDF	CLEAR FINISH	WOOD	CLEAR FINISH	*NATURAL FINISH (VERIFY) ** TILE BACKSPLASH
105	CORRIDOR	GYP	PAINT	GLASS		GYP	PAINT	GYP	PAINT	WOOD	CLEAR FINISH	MDF	CLEAR FINISH	WOOD	CLEAR FINISH	
106	1/2 BATH	GYP	PAINT	GYP	PAINT	GYP	PAINT	TILE	*	WOOD	CLEAR FINISH	MDF	CLEAR FINISH	WOOD	CLEAR FINISH	
107	LAUNDRY	GYP	PAINT	GYP	PAINT	GYP TILE	PAINT **	GYP	PAINT	WOOD	CLEAR FINISH	MDF	CLEAR FINISH	WOOD	CLEAR FINISH	** TILE BACKSPLASH
108	MASTER BEDROOM	GYP	PAINT	GYP GLASS	PAINT	GYP	PAINT	GYP	PAINT	WOOD	CLEAR FINISH	MDF	CLEAR FINISH	WOOD	CLEAR FINISH	
109	HER BATH	TILE		GYP MDF	PAINT	GYP/MDF TILE	PAINT	CABINETRY		TILE		TILE		WOOD	CLEAR FINISH	
110	HIS BATH	TILE		GYP MDF	PAINT	CABINETRY		GYP/MDF TILE	PAINT	TILE		TILE		WOOD	CLEAR FINISH	
111	SCREENED PORCH	WOOD LAP SIDING SCREEN	PAINT	WOOD SCREEN	PAINT	LAP SIDING GLASS	PAINT	WOOD SCREEN	TREATED	TREX	TREATED			WOOD	CLEAR FINISH	
201	CORRIDOR	GYP	PAINT	MDF	PAINT	GYP GLASS	PAINT	GYP	PAINT	WOOD	CLEAR FINISH	MDF	CLEAR FINISH	WOOD	CLEAR FINISH	
202	STUDY	GYP MDF	PAINT PAINT	GYP MDF	PAINT PAINT	STEEL RAIL GYP	PAINT PAINT	STEEL RAIL GYP	PAINT PAINT	WOOD	CLEAR FINISH	MDF	CLEAR FINISH	WOOD	CLEAR FINISH	*VERIFY MDF FINISHES
203	BEDROOM	GYP GLASS	PAINT	GYP GLASS	PAINT	GYP	PAINT	GYP GLASS	PAINT	WOOD	CLEAR FINISH	MDF	CLEAR FINISH	WOOD	CLEAR FINISH	
204	GUEST BEDROOM	GYP GLASS	PAINT	GYP	PAINT	GYP	PAINT	GYP	PAINT	WOOD	CLEAR FINISH	MDF	CLEAR FINISH	WOOD	CLEAR FINISH	
205	BATH	GYP TILE	PAINT *	TILE	*	GYP TILE	PAINT *	GYP TILE	PAINT *	TILE		TILE		WOOD	CLEAR FINISH	*TILE TO 6'-8" AFF

Sample finish schedule

Water efficiency (WE) components can be described and scheduled in the plumbing documents if sufficiently detailed and prepared by a team member well versed in LEED for Homes requirements.

18. *Mechanical drawings*: The heating, ventilating, and air-conditioning systems are described on these drawings, and, as with plumbing drawings, are often submitted separately for permitting. Mechanical drawings must always show proof of meeting model energy codes, and incorporate locations for major equipment, ducting layout, diffusers, return-air grilles, and exhaust fans. Drawings often include systems specifications and other such typical items as:

• Plans showing the size, type, and layout of ducting

• Diffusers, heat registers, return-air grilles, dampers

• Turning vanes, ductwork insulation

• HVAC unit: type, quantity, location

• Thermostats: type, quantity, location

• Smoke detectors: quantity, location

• Electrical, water, or gas connections

• Ventilation and exhaust fans

• Symbol legend, general notes, and specific key notes

• Heating and/or cooling load summary

Other information, depending on the project:

• Connection to existing systems

• Demolition of part or all of existing systems

• Smoke detector

• Thermostat programming

• Heat loss and heat gain calculations

• Details: round ducts, turning vanes, diffusers

• Special conditions—for example, seismic restraints

Of all the engineering disciplines, mechanical drawings may provide the greatest opportunity for effective description of LEED products and systems. Indoor environmental quality (IEQ) requirements are extensive and can best be planned if designed and coordinated by a professional familiar with LEED for Homes.

19. *Structural drawings*: These consist of all the drawings and details that describe the structural members of the house and their relationship to each other. Basic working drawings for houses often do not include structural drawings, and may even depend on the builder or framing crew to size joists, rafter, and structural members; as a result, material inefficiencies often result. Builders rely on manufacturers for the design of trusses. In LEED for Homes, points are available for structural systems employing efficient use of materials. Structural drawings can include the following:

• Foundation plans and details

• Framing plans and details for each floor and roof

• Wall sections, column and beam details

• Schedules describing structural components

• General notes, which should include, where applicable: roof, floor, wind, seismic, and other loads; allowable soil pressure or pile-bearing capacity; and allowable stresses of materials used in the design

From a LEED for Homes standpoint, important considerations for structural drawings involve Materials and Resources (MR) considerations such as Material Efficient Framing, EPPs and perhaps preproject considerations for Waste Management.

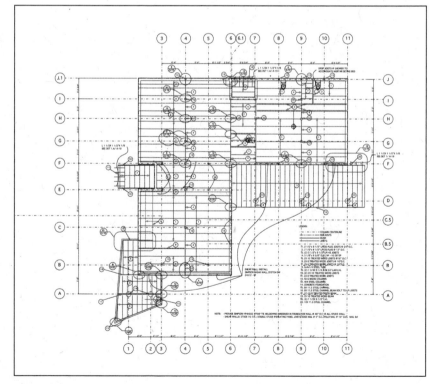

Sample structural plan

Aspects of various structural systems offer LEED for Homes considerations, among them:

- *Wood*: Can be FSC-certified, salvaged, or locally or site-harvested. EPP is the focus of MR1.1 Material Efficient Framing, and any waste can be chipped and used as mulch in compliance with MR Waste Management.

- *Steel*: Many American minimills produce steel with 100 percent recycled content. In some regions, almost all tubing, reinforcing bars, and other specialty shapes are produced by minimills, and most mills are eager to document their compliance with LEED requirements. Not so with fabricators. Minimills are successful because of the amount of steel out there waiting to be salvaged. Creative use of salvaged steel on your project can eliminate the trip to the minimill, save energy, and may be a consideration for LEED Innovation and Design Process (ID) credits.

- *Concrete/masonry/precast*: Think fly ash and slag as major ingredients and 100 percent recycled steel reinforcing.

- *Structural insulated panels (SIPS)*: The poster child for LEED for Homes structural systems. SIPS can be slightly more expensive, but perhaps not if used creatively.

PREPARING THE SPECIFICATIONS

Specifications evolve as the working drawings evolve. Each material, system, product, desired result, or equipment decision made during the working drawing process should be documented and filed in a three-ring binder set up with specification division inserts for incorporation into the specifications written during the last phase of producing the CDs. An excellent method of organization is to reproduce (two-sided) the technical literature for each decision at the time it is made, note the particular characteristics (color, size, accessories, etc. chosen), and file in the appropriate division of the binder.

Specifications are organized into standard divisions relating to types of products used in con-

struction. Each division is further subdivided into individual sections as follows, for example:

Division 7	Thermal and Moisture Protection
07050	Basic Thermal and Moisture Protection Materials and Methods
07100	Dampproofing and Waterproofing
07200	Thermal Protection
07300	Shingles, Roof Tiles, and Roof Coverings
07400	Roofing and Siding Panels
07500	Membrane Roofing
07600	Flashing and Sheet Metal
07700	Roof Specialties and Accessories
07800	Fire and Smoke Protection
07900	Joint Sealers

For specialized products or systems, further subdivision of specification sections not covered by the generic sections can be created, such as 07320 Roof Tile or 07330 Roof Covering (sod or thatched). Go to www.constructionnotebook.com/ipin2/CSIDivisions.asp or http://en.wikipedia.org/wiki/MasterFormat for additional information on specification divisions and subdivisions.

Coordination with Working Drawings

It's essential to coordinate specifications and working drawings. A common tendency is to overdescribe materials in working drawings. For example, a project may utilize a variety of flashing types. Flashing on the drawings should be generically noted as flashing, and the various types of flashing thoroughly described in the specifications. Also, the nomenclature on the drawings should be reflected in the specifications. Concrete masonry units in the specifications should not be called concrete block on the drawings.

Types of Specifications

Specifications, when employed on residential projects, are often given in outline form and can be brief. Specifications for projects to be bid or seeking the highest quality or classification may use longer formats. The MASTERSPEC Web site (www.arcomnet.com/masterspec/masterspec_asc.php) has examples of prewritten specification sections in full-length, short-form, and outline formats. Specifications in outline format can be

placed on the working drawings. Those in short or full-length format are often bound into separate documents as a part of the project manual.

LEED Coordination

Specifications provide an excellent CD vehicle for describing LEED project criteria. MASTERSPEC, a proprietary specifications system and an active member of the USGBC, for example, incorporates many green building considerations in its specifications formats (www.arcomnet.com/users/spec_resources_leed.php). In addition to three Division One LEED-related sections (covering Sustainable Design Requirements, General Commissioning Requirements, and Construction Waste Management and Disposal), MASTERSPEC provides more than 350 sections, with LEED requirements text and commentary, discussions in supporting documents, and a reference book/CD-ROM on specifying LEED requirements. Within individual specification sections, MASTERSPEC describes LEED Submittal and Quality Assurance requirements, both in short and full-length formats. For example, see www.arcomnet.com/pdfs/mss95/09640fl_.pdf for LEED Submittal and Quality Assurance options for Section 09640 Wood Flooring. Building Systems Design, Inc.'s SpecLink offers similar LEED specifications aids. Go to www.bsdsoftlink.com/speclink/sl_LEED.htm.

GreenSpec, an invaluable proprietary source for green products, has introduced four Division 01 specification sections designed to be modified for particular project requirements (www.buildinggreen.com/guidespecs/index.cfm). Note, however, these sections were created for use in the four currently official LEED rating systems and do not necessarily reflect the LEED for Homes program.

Environmentally preferable products (EPPs) under MR2-B of the LEED manual can be a considerable contributor to certification points. Organizing, tracking, and ensuring documentation of products is critical. The example here shows an expanded version of the LEED Manual EPP spreadsheet exhibit adapted for an actual project and used as a summary in the General Conditions Sections of specifications and for coordination throughout a project.

CONSTRUCTION ADMINISTRATION

For LEED and many other projects, construction documents are not complete until the project is finished, occupied, commissioned, and certified. During bidding and negotiation, addenda issued to further describe the project become part of the construction documents. Drawings issued as addenda should be bound into the field and office sets of the CDs. Specifications issued as addenda should similarly be bound into the appropriate specifications divisions of the field and office copies.

During construction, additional information regarding drawings and specifications issued as part of Supplemental Instructions (changes or information not affecting the contract sum) or as Change Orders (changes or information that affect the contract sum) should be incorporated into all field and office copies of the CDs.

Conclusion

As a collaborative initiative, the LEED for Homes program offers powerful tools to influence residential construction methods. By recognizing sustainable design, construction, and operational practices in homes nationwide, LEED-Certified Homes will establish themselves in the minds of homeowners and buyers as a recognized brand identifying the best in high-quality green construction and performance. For those of us (whether buyers, owners, builders, developers, or others) who are or become involved in the design and construction process, LEED for Homes defines criteria for judging whether a home reaches various defined levels of sustainability, but it does not define the process used to get there. Therefore, the following are guidelines to assist in organizing the effort:

1. *Name a project manager (PM) for the project.* Well-crafted construction documents are one of the key components in organizing LEED for Homes efforts. Critical to the delivery of a successful project is that all team members work together to embrace the scope, schedule, and budget, and be responsible to keep these in focus when making decisions, then document those decisions in well-crafted and easily

understood construction documents. For the team to be effective, one person must be defined as the PM. In general, the PM should allow everyone to talk to everyone else but must be informed about all communications and give final approval on all decisions. To successfully integrate LEED for Homes into the construction documents, the PM must:

- Gain in-depth knowledge of the LEED for Homes manual.

- Create spreadsheets to assist tracking criteria.

- Work closely with the builder in making decisions.

- Understand how points may be lost through poor coordination and planning.

- Create an interaction matrix of team members indicating LEED credits within their range of expertise, with credit status updated on a scheduled basis.

2. *Plan the construction documents.* The key to successful construction documents is planning the documents before starting the CD process. A few suggestions:

- Identify and educate the project team, and specify responsibilities, tasks, and goals for each project team member. Assign a project manager with central responsibilities for coordination and decisions during the construction document process.

- Organize your thought processes to go from the general to the specific as the process evolves, so you don't get lost in minutiae in the early stages.

- Review, understand, and document code and jurisdictional requirements prior to initiating the construction documents.

- Create a LEED for Homes task chart defining LEED tasks and coordination for each team member.

- Create a LEED for Homes EPP and innovation chart and update it for each project team meeting

An expanded version of the LEED Manual EPP spreadsheet exhibit adapted for an actual project

- Carefully review all of the potential components of the complete set of CDs and decide which ones are to be produced (refer back to the CD Terminology sidebar and the Process section earlier in the chapter).

- Organize binders in which to document your decisions so you don't have to revisit them time and time again.

- Organize the materials required for working drawings and specifications. Consider creating binders into which cutsheets and other information can be inserted for continuing reference and documentation of decisions.

- Plan to incorporate LEED decisions into project documents in the design phase, construction documents phase, and construction phase.

- Create checklists and adhere to redlines and reviews at regular intervals.

- Resolve all contractual issues as soon as possible and integrate the decisions into the documents.

- Consider making 8½ x 11-inch maquettes of each sheet of working drawings in the construction documents set.

- Write an initial outline specification for continual revision and notation during the working drawing process.

- Reference applicable LEED Resource categories and EPPs in the working drawings and specifications.

- Include or reference commissioning requirements in the specifications.

- Review and coordinate the construction documents and LEED decisions at scheduled stages during the production of the working drawings and specifications. For example, conduct 30, 60, and 90 percent complete reviews.

- Thoroughly review the content, coordination, and cross-referencing of the construction documents prior to issuing for pricing or construction.

- Incorporate into the final construction documents clear explanations of all LEED credits under consideration. Resolve all credits and define material and construction methods (where required).

- Check your work. Consider using a third party to help catch the issues you might miss.

- After producing your well-crafted CDs, prepare to enjoy the rewards!

Resource Summary

Example Specifications
www.constructionnotebook.com/ipin2/
  CSIDivisions.asp

http://en.wikipedia.org/wiki/MasterFormat

www.arcomnet.com/masterspec/masterspec_asc
  .php

www.arcomnet.com/users/spec_resources_leed-
  .php

www.arcomnet.com/pdfs/mss95/09640fl_.pdf

www.buildinggreen.com/guidespecs/index.cfm

Supplementary Conditions Guide
www.aia.org/docs_free_paperdocuments

AIA Documents Summary
www.aia.org/SiteObjects/files/docs_paper-
  pricelist.pdf

LEED for Homes Agreement for Home Builders
www.contects.com/pdf/leedsteps/2007 Builder
  Agreement.pdf

LEED for Homes
www.usgbc.org/DisplayPage.aspx?CMSPage-
  ID=147

GreenSpec Products
www.buildinggreen.com/menus/

Greenguard Environmental Institute Products
http://greenguard.org

Energy and Environmental Building Association Builder's Guide
www.eeba.org/bookstore/books.asp?CatID=1

Building Science Press Builder's Guide
www.buildingsciencepress.com/books.asp?
  CatID=1

Working Drawing Manual by Fred A. Stitt (printed on recycled paper)
Author: Fred A. Stitt; Format: Paperback (Illustrated), 352 pages. Publication Date: May 1998. Publisher: McGraw-Hill.

Architectural Graphic Standards
www.wiley.com/WileyCDA/Section/id-
301525.html

Residential Green Architecture Checklist
http://doerr.org/checklists/Green-
  Residential.pdf

Residential Interiors

■ Michelle Timberlake, ASID, and William Carpenter, FAIA, PhD

THE RESIDENTIAL INTERIOR design profession is a multifaceted one, providing research and programming services, schematic design, development of conceptual studies, and the execution of construction documents and plans for the interior home environment. As defined by the National Council for Interior Design Qualification, the objective of the interior designer is to "improve the quality of life, increase productivity, and protect the health, safety, and welfare of the public." As interior designers, we must take this objective a step further. While the objective is to design interior space for our clients that is safe and healthy, we must also be sure that we are integrating methodologies that interface with the architectural intent, the site, the community, and, most importantly, our clients' need for "home." The residential interior designer adheres to a logical and systematic series of steps throughout the design process, always returning to the research and the analysis of that information, to ultimately assimilate it into the appropriate design of a creative interior space.

While the design process for residential interiors has a seemingly esoteric approach, a collective of psychological and physiological information gathering, it should always also be acutely creative, always questioning, "What is *good* design?" Clients may or may not wish to be educated on this topic; they may or may not wish

to have a full understanding of the design process; but they do deserve an interior designer who understands the "rules," and understands, too, which rules may be broken.

The modern residential interior designer is responsible on a very intimate level to the client. The interior designer is the client's advocate. The role of the designer goes beyond engaging a client and listening to his or her dreams and vision for "home"; the interior designer must constantly refer to the objective, asking: "Is this design improving the quality of life for my client? Is this design protecting the health, safety, and welfare of my client?"

Sustainability in architecture has been gaining momentum in recent years, as has the awareness of eco-friendly design in interior spaces. Since the early nineties, the commercial interior design sector has been sentient to the need to have healthier interior environments; but, now, green residential interior design is quickly becoming a modus operandi.

In this chapter focusing on sustainable interior design practices, the intent is threefold: (1) to inform about the history of the sustainable design movement as it relates to interior design and decorating; (2) to present information and guidelines for designing with an eco-friendly-based checklist; and (3) to open a dialogue to bridge the fields of architecture, landscape design, and interior design, while maintaining a green sensibility.

Always design a thing by considering it in its next larger context—a chair in a room, a room in a house, a house in an environment, an environment in a city plan.

ELIEL SAARINEN

Opposite:The home was constructed around the three large trees that were already on-site; the roof conforms to the tree. (Steven Ehrlich, FAIA)

Above: View from the hearth toward the loft wall and kitchen space. (Bush Residence)

Left: Kitchen view toward floating cabinet. (Bush Residence)

How History Launched a Movement

IMPACT OF THE INDUSTRIAL REVOLUTION

What is *sustainable interior design*? To answer this question, we must first consider the history of interiors going back to the Industrial Revolution, which catapulted Western countries into a new age. The late eighteenth and early nineteenth centuries saw an almost immeasurable shift in technology and socioeconomic conditions that continues today. Nearly every facet of daily life in this century has been touched and influenced by

"There is no excuse which I have heard that can compensate for a poorly designed building. The only thing that I can say about an individual who takes no responsibility for his ideas is either lazy or a truly uncaring person."

FRANK LLOYD WRIGHT,
The Natural House

the impact of this turning point in history, right down to the kitchen you wash your dishes in and the detergent you wash them with. Some say that the onset of the Industrial Revolution, which started in Britain, led to effective border controls, which helped to reduce the spread of disease, which in turn helped to prevent epidemics. This directly affected the workforce because more children were living past infancy; hence, more people were then available to join the workforce. And as food production became more efficient, people were able to find employment in other venues.

Of course, it was the technological advancements that really added fuel to the Industrial Revolution fire, in particular the invention of the steam engine. The textile industry was changed dramatically by steam-powering the machinery that not only produced the material but also improved the efficiency of production. Machine tools for working wood and metal speeded the mass production of building materials, furnishings, and equipment. The metals industry was changed during this period, too, when organic fuels (e.g., wood) were replaced with fossil fuels (e.g., coal). The production of chemicals such as sodium carbonate and calcium hypochlorite (bleach powder) were notable advancements as well. Sodium carbonate made the manufacture of textiles, paper products, and soap a more controllable process, as well as cost-effective. Bleach powder replaced the traditional process of sun-bleaching textiles after soaking them first with sour milk, substantially reducing the time to produce a finished product. During the latter part of the Industrial Revolution, gas lighting was introduced, an invention that had an impact not only on industry—factories and stores could remain open longer—but also on society and the economy— cities could now offer nightlife.

INFLUENCE OF OTHER DESIGN MOVEMENTS

What does the Industrial Revolution have to do with sustainable interior design? For a short time after this period, in response to the excesses of the Victorian Age, the aesthetic movement emerged, lasting until the 1880s. The objective of this movement was to bring back the craftsmanship and the honesty of materials, lost when the machines of the Industrial Revolution replaced the woodworkers and craftsmen. The aesthetic movement bridged the gap between the Victorian eras (gothic, rococo, and the Renaissance) with the arts and crafts movement (1860s–1890s). Designers like William Morris strived for a return to craftsmanship, handmade construction, and inspiration from nature. In America, designers would use machines to their advantage by constructing a product with the machine first and then hand-finishing it.

The arts and crafts movement evolved into art nouveau, which many consider the first "modern" style. The designs from this period emphasized asymmetry, free forms, and natural figures. Art nouveau was the first design aesthetic to be applied not only to architecture and design but also to industrial design, jewelry, fashion, and graphic design. The zenith of art nouveau may have been the 1902 exhibition at the Esposizione Internazionale d'Arte Decorative Moderna in Italy, a veritable trade show where designers of the period presented the latest in the modern style, which made use of nineteenth-century technologies, such as the use of exposed iron, and instilled a hand-finishing technique. This was all in contrast to the Industrial Revolution, not to mention the historical designs of the century.

By the beginning of the First World War, the writhing plant forms and highly stylized designs typical of art nouveau, which were expensive to produce, began to lose popularity, in favor of more rectilinear and streamlined styles that were less costly, and thought to be more faithful to the industrial aesthetic of the art deco movement of the early twentieth century. Initially called style moderne, art deco was essentially a collective of many different styles and movements including cubism, modernism, Bauhaus, and art nouveau. Whereas most movements are influenced by political and philosophical influences, art deco was solely decorative, utilizing materials such as lacquer, inlaid wood, aluminum, and zebra skin, in stepped forms and sweeping curves considered ultra modern. Seemingly omnipresent chevron patterns and the sunburst motifs were used in industrial design (e.g., automobile radiator grilles), fashion design, and architecture (e.g., the Chrysler Building).

Emerging as the art nouveau movement faded was modernism, and with it Frank Lloyd Wright. One of Wright's trademarks in all his work was the detailed attention he paid to the interior space planning of his projects. He utilized built-in furnishings that made smaller spaces seem larger; kitchens, while small were efficient; interior colors were derived from the natural surroundings of the site. Wright's Prairie-style houses are said to be the first examples of an "open plan" architectural footprint, where the kitchen was more accessible to the living and dining areas, to allow for more social interaction. Wright also coined the term *organic architecture*, to promote accord between nature and the human environment through design. The goal of organic architecture was to integrate the design with the site to form a unified composition.

In the 1930s, Wright practiced what by today's standards would be considered a sustainable concept. He began designing the Usonian home, a small, simple, usually single-story structure intended to be a cost-conscious dwelling for his middle-class clients. He deemed that the Usonian house would be constructed of native materials, utilize passive solar heating and cooling methods, and ensure an abundance of natural light through the use of clerestory windows. Visual connections would be made between inside and outside, such as living space opening up to an exterior terrace.

In contrast to art nouveau and art deco, which introduced the concept of ubiquitous design in society, Frank Lloyd Wright promoted the concept of organic architecture, in conjunction with the ideal of fully integrated and designed architectural interior spaces. Interior design today still feels the influence of Wright's philosophies, as seen in his Usonian and Prairie designs.

INFLUENCE OF FASHION AND CELEBRITY CULTURE

Today, interior design is greatly influenced by the trends—the colors, fabrics, and styles—dictated by the fashion industry and paraded on the fashion runways each new season. How? For one thing, as fashion designers begin to create and produce clothing made from organic and eco-friendly materials, the home goods sector is taking notice. Even more noticeable are the number of celebrities jumping on the green bandwagon. Here are just a few of many examples:

- On November 29, 2001, *USA Today* reported that the actor Woody Harrelson had worn a Giorgio Armani tuxedo made of hemp to the 1997 Golden Globe Awards. It was also noted that Armani had begun to manufacture recycled jeans and organic cotton shirts.

- The clothing designer prAna, a member of the Organic Trade Association, states it "is continually increasing the use of organic cotton, as well as sourcing other natural fibers and innovative recycled/upcycled materials."

- In the May 2007 issue of *Vogue* magazine, Los Angeles-based Viridis Lux was profiled for its earth-kind and chic hemp and bamboo fashions, and its philosophy that "designing is part of the solution." Celebrities such as Eva Mendes and Catherine Zeta-Jones are wearing clothes from the Viridis Lux line, helping to spread the word and bring notoriety to sustainable concepts in the design industry.

- In August 2007, Warner Independent Pictures released *The 11th Hour*, narrated by actor and environmental activist Leonardo DiCaprio. The film asks the question: "Are the environmental changes on this earth permanent or can they be reversed?"

- In 2007, Robert Redford launched *Big Ideas for a Small Planet*, *Ecobiz*, and *Ecoists* on his Sundance TV channel.

In a July 2003 article in *GRIST* actress Julia Louis-Dreyfus discussed her ocean-front home north of Santa Barbara, and how she and architect David Hertz, of Syndesis, went about planning and developing an eco-friendly home. In short, we can thank celebrities for using their public platforms to campaign for a more sustainable world. But what about those of us who work in the building industry? It is said that the building industry is one of the largest contributors to greenhouse gases. Who is leading the cause in our world? How do we as designers and architects help to transform the sustainable design movement from a grassroots campaign to a sustainable practice?

"So here I stand before you preaching organic architecture: declaring organic architecture to be the modern ideal and the teaching so much needed if we are to see the whole of life, and to now serve the whole of life, holding no traditions essential to the great TRADITION. Nor cherishing any preconceived form fixing upon us either past, present, or future, but instead exalting the simple laws of common sense, or of super-sense if you prefer determining form by way of nature of materials..."

FRANK LLOYD WRIGHT,
An Organic Architecture, 1939

The Importance of Practicing Sustainable Interior Design

The American Society of Interior Designers (ASID) states:

> Green design is design that goes beyond being just efficient, attractive, on time, and on budget. It is a design that cares about how such goals are achieved, about its effect on people and on the environment. An environmentally responsible professional makes a commitment to constantly try to find ways to diminish design's impact on the world around us.

In *Sustainable Residential Interiors* (John Wiley & Sons, 2006), the authors (Associates III: Kari Foster, Annette Stelmack, and Debbie Hindman) credit Rachael Carson with launching the environmental movement in her 1962 book *Silent Spring.* "In it," they write, "she made a radical proposal: that, at times, technological progress is so fundamentally at odds with natural processes that it must be curtailed. Prior to the book's publication, conservation had never before raised much broad public interest, for until then few people had worried about the disappearing wilderness."

As professional interior designers, we must do more than jump on the green bandwagon; we must be agents for change. We must maintain a growing awareness of why it is essential to design interiors that are conscientiously designed, with the safety and welfare of the inhabitants in the forefront of our minds. Most people today spend the majority of their days in buildings of one sort or another. Clearly, then, indoor air quality can dramatically affect our lives, which means it should dramatically influence the way we go about designing interior spaces. As interior designers and architects, we are not bound by an oath or by law to design with indoor air quality in mind, but we should be bound by conscience to design healthy spaces for our clients.

HEALTH EFFECTS OF POORLY DESIGNED INTERIOR SPACES

In an October 2000 National Institutes of Health (NIH) *Record* article, Roland Owens quotes Dr. Floyd Malveaux, a nationally recognized expert on asthma and allergic diseases. Dr. Malveaux explained that asthma is a chronic inflammatory disease of the lungs and that, at the time, there were approximately 17 million asthmatics in the United States. Triggers of asthma can include air pollutants, paint and finish odors, and smoke. Malveaux said, "The smart expenditure of resources is in prevention, rather than...managing crises." The volatile organic compounds (VOCs) found in paint, fabrics, and carpeting can perpetuate and exacerbate asthma, as well as other upper respiratory afflictions such as bronchitis.

Poor indoor air quality also has been shown to cause other health problems, ranging from minor irritations to life-threatening illnesses. So problematic has this become that the United States Environmental Protection Agency (EPA) has defined two categories of health issues connected with buildings: sick building syndrome (SBS) and building-related illnesses (BRI).

SBS is the term used to refer to the health complaints of occupants of certain buildings that appear to be linked to time spent in the buildings but for which no specific illness or cause can be identified. The complaints may be localized to a particular room or zone, or may be widespread throughout the building. Indicators of SBS include:

- Acute discomfort; for example, headache; eye, nose, or throat irritation; dry cough; dry or itchy skin; dizziness and nausea; difficulty in concentrating; fatigue; and sensitivity to odors.

- The cause of the symptoms is not known.

- Most of the complainants report relief soon after leaving the building.

BRI refers to diagnosable symptoms and/or illnesses that can be attributed directly to airborne building contaminants. Indicators of BRI include:

- Cough; chest tightness; fever, chills, and muscle aches

- The symptoms can be clinically defined and have clearly identifiable causes.

- Complainants may require prolonged recovery times after leaving the building.

A 1984 World Health Organization (WHO) Committee report suggested that up to 30 percent of new and remodeled buildings worldwide may be the subject of complaints related to poor indoor air quality (IAQ). Often, the condition is temporary; but some buildings have long-term problems, frequently resulting when a building is operated, maintained, or used in a manner that is inconsistent with its original design or prescribed operating procedures. But sometimes indoor air quality problems are the result of poor building design.

It is important to note that complaints from building occupants may, of course, result from other causes. These may include an illness contracted outside the building, acute sensitivity (e.g., allergies), job-related stress or job dissatisfaction, and other psychosocial factors. Nevertheless, studies show that symptoms may be caused or exacerbated by indoor air quality problems.

Another condition called multiple chemical sensitivity (MCS) is a major cause for concern related to IAQ. To that end, the Interagency Workgroup on Multiple Chemical Sensitivity (MCS), referenced by the National Institute of Environmental Health Sciences (NIEHS), developed a "predecisional draft" in August 1998 on MCS, stating:

> Multiple chemical sensitivity (MCS) is the term most commonly applied to a condition that challenges patients, health-care providers, and health and environmental agencies alike. Persons reported as suffering from MCS present with outcomes that range from minor discomfort to severe disability. However, many scientists and medical specialists continue to debate the validity of MCS as a distinct disease entity.

> In 1995, because of concern for the health and well-being of persons with symptoms of MCS and because MCS presents challenging policy issues, several federal agencies that conduct or sponsor environmental programs formed

the Interagency Workgroup on Multiple Chemical Sensitivity (referred to as "the workgroup" in this report). The workgroup reviewed relevant scientific literature, considered recommendations previously issued by various expert panels, reviewed current and past federal actions, and developed technical and policy recommendations concerning MCS.

The report was evaluated by experts in occupational and/or environmental medicine, toxicology, immunology, psychology, psychiatry, and physiology. The intention of the report was *not* to provide guidelines for the clinical management of those with symptoms of MCS or to appraise diagnostic tests or methods of treatment of MCS. In basic terms, it was to recommend that a number of federal agencies consider MCS, among them the Department of Defense, Department of Energy, Department of Health and Human Services, Department of Veterans Affairs, and the U.S. Environmental Protection Agency. The consensus of this draft report seems to be that more research is needed in order to deem MCS a valid condition; however, it made clear there is a need to inform the healthcare community about MCS.

The symptoms of MCS, often occurring following exposure to certain VOCs, can affect more than one body organ system and can occur, recur, and disappear, depending on the level of exposure to low levels of chemicals containing VOCs. Because MCS is difficult to study and define, its actual existence is still disputed. Some think that the health indicators of MCS are psy-chological, while others believe they are physiological; still others purport the symptoms are indicators that MCS is both psychological and physiological.

Researchers have identified six criteria used in the diagnosis of MCS:[1]

1. Symptoms are reproducible with repeated (chemical) exposures.

2. The condition has persisted for a significant period of time.

3. Low levels of exposure (lower than previously or commonly tolerated) result in manifestations of the syndrome (i.e., increased sensitivity).

4. The symptoms improve, or resolve completely, when the triggering chemicals are removed.

5. Responses often occur to multiple, chemically unrelated substances.

Symptoms involve multiple-organ symptoms (e.g., runny nose, itchy eyes, headache, scratchy throat, earache, scalp pain, mental confusion or sleepiness, palpitations of the heart, upset stomach, nausea and/or diarrhea, abdominal cramping, aching joints).

Claudia Miller, MD, University of Texas Health Science Center, has defined MCS as "sensitivities to extraordinarily low levels of environmental chemicals" appearing "to develop *de novo* in some individuals following acute or chronic exposure to a wide variety of environmental agents including various pesticides, solvents, drugs, and air contaminants," including those found in sick buildings.[2]

And Pamela Reed Gibson, PhD, in her book *Understanding and Accommodating People with MCS* lists the following as indicators of MCS:[3]

• Anaphylactic shock

• Chest pains

• Asthma

• Skin sensitivity and irritation

• Headaches

• Short-term memory loss

• Weakness

• Seizures

• Visual impairment

• Nausea

• Dizziness, and joint and muscle pain

Some of the VOCs emitted by interior materials (petrol-based wood preservatives, polyurethanes, glues, painted finishes, etc.) include:

• Household cleaning detergents

• Fiber shed from textiles and insulation

• Biological materials and gases (molds, fungi, bacteria)

• Dust particulates

• Air fresheners and scented chemicals

• Bleach, fabric softeners, and laundry agents

Case Study: Designing a Healthy House

Carter+Burton Architecture was approached in the late nineties by a couple moving from the Washington, DC, area. Their goal was to find a design firm that could create for them a modern home that was also a healthy home. The latter was particularly important because Mrs. D. was suffering from MCS and was predisposed to allergies triggered by fragrances and many odors.

Ironically, Mrs. D. had worked for the EPA for many years, during which time the building where she worked was renovated, to replace deteriorating carpet, do periodic painting, and install new systems furnishings with fabric panels, and so on. As a result, the indoor air quality in her office building became so toxic from off-gassing of the furnishings and finishes that her health began to deteriorate rapidly. She and her husband began to research and plan the construction of a healthy house where she could lead a relatively normal life.

They contacted Carter+Burton, whose team welcomed the opportunity to design one of the first known healthy houses in Virginia's Shenandoah Valley. The firm had already begun practicing passive-solar design, and had a modern aesthetic, but from the get-go collaborating with a client with MCS presented a new challenge for them. Even meetings had to be held outside their office because the fumes from the blueprinting machine made Mrs. D. very ill. Very quickly, MCS, which was something they had only read about, became very real. They had conducted research into the syndrome in preparation for working with Mrs. D, whose symptoms included slurring of speech, weakness, severe headaches, memory lapses, and dizziness. The designers, who had also conducted research on building materials, began to understand why: plywood was treated with formaldehyde, paints contained volatile organic compounds, and wood floors were often sealed with oil-based polyurethane. It seemed, in fact, as if every building material had an ingredient list topped by the word *petrochemical*.

Carter+Burton was also called on to provide the couple with interior design services. Fortuitously, the interior designer assigned to work with them had experience in the commercial sector prior to joining C+B and, coincidentally, had firsthand experience with the building Mrs. D. had worked in. She was aware it was devoid of ample daylighting, that entrants to the building had to pass through a lobby where smoking was permitted, and that the systems furnishings at the time were not yet on par with current standards. Formaldehydes and glues were commonplace in the production of the goods used in the systems and, worse, they had been installed as soon as they came off production lines, meaning they offgassed into an already toxic environment. The designer, who was very aware of sick building syndrome, was not surprised to hear that her new client was suffering from MCS.

The dining room view at Boxhead, architect Jim Burton's (Carter + Burton Architecture) own home, showing the room as a discreet interior volume.

The kitchen view at Boxhead, showing the stained concrete floor and the strong horizontal window.

Above: The Boxhead living room, with its double-height space and high clerestory.

Left: Another living room view at Boxhead.

The loft space above the living room at Boxhead serves as a home office.

Boxhead's master bath, with its elegant built-in tub and sink.

Before beginning the space planning process, the interior designer reviewed with her clients their existing furnishings that they wanted to use in their new home; they also outlined goals and requirements for new furnishings and finishes. The most challenging space was the main living area. It featured views on three sides and would require two seating arrangements; at the same time, it had to be capable of being unified for entertainment purposes. And the items in the space had to be healthy *and* relate to the architecture. Together, Mr. and Mrs. D. and the designer decided that a large, custom-sized and custom-colored and patterned Tuffenkian wool rug was the best solution for the floor covering. It allowed for the perimeter of the room to remain free of furnishings, making it easy to meander the perimeter to enjoy the views, so that the concrete floor could absorb the sun's warmth during the cooler winter months. The design of the rug also delineated the space for the two seating areas, and served as a wayfinder to the door, leading to a walled sculpture garden outside. The challenge was to ensure that the dyes used in the rug were not chromium-based, but vegetable dyes, and that the wool was not stripped of its natural lanolin only to be treated with a petro-chemical stain repellent. It was also important that the rug be dense enough to preclude the need for a rug pad, and that the backing be of natural fibers, not poly-based. The designer also had to verify that no known chemical cleaners would be used during the washing process.

ECO-RATING SYSTEMS: LEED AND CRADLE TO CRADLE

LEED

As SBS, BRI, and MCS became widely understood in the commercial design sector, the National Resources Defense Council (NRDC) began to organize Leadership in Energy and Environmental Design (LEED). Launched in 1996, initially LEED was used as a rating system for commercial architectural and interior design projects; now it is beginning to cross over into the private sector. The growth of sustainable projects, both commercial and residential, certainly can be linked to the U.S. Green Building Council's (USGBC) influence. With the establishment of LEED for Commercial Interiors (CI) and LEED for Homes (LH), it is no surprise that this is one of the fastest-growing sectors in the architecture, design, and building industry. To quote from the USGBC Web site:

> LEED for Commercial Interiors is the green benchmark for the tenant improvement market. It is the recognized system for certifying high-performance green interiors that are healthy, productive places to work; are less costly to operate and maintain; and have a reduced environmental footprint. LEED for Commercial Interiors gives the power to make sustainable choices to tenants and designers, who do not always have control over whole building operations.
>
> LEED for Homes is a rating system that promotes the design and construction of high-performance green homes. A green home uses less energy, water, and natural resources; creates less waste; and is healthier and more comfortable for the occupants. Benefits of a LEED home include lower energy and water bills; reduced greenhouse gas emissions; and less exposure to mold, mildew, and other indoor toxins. The net cost of owning a LEED home is comparable to that of owning a conventional home.

Residential interior designers today have the opportunity to utilize environmentally friendly materials and furnishings that have a positive health effect on their clients, which in turn benefits the earth, when specified in a new design or remodel of a residence. Designers now have resources that were not available even five years ago for designing sustainable interiors for their clients. To advance the implementation of these resources and materials, the USGBC has partnered with ASID to initiate REGREEN, a set of guidelines—the nation's first—for green residential renovations and remodels. The guidelines aim to increase the understanding of sustainable renovation project procedures while benefiting

Operable windows are located to allow hot air to rise and pass through, and for natural cross-ventilation through the home. The windows along the south façade are also shaded by a series of abstract fins. (Solar Umbrella—Pugh + Scarpa)

Solar panels were installed on the roof; they also wrap down the west building façade to illustrate that the panels can be beautiful as well as functional.

the homeowner, the design professionals, and the product suppliers, and ultimately supporting the demand for green building and renovation practices and materials.

As yet, there is no LEED for residential interior design, but designers can certainly use the rating systems set forth in LEED for Homes and LEED-CI and the REGREEN guidelines as tools for making the interior spaces they design more eco-friendly and healthier for the end user. They will find checklists for specifying green finishes such as paints, plasters, and coatings; eco-friendly plumbing fixtures and supplies; flooring and floor coverings; lighting; and appliances. For now, however, when it comes to furnishings (furniture, window treatments, area rugs, and accessories), interior designers will have to rely on their own research and on the veracity of manufacturers' claims about those goods until stringent guidelines are set forth. In the case of the latter, interior designers and decorators would be wise to remain wary of "greenwashing," the unethical practice of touting products as "green" that do not, in fact, offer health or environmental benefits.

Cradle to Cradle

William McDonough's book, *Cradle to Cradle: Remaking the Way We Make Things*, written with his colleague, Dr. Michael Braungart, calls for the transformation of industry through ecologically and environmentally intelligent design. The authors provide facts about the history of the Industrial Revolution and the unintended consequences that we face today as a result of opportunistic design and manufacturing that was set in motion during that period of commerce. They explain that if designers make use of natural systems (e.g., local materials, solar energy, wind energy, nutrient cycling) products can be created and manufactured that will enable commerce to prosper, along with the health of the planet and its inhabitants.

To that end, in 1995, McDonough and Braungart founded their firm, McDonough Braungart Design Chemistry, LLC (MBDC), "to promote and shape the *next industrial revolution* through the introduction of a new design paradigm called Cradle to Cradle Design, and the implementation

of eco-effective design principles." Cradle to Cradle (C2C) Certification is "a means to tangibly, credibly measure achievement in environmentally intelligent design, and helps customers purchase and specify products that are pursuing a broader definition of quality." Cradle to Cradle Certification, which labels products that meet the C2C guidelines, is an essential resource for interior designers. MBDC has encouraged manufacturers of building materials and interior products to develop products in which every ingredient is safe and either biodegrades naturally or can be recycled into quality materials for future products.

The certification of these goods is based on the evaluation of five criteria established by MBDC:

1. Materials

2. Material reutilization/design for the environment

3. Energy

4. Water

5. Social responsibility

Products meeting certain criteria within these categories are awarded certification at three levels: silver, gold, or platinum. The Cradle to Cradle certification program has certified and rated a wide range of materials and products, from diapers and cleaning solutions to surface coatings, window shades, and office furnishings.

The exterior is clad in stucco that has been incorporated with colored pigment to preclude the need to repaint. (Solar Umbrella—Pugh + Scarpa).

Conclusion

Interior designers and decorators must be prepared to research the products and furnishings they specify for their clients, so that they may reliably recommend these materials as green. Although LEED and Cradle to Cradle Certification offer the means to evaluate the "greenness" of building materials, they have yet to fully establish criteria to do so for home goods and furnishings. Therefore, to conclude this chapter, three green product directories are listed for specifying interior finishes, furnishings, and equipment, and, perhaps, for cross-referencing with programs like LEED. Note that neither ASID nor the USGBC endorses these directories, but they can serve as a starting point for designers and architects alike.

- *Greenspec Directory*: An online directory that lists products for environmentally preferable goods. The products are selected by the editors of *BuildingGreen*.

- *The Green Guide*: National Geographic's directory offers staff reviews of building materials, residential furnishings, and appliances.

- *Green2Green*: This online directory offers information and comparisons of products using environmental, economic, and technical criteria.

Finally, here are some final thoughts on "going green" in your practice:

- Make an ecologically sound choice of wood by patronizing suppliers that can verify through a chain of custody that the original trees they use came from an ecologically sustainable forest managed under guidelines of the Forest Stewardship Council.

- Specify green paint and other finishing materials that have documented levels of volatile organic compounds (VOCs), that contain chemical-emitting materials at the lowest levels possible, and that the rate of emissions, or dissipation, is as fast as possible.

- Specify paints and finishes that do not contain formaldehyde, a known carcinogen.

- Specify sustainable fabrics that support the use of materials from rapidly renewable, postconsumer or postindustrial sources.

- Use rapidly renewable flooring products such as bamboo or linoleum to help reduce the amount of land and resources dedicated to producing construction materials.

- Specify energy-efficient appliances such as dishwashers and refrigerators with the ENERGY STAR rating.

- Design around standard product sizes to reduce material waste.

- Consider the recyclability of all materials used to redirect their "next life" away from landfills.

The Sustainable Modern Home:
Case Studies

Vanguard Sustainable Homes

THE CASE STUDIES DESCRIBED IN this chapter represent a group of vanguard projects that delineate the current best practices in sustainable residential design, beginning with incorporating sustainable principles early in the design process. These projects also illustrate the convergence of the eco-modern movement and the modernist ethos; and each of the projects construes the notion of universal space. Finally, these projects direct us to a future where sustainable design is part of the "DNA" of architecture, one in which each decision contributes to the overall design of the home—the landscape, the interior, and exterior.

Best practices you'll see addressed in the case studies in this chapter include:

- Sustainable site planning
- Use of healthy building materials
- Attention to indoor air quality
- Energy conservation and efficiency
- Maximized efficiency of interior spaces

In short, here you'll read about some of the best examples of residential architecture in the world, produced by some of the most talented architects in the sustainable modern design movement. This is a movement that has grown dramatically over the past 10 years and that will no doubt continue to evolve over the next 10. To borrow from Malcolm Gladwell, we have reached a "tipping point" in architectural practice, participating in the meeting between eco-design and modernism.

Black House, Prickwillow, England

Designer/Architect: Meredith Bowles, Mole Architects

■ By Wesley Thiele and William Carpenter

I N 2001, MEREDITH BOWLES, PRINCIPAL of Mole Architects, completed his home and studio in Prickwillow, a small village near the town of Ely, England. Designed to accommodate both his growing architectural practice and his family of four, the home constitutes three floors of living space, and five bedrooms (two of which previously served as a work studio). At 150 square meters, or just over 1,500 square feet, the home seems to encompass a significant amount of living space within its relatively small stature. The structure is oriented on its site so as to maximize all that the surrounding landscape has to offer, and to spotlight its shed-like qualities, a form that inspired Bowles in the design of the house.

OVERVIEW

In the small village of Prickwillow, some 80 miles outside of London, the Black House sits along a small road lined with other houses, nestled against a rural backdrop. Adjacent houses are typical brick developer style, mixed with older, semidetached houses. "Fairly mean-spirited, all of them" is how Bowles describes the structures. This is a very scenic part of eastern England, in the Fens, a historically rich area of reclaimed wetlands and salt marshes that have been drained for centuries, and entirely by the early nineteenth century, for agricultural purposes. For Bowles, the agricultural nature of the landscape was the most intriguing aspect of the design proposition. The working agricultural sheds that dot the immediate surrounding were fascinating to the architect, as evidenced by his extensive photograph collection of sheds from around the world. More specifically, these buildings became the formal point of departure for Bowles's modern rendition, "The landscape almost demands it," he says, in response to the

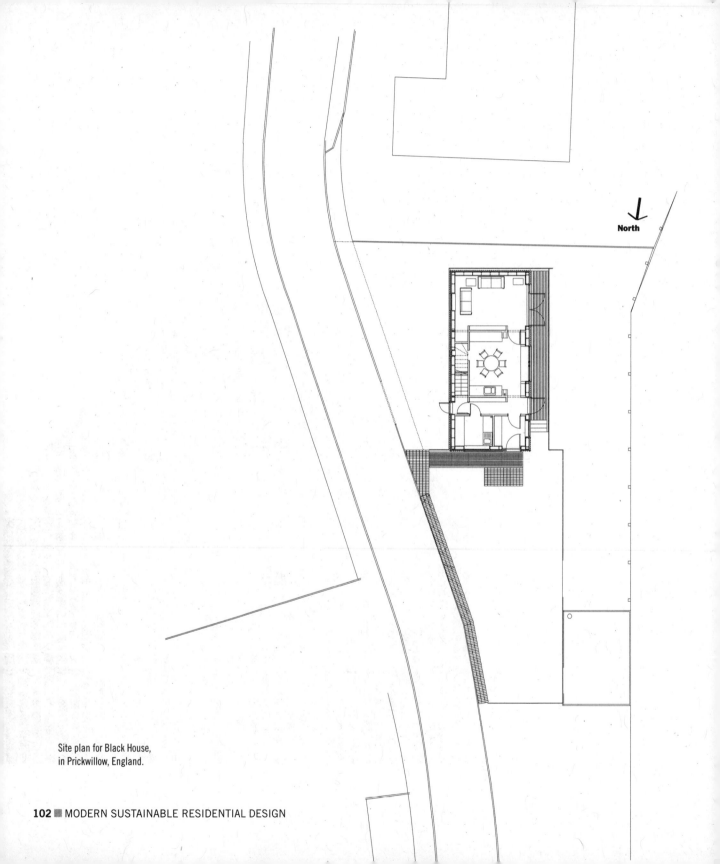

North

Site plan for Black House,
in Prickwillow, England.

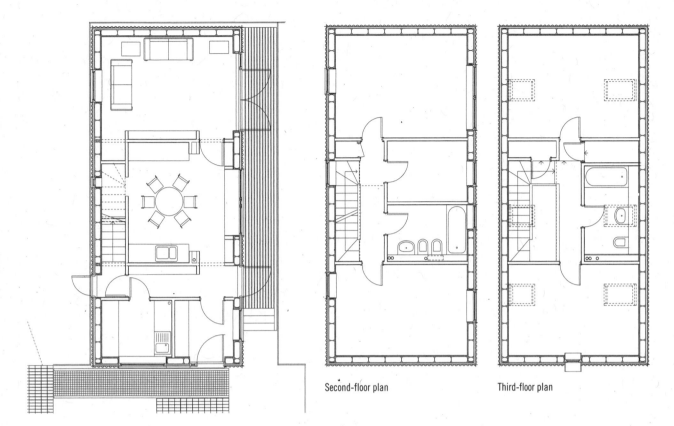

Second-floor plan

Third-floor plan

First-floor plan

question whether it was always his intention to design his home with a shed-inspired styling.

As noted, the site is small—only 15 meters by 25 meters (82 feet by 50 feet). The house expands beyond the official property line by, as Bowles explains, "relying on the borrowed landscape from the surrounding fields, without a fence between them and us." This was one of the motives behind the westerly orientation of the house, which offers a twofold benefit: It yields a view of the historically significant twelfth-century Ely Cathedral and enables solar gain in the winter months, which helps to heat the home with minimal supplementary energy usage. The east-west orientation also gave the best quality of light inside, and was the most efficient option, as a southern orientation was just not possible.

DESIGN DETAILS

The Black House is compositionally long and narrow, both in plan and in section, so as to resemble as closely as possible the vernacular sheds that so captivate Bowles. At three floors, the home is both taller and narrower than its single-story predecessor, yet it retains its formal characteristics in a modern and sophisticated way. The long and narrow frame of the dwelling allows natural light to penetrate rooms from both sides. The western façade, which is highly glazed, is treated with external thermal canopies to the ground floor and reflective coatings on the first-floor windows.

Spatially and formally the plan is simple and unassuming. On the ground floor, the kitchen and dining room serve as the dual focal point, the

heart of the home. Said Bowles, "We wanted spaces that joined together but that could be separated, as kids and parents have different priorities." The stairway stands as the constant element on all floors, opening up to all three levels of the home while permitting morning light to pierce the skylight and fill each floor with natural light. The stairway also acts as a heat chimney in the afternoon, to draw air through the house and out the roof window—a utilitarian yet sustainable solution to a required programmatic element.

The corrugated metal skins covering the entire structure cast a black hue and are the most noticeable feature of the home, giving it its name. Though standing in stark contrast to its context, the style of Black House is site-specific and con-

Side elevation

Side elevation

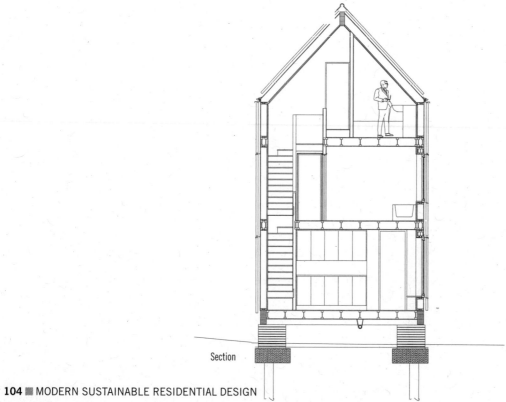

Section

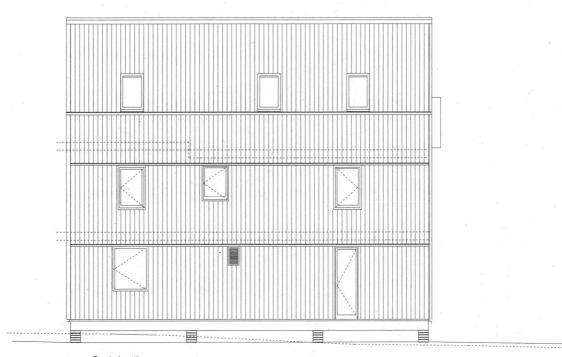

Front elevation

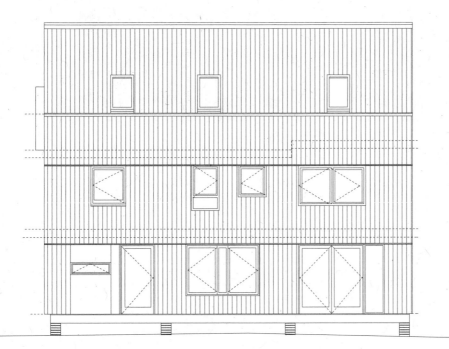

Rear elevation

Black House sits on a small lot and makes use of the surrounding fields to expand beyond the official property line.

ceptually driven. The vernacular shed design is reinforced in this modern interpretation, recalling the same color scheme and exterior cladding. The color also relates to the black peat soil of the surrounding fields. Notably, the black color was more than a stylistic choice; it was a result of the manufacturing process inherent in making the material, a result of the weatherproof coating applied to the cement-fiber cladding. The use of metal cladding was dictated by the shed concept, as the material resembled the qualities and characteristics inherent in these buildings. The dark

exterior of Black House is offset effectively by the Scandinavian softwood windows and floors, which act as a visual foundation and provide a playful touch to the exterior façade.

In 2004, Black House received the New House of the Year Award from the Royal Institute of British Architecture. It has received more mixed reviews from the neighborhood, however, varying from vague remarks that "so and so doesn't like it" to enthusiastic responses from interested parties who stop by to ask about the design and to take photos.

CONSTRUCTION DETAILS

One of the more evident and unique features of Black House is its raised "posture," which attracts the eye at first glance. Primarily a reference to the sheds that inspired Bowles, the feature has practical implications as well. For one, it precluded the need to provide a damp coarse, a plastic membrane between the structure and the ground, and allows any drainage to flow underneath the house to the closest drain.

To raise the structure, the architect chose to use glu-laminated (glu-lam) beams, as opposed

The side elevation proves
a clear resemblance to
the agricultural sheds of
the region.

Opposite: Black House is raised on concrete piles to reinforce the notion of the shed, as well as to allow any drainage to flow underneath the home.

Above: The corrugated metal cladding was selected for its resemblance to the working agricultural sheds found along the landscape; the black color is the result of the weatherproof coating applied to the cladding.

The interior view outlines the direct link between the entry, kitchen, and living area.

to the conventional concrete ring beams; this meant minimal concrete foundations were necessary, with a concomitant reduction in weight. The glu-lam beams are either half-lapped or third-lapped at each junction, with bolts fastening through each member to the pile caps using high-tensile-strength stainless steel rods; the beam ends are protected with galvanized plates. The brick-faced concrete piers, 9 meters deep (27 feet), act as a plinth on which the beams rest, much like its shed ancestors. Laminated timber trusses that form the visible link between the structural framework and the foundation are anchored to the foundation poles with steel cables.

Prefabrication was an important strategy in the design of the house, one that greatly reduced the disturbance of existing site conditions while significantly shortening construction time. Erected in only five days, the entire construction period lasted a mere eight months. Timber studs, joists, and rafters were made as I-sections from timber waste material, which could be fabricated off-site and so caused minimal environmental impact. The resulting structure contained lightweight yet strong beams, which reduced the overall weight of the home. This, then, had a direct effect on the number of piles need in the foundation, and minimized the amount of concrete, and thus energy, needed for construction.

The black profile cladding (composed of fiber-cement slates by Eternit, Inc.) used on the exterior not only made a design statement but also contributed to the concise nature of the design. Built on the breathing wall principle, with paneling on the interior face and panelvent (a sheathing board) on the exterior face, the plastic membrane on the sheathing was eliminated. And because the material is capable of breathing, it also can be used as a rainscreen and is fireproof.

SUSTAINABILITY

Architect Meredith Bowles and his practice, Mole Architects, were founded on principles of environmentally conscientious design practices and site-specific architecture. These principles served as the guiding light when it came time to design Bowles's personal residence, too.

Black House incorporated many different aspects of this approach, many of which involved making simple and practical decisions—as Bowles says, deciding to be conscious of the surroundings and design with a purpose. The walls in the house are 200 mm thick (7.8 inches), and the floors and roof 250 mm (9.8 inches); both are filled with Warmcel recycled newspapers and old car tires, to provide both acoustics and insulation. This material choice dramatically increased the energy efficiency of the house. The calculated heat loss at –4 degrees is less than 5 kW for the entire house; and the U-value of the walls and

The kitchen tiles are composed of recycled industrial cutting boards and garden furniture. The color scheme was inspired by the pea fields just outside the kitchen window.

The bedroom window overlooks the agricultural fields located just behind the home.

floors are 0.16 (1.72 w/sq. ft.) and 0.14 (1.5 w/sq/ft. w/sqmk), respectively. Windows were specified as double-glazed and have a low-emissive coating that deflects heat back into the house. Sunscreens fitted above the large ground-floor windows cut out overhead midafternoon sun in the summer.

Electricity for the house is generated from a wind farm in the town of Cornwall. It helps to run the air-to-air heat pump that increases the efficiency of the electricity input by almost three times, and provides hot water and warm-air heat-ing. For the heat pump, says Bowles, it was more important to find an alternative to fossil fuels than to increase efficiency or savings, since at the time electricity cost more than gas. A typical heat pump cost around £4K (about $7,000 U.S.) as op-posed to £1.5K (about $2,900 U.S.) for a standard gas boiler. Heat loss throughout the house was reduced in winter with ventilation, provided by a whole-house extraction system that features a cross-current heat exchanger, which produced an 85 percent recovery rate.

Finally, many of the finishes in the house, both on the exterior and interior, were chosen specifically for their low environmental impact. Masonite I-Studs were chosen because their man-ufacturing process is free of formaldehydes. Floor coverings are made from reclaimed wood blocks. The yellow/green interior of the kitchen splashbacks are made from recycled industrial cutting boards and garden furniture, with a color scheme dictated by the pea fields seen from the kitchen windows.

Shenandoah Retreat, Warren County, Virginia

Architect/Designer: Carter + Burton Architecture

■ By James Burton and William Carpenter

ROXANNE FISCHER AND DON ORLIC, a couple who worked for the National Institutes of Health (NIH), commissioned Carter + Burton Architecture, Berryville, Virginia, to design a weekend house as a retreat and gathering place for their family and friends, and as a place where they could pursue their interests in hiking and kayaking. The Washington-area residents had in mind a clean, modern aesthetic that fit with the site, taking advantage of the dramatic views, with minimal obstructions from the architecture, and following green principles of design. They also wanted ample wall space to display their growing art collection.

In conducting research into architecture firms that might fill the bill, they came upon an article in the *Washington Post* describing a local duo who were referred to as being pioneers in contemporary and sustainable house design. Page Carter had studied under Rafael Moneo at Harvard, and Jim Burton was a Mississipi State graduate who had studied under Samuel Mockbee and Christopher Rischer. Their approach was to use an inclusive process to understand the goals and wishes of the couple, at the same time educating them about the options to choose from for designing a home worthy of such a beautiful setting.

The master bedroom wing and the entry hall are built on piers to allow groundwater to flow under the home.

OVERVIEW

The 24-acre property, located on the North Fork of Virginia's Shenandoah River, stretches from a steeply wooded mountainside on the north to a grassy floodplain bordering the river to the south. The structure (two bedrooms, two-and-a-half baths with flex space) "treads lightly" on the site—it is barely visible from the river—and takes advantage of its peaceful, natural surroundings.

In early discussions about the design of the house, the couple said they wanted it to lend a cave-like security, or provide an experience similar to being in a treehouse, with exposures to views and light at high levels. It became clear that it was possible to design sustainably by taking the treehouse approach—in particular to gain the thermal mass benefits that berming into a hillside would allow.

The house was designed as a composition of smaller forms that follow the site contours and accommodate existing trees, which consequently introduced natural light and ventilation to the structure. Carter and Burton had found that houses that are 3000 square feet or larger tend to need to be "stretched" or "pulled apart" in this manner, whereas smaller houses can achieve these effects while maintaining a simple and compact shape.

The scale of the house grows from an open deck area on the west side of the clearing to a four-story tower scaled so as to relate to the tree line on the east. Beyond the tower, the one-story master bedroom wing appears nestled in the woods, for a more intimate setting. The passive solar design allows all main rooms to face south. Angled glass walls are tilted for optimal solar exposure, while north walls provide a thermal barrier against winter winds, as well as privacy screening.

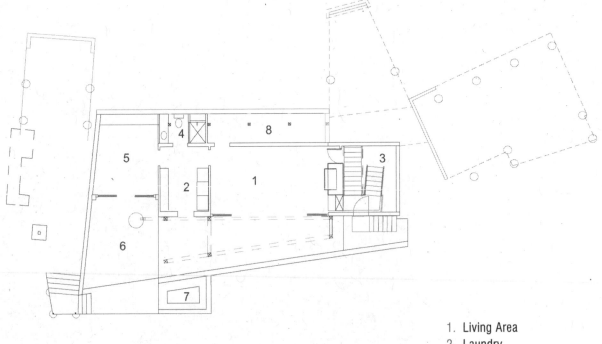

Lower-level plan of the Shenandoah Retreat, Warren County, Virginia.

1. Living Area
2. Laundry
3. Stair Tower
4. Bathroom
5. Bedroom
6. River Rock Drainbed
7. Spa
8. Mechanical Room

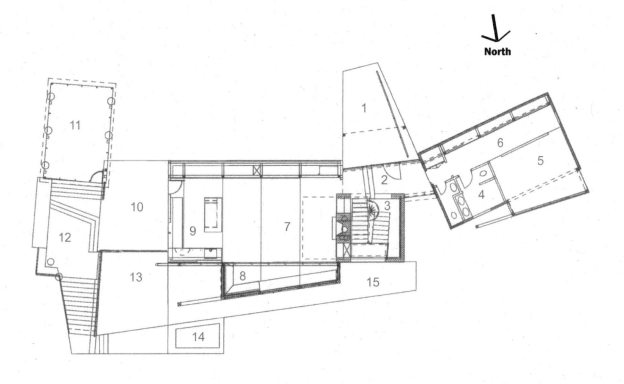

North

1. Concrete Bridge
2. Entry Hall
3. Stair Tower
4. Master Bathroom
5. Master Bedroom
6. Dressing Area
7. Great Room
8. Dining Area
9. Kitchen
10. Upper Terrace
11. Screen Porch
12. Upper Deck
13. River Rock Drainbed
14. Spa
15. Lower Terrace

Main-level plan

DESIGN DETAILS

As one approaches the top of the site, following a winding wooded road, the house seems to frame a view of the mountains. A concrete bridge leads into the entry hall where the stair tower emerges as the central organizing element, separating the house's master bedroom wing from the open kitchen, living, and dining areas of the great room. The master bedroom wing and the entry hall are built on piers to allow groundwater to flow under the house.

Intended as a vertical gallery for the couple's art collection, the tower and its integrated fireplaces create a central hearth element, while its cantilevered loft forms a cozy space within the great room. A custom steel, glass, and wood desk rail system frame the loft. In the great room and master bedroom wings, a bank of closets, a mechanical space, benches, and shelves line the north circulation spine. High clerestory windows above this spine bring in cool north light to mix with the warm southern

light. Along these walls, on giant custom sliding panels, are displayed the paintings done by the couple's son. The tilted south glass wall formed a place for the informal dining area. A built-in dining bench and benches surround a custom-built aluminum foam table, which blends with the aluminum windows and glass wall, creating a minimalist aesthetic warmed by the wood.

The lower level features a large family room, mud room, and guest suite, with glass doors that

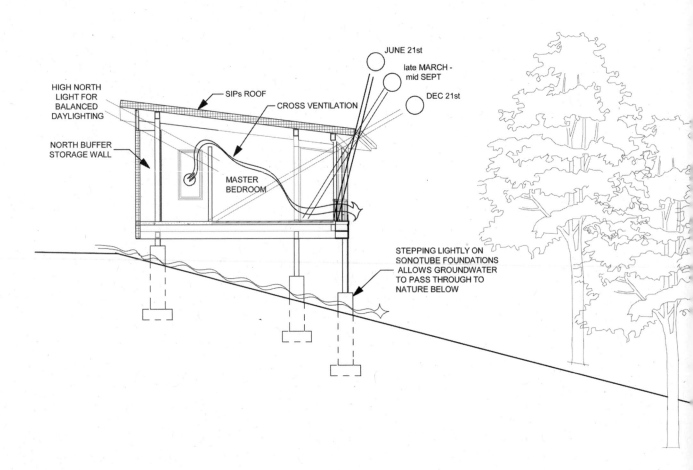

Building section 1

open on to a large terrace, thus creating a strong connection to the outside. By locating the second bedroom beneath the deck, more living space was gained without increasing the scale of the house. The combination wood and concrete deck connects the kitchen area to the screened porch pavilion. The outdoor cooking and entertaining area revolves around a built-in concrete grill center. Interstices are anchored by these items, along with a custom terrazzo ground concrete Jacuzzi located on the lower terrace.

CONSTRUCTION DETAILS

Carter and Burton chose materials and technologies to reinforce their sustainable approach to the project. The thermal mass of the poured-in-place concrete allows the house to be unaffected by the shift in temperature common to this transitional southern climate. The foundation rises to form the base of the house up to countertop height, where the concrete turns in to become the kitchen counters. Retaining walls and the tower are also made of concrete, reminiscent of the fire towers found in the area. Exposed interior concrete walls provide structure and support for a concrete floor. Heat crete was used to form the fireplaces. Stress-skin walls, a steel structural frame, and aluminum windows comprise the house's structure, while vertical exterior cedar siding adds warmth and texture. Jumbo structural stress-skin roof panels span up to the maximum 18 feet, with 4-foot cantilevers, eliminating the need for roof rafters and resulting in a thin profile that documents a new place in time.

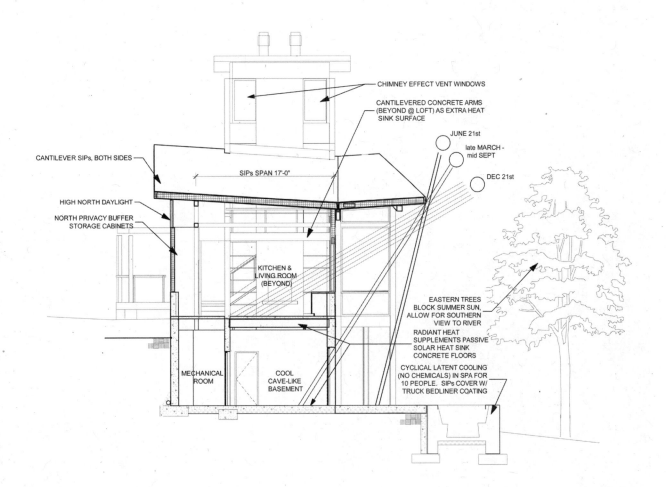

CHIMNEY EFFECT VENT WINDOWS

CANTILEVERED CONCRETE ARMS (BEYOND @ LOFT) AS EXTRA HEAT SINK SURFACE

JUNE 21st

late MARCH - mid SEPT

DEC 21st

CANTILEVER SIPs, BOTH SIDES

SIPs SPAN 17'-0"

HIGH NORTH DAYLIGHT

NORTH PRIVACY BUFFER STORAGE CABINETS

KITCHEN & LIVING ROOM (BEYOND)

EASTERN TREES BLOCK SUMMER SUN, ALLOW FOR SOUTHERN VIEW TO RIVER

RADIANT HEAT SUPPLEMENTS PASSIVE SOLAR HEAT SINK CONCRETE FLOORS

MECHANICAL ROOM

COOL CAVE-LIKE BASEMENT

CYCLICAL LATENT COOLING (NO CHEMICALS) IN SPA FOR 10 PEOPLE. SIPs COVER W/ TRUCK BEDLINER COATING

Building section 2

The four-story stair tower, located just off the entry to the home, separates its private and public functions; the large scale of the tower establishes a relationship to the eastern tree line.

The design of the home was based around the idea of creating multiple smaller forms that follow the site contours and work around the existing trees.

The expansive rear patio space
provides an uninterrupted view of
the nearby mountains.

All of the windows and structural materials used in the house were manufactured or fabricated within 30 miles of the site. The house carries local technologies and craft to their limits of expression, while maintaining a modern elegance. Patronizing local craftsmen supports the local building culture. Culture, after all, is the other half of sustainability and helps to create an evolving sense of place.

ADDITIONAL SUSTAINABILITY TACTICS

The more obvious sustainable aspects of the house are found in the active and passive systems used for heating, cooling, ventilation, and daylighting, which, combined, reduce energy consumption dramatically. When the couple does need to run the HVAC system, they benefit from an energy-efficient geothermal heat pump and radiant floor heating. In the winter months, the living room is warmed by the low sun through the south-facing windows. Exposed concrete floors throughout the home absorb and slowly release this heat. In the summer, large overhangs shade the interior of the house; and windows in the tower can open up to expel heat, using a chimney effect. In addition, the entry bridge has a dogtrot ventilation system for passive cooling. When it is simply too hot to be upstairs, the bermed basement and guest room function as a cavelike retreat from the heat. The couple also beats the heat by cooking outdoors at the built-in concrete grill. The balanced daylighting design also reduces the need for electric lights, another very effective strategy for saving energy and keeping things cool in a southern climate.

The main entrance to the Retreat, shown at night with a view of the glowing vertical tower.

Above: The multilevel rear patio blurs the line between the indoors and outdoors in much of the site.

Opposite: The spa is located just off of the basement-level family room.

The open-plan kitchen and living space illustrate the intent to create a minimalist aesthetic with a clean palette of materials.

Above: The loft space sits cantilevered over the great room, creating a cozy, intimate space within a large open room. The loft is framed with custom steel, glass, and a wood desk rail system.

Left: The lower-level family room with glass doors, which open out to a large terrace with a terrazzo and concrete spa.

By locating the family room beneath the deck, more living space was gained, without increasing the scale of the house.

The northern circulation spine consists of a bank of closets, mechanical space, benches, and shelving. High clerestory windows above this spine bring in cool northern light.

The stair tower serves as a vertical gallery for the family's art collection.

Concrete entry detail at the vertical stair tower.

The one-story master bedroom wing is nestled into the woods, forming a peaceful, intimate setting.

Yoga Studio, Bluemont, Virginia

Architect/Designer: Jim Burton, Carter + Burton Architecture
■ By James Burton and William Carpenter

WASHINGTON, DC, RESIDENTS PAUL and Annie Mahon are practicing Buddhists who yearned for a weekend retreat in the country to fight off the onset of so-called nature deficiency disorder (NDD). Paul is an attorney, and Annie runs a yoga studio for adults and children where she uses the ancient practice as a therapeutic modality for healing anxiety, depression, and other physical and emotional problems. They purchased Studio Loggerheads, a 1,300-square-foot-house from architect Jim Burton of Carter + Burton Architecture; but over time, they realized they needed more space to house visiting friends and family and to serve as a serene, contemplative studio where Annie and her family could practice yoga. Thus, the idea for the Yoga Studio was born.

The Mahons also are committed environmentalists and share a love of modern design. Thus, they wanted the studio to be designed for energy efficiency, using material and products that caused minimal waste or consumption in production, delivery, installation, and maintenance. Their green philosophy matched that of Carter + Burton, and so it became the driving force behind this sustainable design effort. The client/architect team also agreed on the importance of involving local craftsmanship as a way to nurture local culture, the "other half of sustainability."

OVERVIEW

The mountainside site chosen for the yoga studio proved to be a challenge for both the design and construction processes. It is situated behind a craggy stone ridge on a 5-acre lot, 100 feet from the main house. Thus, it is somewhat independent yet remains sufficiently connected for shared functions and systems, reducing the overall impact on the site. The two structures anchor the ends of the 150-foot-long rock ledge.

Above: Section diagram of the Yoga Studio, in Bluemont, Virginia.

Opposite: Deer trails lead the way around the rock outcropping of the site to the back entrance of the Yoga Studio. The site rests behind a craggy stone ridge on a 5-acre lot one hour west of Washington, DC. Native plants were left intact, among them mountain laurel, hardwoods, and more than 1 acre of wild blueberries.

Above: The Yoga Studio by Carter + Burton Architecture is the first LEED Gold home in the southeastern United States. It was awarded this certification after participating in the LEED for Homes pilot program and achieving points for the building's various green features. It is nestled in the hillside on which it sits.

Opposite: The green roof on the Yoga Studio helps to keep water retention on the site.

The view from the road 70 feet below changes with the seasons. The native plants, such as mountain laurel, hardwoods, and over an acre of wild blueberries, were left intact, as were the lichen-covered boulders.

County restrictions on size for a studio—600 square feet—warranted a design that gives the impression of spaciousness yet maximizes efficiency. The organic shape stretches out to take in as much southern light as possible, while still being compact. For circulation, there are doorways at each end. A bermed entrance to the east and the western end sits high, with a deck on the view side. The walls and ceiling curve, to provide an energy-efficient and site-responsive design, while maintaining a modern aspect of form and space

Care was taken in the design of the landscape around the house to allow for the forest to return to its natural state as quickly as possible after construction. And measures were taken during construction to protect the existing trees and control erosion, including covering the topsoil and using erosion fencing to prevent additional dirt from sliding down the steep hill. Permanent erosion measures include planting indigenous trees to absorb water in the meadow formed by the staging area of construction, and a low retaining wall, which scoops out of the hill to form the grill area and front terrace. The driveway does not extend beyond the main house; visitors walk downhill to the Yoga Studio. A living roof with sedums provides a maintenance-free system for the low-pitched structure while saving 20 to 30 percent on energy bills and retaining 70 percent of rainwater to aid with latent cooling and stormwater management on the site. The minimal landscaping, indigenous trees, and succulents on the living roof are noninvasive and drought-tolerant, which also saves on maintenance and water consumption on the site.

Rear courtyard view

Below: The architecture of the Yoga Studio is a response to the site, as well as to the intentions of the clients and how they hoped to use the space. The shape was inspired by the need for maximum spaciousness within the 600-square-foot footprint, squeezing the bathroom, entrance, and laundry space to their smallest proportions, thus leaving the largest space for living.

Opposite: The eastern patio grill center with TMX Active concrete draws pollution out of the air.

The project tested the limits of construction technologies for the area and its tradesmen. The following were incorporated to create unique spaces, details, and functional attributes:

Curved structural insulated panels (SIPs) were used for many reasons, including: structural strength with less material, high R-value, low air infiltration, and use of recycled materials in the OSB and expanded polystyrene bead foam. On a tour of the local SIPs factory 23 miles away, the architect was shown a curved panel sample that another designer wanted to use to build a boat. That let Burton know that curved panels were possible. He also learned that SIPs could provide a clear span of 17 feet over an entire space, rather than be interrupted by rafters, which meant saving on wood resources. This led to the idea of curved roof panels.

Ironically, the simplicity of the diminutive structure required greater attention to detail and materials in order to give the perception of a larger space. This was achieved by customizing

most elements in the project. Both the clients and the designer value the work of local craftspeople and support the local trades and economy; this also enables a higher level of care and craft in the resulting product. All the subcontractors working on the project, including the mechanical contractor, the security contractor, and the electricians were from within 30 miles of the site. The builder and his team spent weeks in his shop constructing all the wood windows and doors.

- The doors have custom steel handles sized to be comfortable for a hand grip, with a narrow profile for the tight spaces.

- The studio doubles as a bunkhouse, so beds were built into the floor diaphragm, with trapdoors to hide them during the day. Bunk beds built out of a steel frame with custom mattresses are located in the loft space. The studio can sleep nine people in a minimal amount of space.

- A custom steel-and-wood ship's ladder saves floor space while allowing natural light to reach all corners; it doubles as access to the loft and as a sculptural piece.

- All the cabinetry in the studio—including a wash closet, shoe storage bench by the front door, bathroom wash basin cabinet, kitchen cabinetry, and a bench and cabinet at the grill center—was built by local craftspeople.

- Maintenance-free galvanized corrugated metal siding creates a rural outbuilding feel. The grain of the wood, extracted from the region, is left exposed inside the studio, highlighting the sense of place.

- An outdoor built-in concrete grill and bench form a retaining wall for steps, at the same time relating to the concrete carport near the main house. TMX Active concrete (the first pour in North America), a pollution abatement system using photo catalytic cement, was used.

- A geoexchange system provides efficient space heating and cooling and all of the studio's hot water needs.

Opposite: The east entry is bermed into the hillside, but as the hillside falls away, the western deck seems catapulted into the dense trees. This peaceful setting is shaded in the summer and a wonderfully warm spot in the winter, protected from the north winds, but exposed to the warm sunlight.

Left: The Jefferson stair serves as access to the loft area, but the openness of the treads and risers allows daylight to penetrate deep into the room. Louvers on the windows control daylighting in the summer by shading the windows and by bouncing light onto the reflective stainless steel ceiling. Dual track lighting, with heads that provide both direct and indirect light off the ceiling, provide ample illumination for the main space.

CONSTRUCTION DETAILS

The Yoga Studio employed many environmentally sound products to satisfy the clients' desire for a healthy interior environment and sustainable materials.

- Twenty-two-inch-wide poplar boards from a sawmill 3 miles away were used to board-form the concrete foundation walls. Soy oil was used as a natural release agent before the boards were air-dried and planed for reuse as flooring and curved wall panels inside the studio. These boards have a richness of pattern that serves as artwork for the structure, while also rooting the project to this place.

- As an alternative to gypsum wallboard and paint, a technique of beeswax/resin mix on canvas pulled over MedEx MDF (no formaldehyde added to the medium-density fiberboard) was used and installed by a local craftsman. No VOC-laden carpet or paint was used in the house.

- Stainless steel ceiling panels were used indoors and on the porch ceilings for indirect reflected lighting and an airy feel. Maintenance-free galvanized corrugated metal siding creates a rural outbuilding feel.

- Colored glass tile lines the bathroom walls and ceiling; a radiant terrazzo ground concrete floor with cast-in-place floor lights covers the bathroom and entry hall areas to produce the sense of a larger space.

- A custom steel handrail at the loft, with resin and grass panels, serves a dual purpose, as safety feature and art element.

- A custom steel-and-wood ship's ladder saves space while allowing natural light to reach all corners under the loft.

- The custom wood windows, fabricated 10 miles from the site by the builder, are low-e with a solar heat gain coefficient high enough to allow for some of the sun's heat to be absorbed by

Three bunk beds are set in the floor. Even though the Yoga Studio is diminutive in size, it can sleep up to nine people.

Blue glass mosaic tiles create sparkle and dimension in the bathroom. A durable concrete floor in the bathroom and hallway makes for easy cleanup.

the building as a passive solar technique in the wintertime. This is offset by custom stainless shading louvers that allow for a curtain-free approach to passive solar light control in the summer, preventing the sun's rays from over-heating the space.

- Built-in floor berths are detailed for storage, or possibly future sleeping bunks.

- Custom-fabricated carbon-fiber stools were de-signed and made to add support in the floor berths for inverted yoga poses such as head-stands. These stools can also be used for addi-tional seating.

- Special lighting concepts include LED track lighting below the loft area and an Artemide Yang light ball, which produces a wash of any color of light using a computer and three fluo-rescent bulbs behind color filters to provide mood and light therapy.

The mechanical system is the most efficient possible without solar panels, which would have been inefficient on the heavily wooded lot. The system consists of a ground-coupled heat trans-fer loop (geoexchanger) connected to a liquid-to-liquid heat pump and a liquid-to-air heat pump. The loop employs vertical and horizontal ground tubing runs, and is sized to heat and cool both the studio and the main house. Heat pumps are limited in their capability to raise and maintain temperature in domestic hot water storage tanks, so the mechanical engineer was concerned about the possibility of biological organisms growing in the tank. For this reason, a thermal storage system (TSS) using an aqueous heat transfer media (HTM) was employed. When a faucet or shower is turned on, cold well water draws heat from the TSS via a parallel-plate heat exchanger. This arrangement allows for continuous heating of the incoming water stream without an imme-diate drop in water temperature, as happens with traditional domestic hot water storage tanks when the hot water runs out. The HTM is heated primarily by the liquid-to-liquid heat pump.

A mixing panel, coupled to the TSS, circulates tempered HTM through a plastic tubing loop em-bedded in the concrete entry and bathroom floors. This assures year-round comfort for bare feet on the floors.

The liquid-to-air heat pump provides space heating and cooling via a forced-air system. A heat recovery ventilator (HRV), along with high-purity air filtration, ensures that indoor air is kept exceptionally clean. When the liquid-to-air heat pump is operating, a desuperheater contained within the unit rejects heat to the HTM. This tops off the overall temperature of the TSS without needing to operate the liquid-to-liquid heat pump. The reduced number of cycles lowers the overall energy consumption and prolongs the life of the equipment. An equally important aspect of the desuperheater function is that the rejected heat is essentially "free" during the cooling operation, because the heat from the building that is normally transferred to the ground is instead transferred to the TSS for later use.

The main house and the studio are a second home for the owners, who take care to minimize energy use while the studio is unoccupied. The TSS is shut down and the space heating/cooling system maintains an "offset" temperature. The owners can remotely switch the systems to occupied mode, so space temperature will be comfortable and the TSS will be able to meet domestic hot water needs when they arrive.

A remote Internet-based monitoring system makes it possible for the owners or a mechanical engineer to observe and control the mechanical system. Interior and exterior temperature sensors and controls allow for reduced interior temperatures without risk of freezing pipes when the house is unoccupied. Temperature settings can be adjusted immediately prior to weekend visits.

Because of the tightness of construction, a heat recovery ventilator (HRV) was installed for energy-efficient fresh-air ventilation. The HRV recovers nearly 70 percent of the heat that would be lost during winter and, conversely, rejects nearly 70 percent of the heat gained during summer, in comparison to a direct ventilation system. In addition, the HRV exhaust airstream is used to ventilate the crawl space below. This dry and tempered air mitigates the potential for mold growth.

ADDITIONAL SUSTAINABILITY TACTICS

The architecture of the Yoga Studio responds to the site and meets the intentions of the clients for use of the space. The strategy enables the structure, exterior surroundings, and the interior furnishings and finishes to act as the artwork for the space. The goals for furnishing the space were to provide visual beauty as well as comfort and flexibility.

The colors, shapes, and textures of the furniture have a strong personality that celebrates design while blending with the unique modern architecture of the building, as well as referencing the use of the space. Each item was selected with the clients' sense of modern panache in mind. While the sofa and chairs add a sense of whimsy, they also exude a feeling of coziness—for example, the sofa, with its kidney shape, envelops those who sit on it. All the furnishings are movable, to allow for flexibility of use within the studio.

The straight beeswax walls form blank canvases on which "art" is displayed: The sunlight through the trees casts dappled shadows, and the Artemide light fixture projects color auras that can be altered based on moods. The sea-blue glass mosaic tiles in the bathroom add a cool contrast that complements the warmth of the poplar shiplap.

In sum, the interior harmonizes with the natural and handmade setting while conveying the fun-loving spirit of the clients.

Specific interior products and materials used in the Yoga Studio are itemized in the following lists.

Living Area

• Karim Rashid Orgy sofa and ottoman

• Pierre Paulin Tongue chairs

• Artemide Metamorfosi Line Yang floor light

• Eames molded plywood coffee table

• Bruck Lighting Boa track

Loft

• Cirrus New Zealand wool round rug

Bathroom

• Valli & Valli hardware (hooks, toilet paper holder, towel rack, etc.)

• Kohler Purist sink

• Waterworks Waterglass mosaic tile

Work Counter

• Elkay Avado Sink with drainboard

• Dornbracht Tara single-hole mixer

Utilizing local craftspeople, as well as experimenting with and using environmentally responsible materials and systems in inventive ways, reinforced sustainable concepts and created an enduring sense of place.

The project was already under construction before the USGBC developed its pilot LEED for Homes program. The owners agreed to have the project graded by LEED. It achieved the first GOLD rating in the Southeast United States.

700 Palms Residence, Venice, California

Owner/Architect: Steven Ehrlich, FAIA

■ By Mike Mcgrath and William Carpenter

AFTER SPENDING SIX YEARS IN rural Africa working in the Peace Corps, Los Angeles-based architect Steven Ehrlich decided to utilize his experience there to inform the design for his family's home. Using a technique that he refers to as "architecture without architects," Ehrlich's goal was to create a sustainable house that fused defined interior and exterior spaces. Transformation was a fundamental concept, particularly with the way the interior spaces permeated into the exterior. As a result, the 700 Palms Residence benefits from this natural ventilation, making air conditioning obsolete. Coupling this with the use of raw, crafted materials, the house brings an energetic presence to an already eclectic neighborhood of homes in southern California.

OVERVIEW

The site Ehrlich selected for his house was a narrow corner urban infill lot, 43 feet by 132 feet. The choice was driven by Ehrlich's desire to live in a walking community, away from the vehicular traffic of Los Angeles. The site featured three large trees that Ehrlich did not want to remove; instead, he strategically worked around them. When asked how he began his process of designing the house, he said that his "first sketches were a study, in plan, of positive and negative space . . . looking at the site, understanding the exposure, understanding the direction of the wind, understanding the trees, where they were, and looking at where there would be enclosed space and where there would be open space."

A 6-foot wall surrounds the site, or what Ehrlich refers to as the "compound." Within this compound he utilizes the whole site, with each exterior space becoming its own unique and carefully defined courtyard. Here's how Erlich describes the three distinct courtyards:

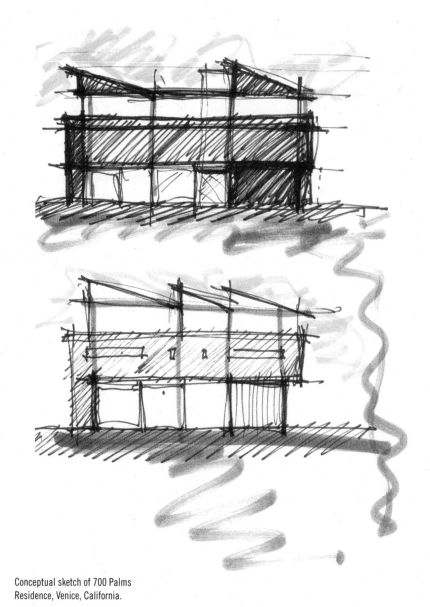

Conceptual sketch of 700 Palms Residence, Venice, California.

You enter the house through the pool court, which includes a swimming pool. I have what I like to call a tree court where I saved this very large 80-year-old pine tree. I have what one might characterize as a family court, where we do outdoor gathering and dining, and it is defined by the guesthouse/studio as well as the main house.

The courtyards connect to the house through a series of sliding and pivoting glass that merge the spaces together, transforming the initially private spaces into an open pavilion, making natural ventilation possible.

Ehrlich used the whole site to build his house, using the courtyards in the voids as a way to fit in as many interior spaces without it becoming too overbearing to the smaller beach bungalows around. This idea was another aspect of the knowledge he gained while living in Africa. "I lived specifically in courtyard houses and I see courtyard houses as a paradigm for increasing density in urban fabric," he explains.

CONSTRUCTION DETAILS

Ehrlich is a firm believer in understanding and seeing the process of construction and the craftsmanship involved. "I appreciate and want to see the craftsman's hand," he says. "I have a number of steel beams in my house that still have the writing from the steel workers." This also explains why none of the interior wall finishes are painted. What appears to be painted drywall is in fact gypsum plaster with a wax cover. The two concrete masonry walls are made with white cement and then shot-blasted by tiny metal pellets to give the walls a highly textured quality.

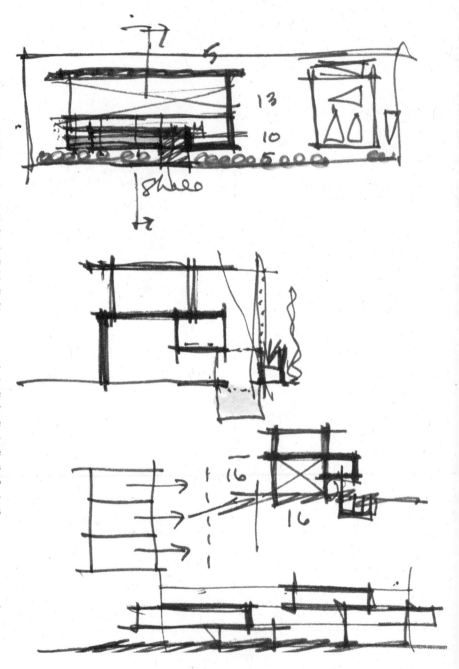

Elevation sketches

Spatial relationship sketches

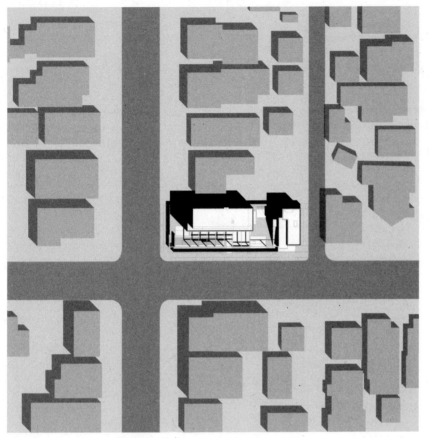

700 Palms site plan in Venice, California

SUSTAINABILITY

The most notable sustainable feature of the house is that there is no air conditioning. The large operable windows run throughout the house, allowing the ocean breeze to naturally cool it during the six warm months of the year. The large steel structure that extends beyond the house supports brightly colored canvas shades that block the warm sunlight from penetrating the rooms on the second floor. The concrete floor contains iron-oxide dust. During the cold winter months, radiant hot water within the concrete heats the house. These features alone cut the cost of the power bill dramatically.

Naturally weathering materials line the outside of the house, giving it not only an aesthetically raw appearance but also allowing for low maintenance. Cladded corten steel rests on the street-facing façade. Over time, it will begin to rust to its own patina. The Trex siding that covers the exterior of the second floor is made up of recycled sawdust and plastic. Special stucco, called Flexirock, that wraps around the back exterior of the house has the capability, if installed properly, to not crack. These low-maintenance materials age with the house, hence, reducing the cost of replacements. Photovoltaic panels were also installed to help convert solar energy into electricity.

When asked if there was anything he would change about the house, Ehrlich said there were some minor details, such as better lighting above the barbecue; but overall he is quite happy about the house. The neighbors are, as well. Although the design is not the stereotypical American dream house with large front lawns and white picket fences, this modern sustainable house creates an exciting dichotomy between the beach bungalows that once dominated the area. With the addition of this contemporary building in the area, Venice is sure to have many more modern buildings on there way. Ehrlich says, "Venice has been called the Petri dish of contemporary design." The 700 Palms Residence is definitely an example of this trend. The project follows a long lineage of Los Angeles modernism, from Wright to Schindler to Neutra to Gehry to Morphosis, and Ehrlich's contribution is lasting and meaningful.

1. living space
2. pool
3. entry
4. powder room
5. dining room
6. kitchen
7. laundry
8. storage
9. garage
10. bridge
11. bedroom
12. bathroom
13. deck
14. library
15. closet
16. master bathroom
17. master bedroom
18. kitchenette

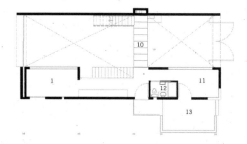
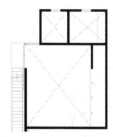

mezzanine plan

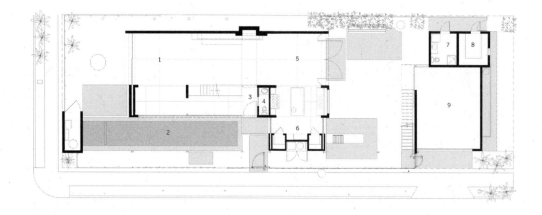

first floor plan

Floor plans

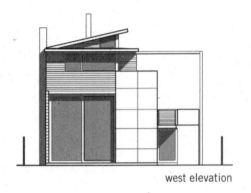

west elevation

east elevation

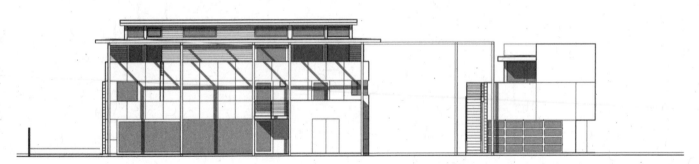

south elevation

Elevations and building section

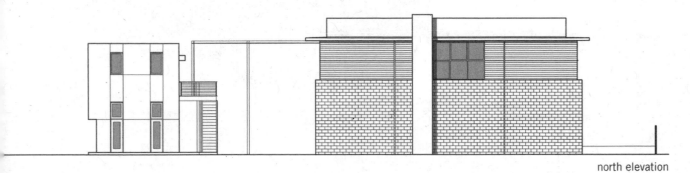

north elevation

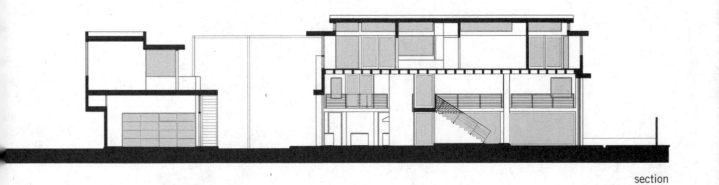

section

Opposite: Naturally weathering materials were used to clad the home's exterior, giving it not only an aesthetically raw appearance but also allowing for low maintenance. Cladded corten steel rests on the street-facing façade. The Trex siding that covers the exterior of the second floor is made of recycled sawdust and plastic.

Above: The casual courtyard space appears as an extension of the living area and is defined by the guesthouse/studio space and the main house.

The long and narrow pool is situated perfectly between the living area and the privacy fence.

The casual living space opens directly out to the pool, with large storefront doors and movable fabric sunshades.

Left: The canvas sunshades provide protection for the second-floor windows, while the steel columns extend down to define the space around the pool.

Above: The second-floor patio wraps around the rear and side of the home to overlook the pool.

Left: The master suite incorporates a private patio just off the bedroom, with large sliding doors to allow for natural ventilation.

Above: Wood shelving appears as though it is carved into the side of the stairwell leading to the guest room, making a distinct contrast to the primarily steel and glass stairs to the master suite.

Opposite: For privacy, the guest quarters are located on the second floor; it is necessary to cross the glass bridge to continue on to the master suite located on the third floor.

Left: The wood, steel, and glass stair and bridge assembly appear to float over the open living area.

The large pivoting doors blur the boundaries between the dining area and the outdoor courtyard space.

The master bath is tucked under the operable canvas shading device, thus providing a sense of privacy.

Trinity Apartments, Auckland, New Zealand

Architect/Designer: Patrick Clifford, Architectus

■ By Lee Cuthbert and William Carpenter

BUILDING WITH ENVIRONMENTAL awareness isn't difficult and it doesn't have to be astronomically expensive. A few hours with Google, a willingness to learn, and a notepad can make a green Eliza Doolittle out of just about anyone. Working with the sun and the wind, not against it, simple as it may seem, can make any building drastically more efficient. In the case of Auckland, New Zealand's Trinity Apartments, 32 domiciles benefit from a well-planned modern design that anticipates the area's South Pacific climate. Units are designed with extra-large windows and outdoor living areas to usher in natural light and breezes, making them comfortable and efficient and connecting them to the surrounding neighborhood.

OVERVIEW

Completed in May 2005, the Trinity Apartments sit on one of the highest points in Auckland's oldest suburb, Parnell, a trendy neighborhood of shops and restaurants and historical buildings. Next door is the Cathedral of the Holy Trinity, and the apartments feature views of the inner harbor and Auckland Domain, the city's oldest park. Developed by New Zealand's McConnell Property, the multilevel building forms an L-shape and shelters a large private garden with reflecting and lap pools; parking is underground.

Each owner-occupied unit features deep patios, bright modern interiors, and a variety of operable screens and shades to help control solar gain, including sun filter blinds at balcony edges.

The large glass panels run vertically along the street side to provide a screen between the building and the street below.

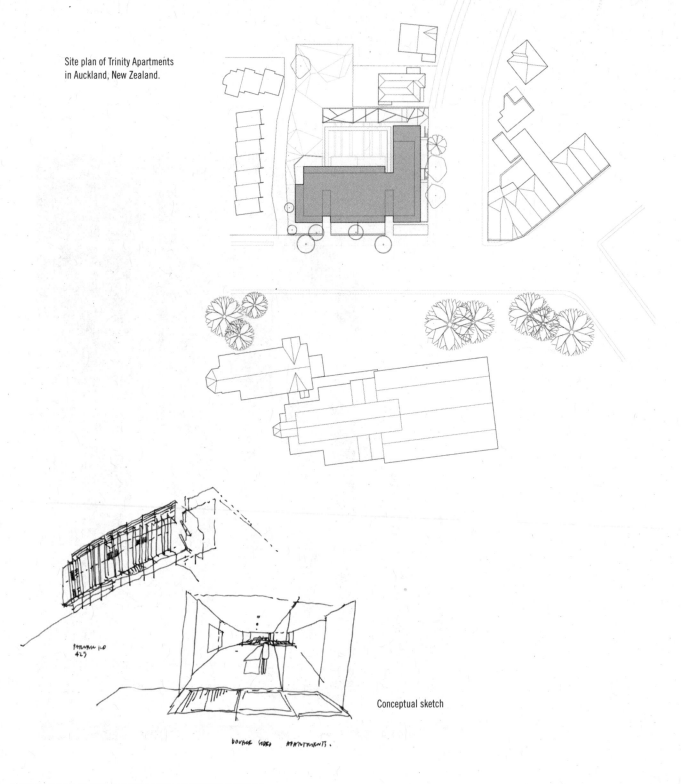

Site plan of Trinity Apartments in Auckland, New Zealand.

Conceptual sketch

On courtyard-side patios, timber shutters may be completely open or closed tight to keep out direct sun. Most units are through-plans, extending straight from the garden side of the unit to the street side. Opening up the apartment from either end results in a strong draw of fresh air.

The building itself is concrete (site prepared and precast with concrete block and exposed aggregate panels) and glass with cedar accents. Its high thermal mass helps minimize temperature fluctuations, as it delays and reduces solar heat gain. Two ground-floor lobbies provide access to resident elevators and act as thermal chimneys, drawing warm air in and up into stories-high glass atria.

Designed by Patrick Clifford of Architectus, a 160-person New Zealand firm with offices in Australia and China, Trinity Apartments won a coveted architecture award in 2007 from the New Zealand Institute of Architects (NZIA). His plan for the building allows each unit to control the sun and breezes that pass through it, reducing the need for mechanical heat and cooling. Even the pools in the garden provide evaporative cool-

ing around the building. Clifford attributes much of the building's efficiency not only to the materials it is made of, but to the implementation of effective shading strategies.

Judges for the NZIA Resene New Zealand Award for Architecture (Resene Paints Ltd. is a sponsor of the program) praised the project for the thoughtfulness of its design, noting, "This is a very successful urban response to apartment street typology, offering appropriate connectedness to the public realm while subtly protecting the privacy of its occupants."

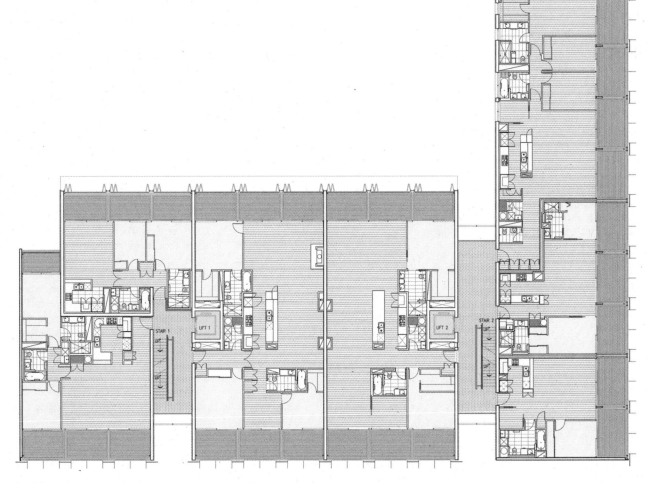

First-floor plan

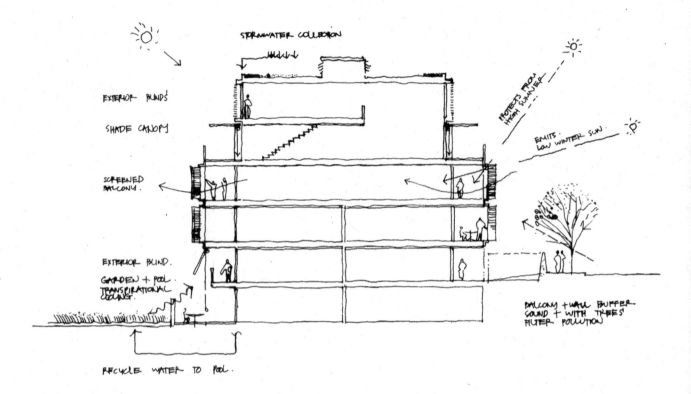

STORMWATER COLLECTION

EXTERIOR BLINDS

SHADE CANOPY

SCREENED BALCONY.

EXTERIOR BLIND.

GARDEN + POOL TRANSPIRATIONAL COOLING.

RECYCLE WATER TO POOL.

PROTECTS FROM HIGH SUMMER

EMITS LOW WINTER SUN.

BALCONY + WALL BUFFER. SOUND + WITH TREES' FILTER POLLUTION

Above: Section diagram drawing

Opposite: The residence includes eight penthouse units on the top floor of the building; they are inset slightly from the building façade. Their second-story bedrooms are enclosed by aluminum louvers that provide shading, with internal blinds and operable windows.

DESIGN DETAILS

Apartment units range in size from 750 to 2,350 square feet, with patios adding another 325 to 1,000 square feet. The nearly subtropical climate of the area brings hot, humid summers and warm and wet winters. In the summer, keeping sun out is paramount; in the winter, welcoming it takes priority. Opening units to breezes is beneficial year-round. Architect Clifford provided flexibility in a number of ways. The sheer size of the verandas attracts cooling cross-drafts across the building, while the lobby, atria, and gardens draw air through it. Eight penthouse units occupy the top floor of the building, inset from its façade. Their second-story bedrooms are surrounded by aluminum louvers for shading, with internal blinds and opening windows underneath. Running vertically along the street side, large glass panels do double duty. "They provide a screen to the street, especially when seen obliquely," says the architect, "as well as enriching the façade."

The Trinity Apartments are situated between the Cathedral of the Holy Trinity and Auckland Domain, the city's oldest park, providing magnificent views all around the building.

SUSTAINABILITY

Trinity Apartments are the result of a commitment to sustainable design on the part of the architect, and less commonly, the developer. McConnell Property has been pursuing site-appropriate, well-planned, and designed communities since it started in 1988.

Featured prominently on the company Web site, a bold philosophy of development is espoused: "Exploring new possibilities and designing with imagination is helping us break a New Zealand property cycle of poor design, mediocrity, and conforming to minimum standards. Taking the easy road is not an option as far as we're concerned." The company developed its own 10-point sustainability framework (available at www.mcconnellproperty.co.nz) and continues to pursue projects that support local economies and energy conservation while providing a sense of community to residents.

The Architectus site (www.architectus.com.au) has a page devoted to its environmental policy, which states the firm's philosophy and commitments. Among these, the firm pledges to: "Place environmental and social sensitivity and sustainability at the core of our practice and professional responsibilities." Clifford notes that building sustainably does not add significant expense when considered from the earliest stages of the design. "It's not more if the design elements are thought about at the outset of a project, rather than attaching or adding them later," he says. Do clients come to Architectus for environmentally friendly design? "Yes," says Clifford, adding "as well as generally excellent buildings, I hope!"

The Trinity Apartments project was completed for roughly $17 million NZD (about U.S. $13 million) and sold out quickly. It is efficient, modern, and easy to live in and it gives residents pedestrian access to the neighborhood. Without a doubt its success gives the architect and the developer impetus to continue setting a higher standard for New Zealand building.

Below: The apartments are constructed of concrete block with exposed aggregate panels, and extensive glass with cedar accents. The building's high thermal mass helps minimize temperature fluctuations, as it both delays and reduces solar heat gain.

Opposite: The apartments are situated on one of the highest points in Auckland's oldest suburb, Parnell, surrounded by trendy shops, restaurants, and historical landmark buildings.

The clean palette of materials proves to be a successful response to urban apartment typology, establishing a relationship with the public street while maintaining the homeowner's privacy.

The patios located on the courtyard side of the building include timber shutters that may be completely opened or closed, depending on outdoor conditions.

Most units are designed with through-plans, which extend from the garden side of the unit to the street side. Opening up the apartment on both ends results in a strong draw of fresh air.

The reflecting pools located in the garden provide evaporative cooling around the building.

An additional view of the reflecting pool that wraps around the building, with distant framed skyline views.

Left: Each unit is designed with large windows and outdoor living areas to bring in natural light and breezes, making them comfortable and efficient while providing a connection to the surrounding neighborhood.

Below: The deep balconies allow for a cooling cross-draft to infiltrate the building, providing natural ventilation through the apartments year-round.

The glass panels give a sense of weightlessness to the building's façade.

The vertical glass panels appear to take on different hues when viewed at an angle.

Each owner-occupied unit features a bright modern interior.

Solar Umbrella House, Venice, California

Architect/Designer: Lawrence Scarpa, AIA, and Gwynne Pugh, AIA, ASCE, Leed AP, Pugh + Scarpa,

■ By Monique Birault and William Carpenter

OVERVIEW

Nestled amidst a neighborhood of single- and two-story bungalows in Venice, California, the Solar Umbrella Residence boldly establishes a precedent for the next generation of California modernist architecture for the architects/owners and their six-year-old son. The parameters of the project are as follows:

- Single-family residential

- 60 percent new

- 40 percent renovation

- 3 permanent occupants, 105 hours/week

- 15 visitors/week at three hours per visit, average

- Total project cost excluding land: $390,000

Inspired by Paul Rudolph's Umbrella House of 1953, the Solar Umbrella provides a contemporary reinvention of the solar canopy. Taking advantage of the unusual through-lot, the addition shifts the residence 180 degrees from its original orientation. What was formerly the front and main entry at the north becomes the back, as the new design reorganizes the residence towards the south. This move allowed the architects to create a gracious introduction to their residence and optimizes exposure to energy rich southern California sunlight. Conceived as a solar canopy, these panels protect the body of the building from thermal heat gain by screening large portions of the structure from direct exposure to the intense southern California sun. Rather than deflecting sunlight, the solar skin absorbs and transforms this rich resource into usable energy, providing the residence with 95 percent of its electricity. Like many design features at the Solar Umbrella, the solar canopy is multivalent and rich with meaning—performing several roles for functional, formal, and experiential effect.

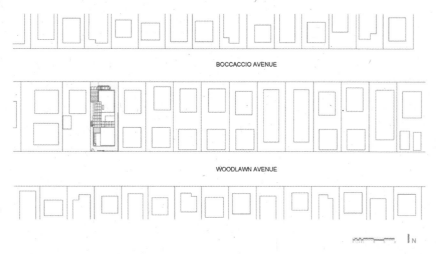

BOCCACCIO AVENUE

WOODLAWN AVENUE

Opposite: The site is located on a through-lot; the garage located along the rear avenue was demolished while the existing single-story structure on what is considered the front avenue was remodeled to incorporate a carport, complete with charging ports for the owners' electric car.

Left: Site plan of Solar Umbrella House in Venice, California

SUSTAINABLE DESIGN
INTENT AND INNOVATION

Green buildings tend to drum up visions of science fairs and survivalists, but the Solar Umbrella defies such stereotypes, giving sustainable living a much-needed modern point of view. The biggest problem in the green building legacy isn't the technology but how little design innovation goes into the architecture. Pugh + Scarpa are interested in developing a new language through the use of sustainable materials environmental concerns.

The architects found inspiration when they were in graduate school, then became more intrigued by the shotgun and other vernacular houses of central Florida—their built-in natural air circulation and shaded porches that are inherently energy efficient and sustainable. The Solar Umbrella is organized so that over 90 percent of the glazing is on the north and south façades. The south and west façades are shaded by a series of abstract fins and solar panels.

In accordance with what the architects call "global regionalism," they picked up on the Cali-fornia modern aesthetic and fluid connections between inside and out, which cropped up around Los Angeles beginning in the 1920s, and mixed it with twenty-first-century technology. The project is a rich collage of interlocking spaces using recycled and sustainable materials in unconventional ways.

A building should take some responsibility for the environment, however; you can't have a really sustainable building if it's not good design. People won't want to live in it. Playful elements are as important as avoiding waste and living responsibly.

First- and second-floor plans

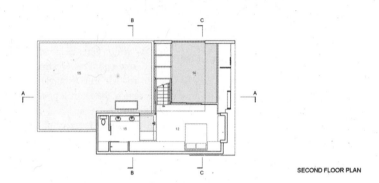

SECOND FLOOR PLAN

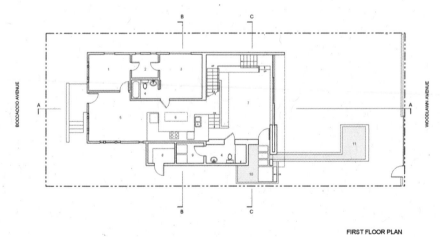

FIRST FLOOR PLAN

1 STUDY	9 LAUNDRY
2 CLOSET	10 FISH POND
3 BEDROOM	11 JACUZZI
4 BATH	12 MASTER BEDROOM
5 DINING ROOM	13 MASTER BATHROOM
6 KITCHEN	14 PATIO
7 LIVING ROOM	15 ROOF BELOW
8 UTILITY CLOSET	

SCALE IN FEET

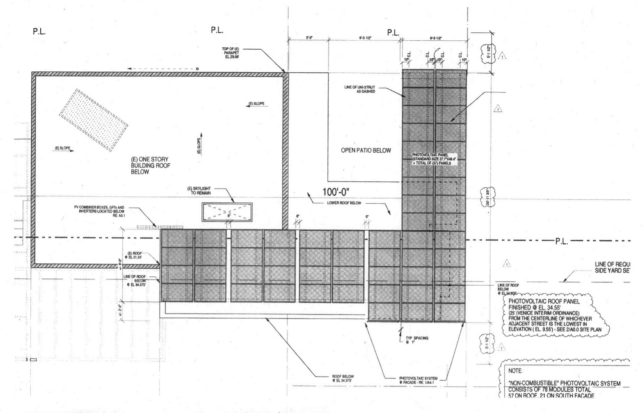

P.L.

P.L.

P.L.

TOP OF (E)
PARAPET
EL.23.08'

(E) SLOPE

LINE OF UNI-STRUT
AS DASHED

(E) SLOPE

(E) ONE STORY
BUILDING ROOF
BELOW

(E) SLOPE

OPEN PATIO BELOW

PHOTOVOLTAIC PANEL
STANDARD SIZE 27.7"x48.4"
= TOTAL OF (57) PANELS

(E) SKYLIGHT
TO REMAIN

100'-0"

PV COMBINER BOXES, GFIs AND
INVERTERS LOCATED BELOW
RE: A3.1

LOWER ROOF BELOW

P.L.

(E) ROOF
@ EL 21.33'

LINE OF ROOF
BELOW
@ EL 34.375'

LINE OF REQU
SIDE YARD SE

LINE OF ROOF
BELOW
@ EL 34.55'

PHOTOVOLTAIC ROOF PANEL
FINISHED @ EL. 34.55'
(25' (VENICE INTERIM ORDINANCE)
FROM THE CENTERLINE OF WHICHEVER
ADJACENT STREET IS THE LOWEST IN
ELEVATION (EL. 9.55') - SEE 2/A0.0 SITE PLAN

TYP. SPACING
@ 1"

ROOF BELOW
@ EL 34.375'

PHOTOVOLTAIC SYSTEM
@ FACADE - RE: 1/A4.1

NOTE:
"NON-COMBUSTIBLE" PHOTOVOLTAIC SYSTEM
CONSISTS OF 78 MODULES TOTAL
57 ON ROOF, 21 ON SOUTH FACADE

Above: Solar hot water panels are located on the roof. One is utilized to preheat the domestic-use hot water before it goes to the gas-fired hot water heater; the other panel is used to heat the pool.

Left: The solar panels extend out over the open balcony space, to absorb sunlight and provide shading for the outdoor space.

REGIONAL/COMMUNITY DESIGN AND CONNECTIVITY

This project is located on a block that is dominated by through-lots, with public streets on two sides of the property. Most houses on the block treat Boccaccio Avenue as the front of the house and Woodlawn Avenue much like an alley, detracting from the neighboring homes across the street. The addition and remodel to the existing house creates living spaces and porches on both sides, addressing both streets equally. All services are concealed in the side yards, to further enhance the quality of the street. Bike racks are located at the property entry gate to provide easy access to neighborhood shops located within just a couple of blocks of the site.

The existing single-story structure located along Boccaccio was retained and remodeled; the garage located on Woodlawn Avenue was demolished and replaced by a new entry and living space, in doing so transforming the pedestrian character along Woodlawn Avenue. A variance was granted for a 13-foot-wide carport (charging ports were provided for the owners' electric car) on Boccaccio Avenue in lieu of a code-required enclosed two-car garage that would have dominated the small 40-foot-wide street frontage. Sixty-six percent of the building population uses transit options other than single-occupancy vehicles; there are 0.33 parking spaces per person.

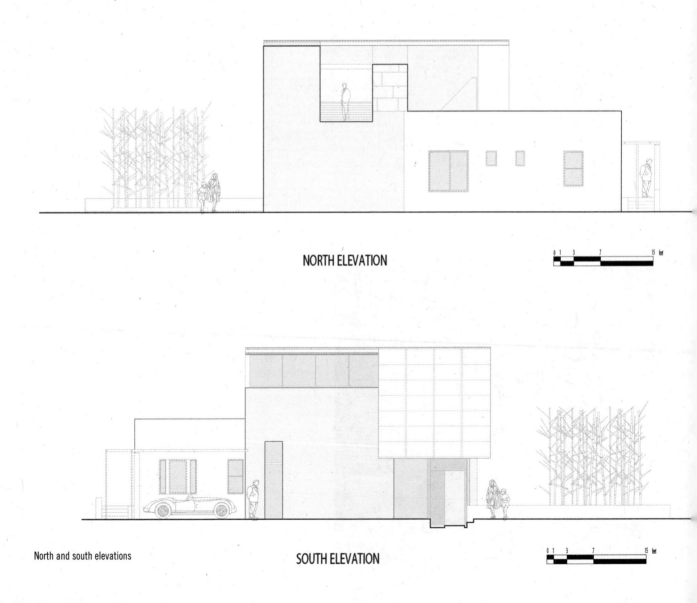

NORTH ELEVATION

North and south elevations

SOUTH ELEVATION

LAND USE AND SITE ECOLOGY

Specific variations from the regional climatic conditions were studied, incorporating the microclimate with regional strategies; proper orientation, natural light, and ventilation; and regional materials with global technologies such as solar panels for energy generation, in-floor heating; and sustainable building materials, which allowed the resultant building to be virtually energy neutral.

The existing 600-square-foot structure built in 1923 was retained and remodeled despite being considered a teardown. The existing garage was torn down and replaced with a smaller carport. Even though the completed structure is three times its original size, the net increase in lot coverage is less than 400 square feet.

The project also has its own stormwater retention system and retains 80 percent of roof stormwater on-site, virtually unheard of for a proj-

ect in the area. In contrast to most structures in the area that cover as much as 90 percent of the site with nonpermeable surfaces, this project maintains over 65 percent of the site unpaved or landscaped on a lot that is only 4100 square feet, dramatically reducing heat island effects and runoff.

Permeable gravel is used in most places (including the carport and driveway) that would normally be covered with nonpermeable surfaces. All landscaping is drought-tolerant native

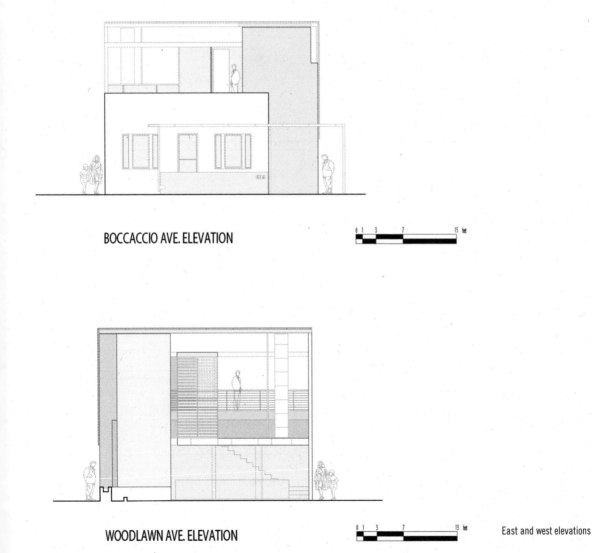

BOCCACCIO AVE. ELEVATION

0 1 3 7 15 feet

WOODLAWN AVE. ELEVATION

0 1 3 7 15 feet

East and west elevations

planting that requires little or no maintenance. Much of the planting was selected to attract an unusually high concentration of hummingbirds in the area. Composting was included as part of the landscape design.

BIOCLIMATIC DESIGN

The Solar Umbrella was designed to passively adapt to the temperate arid climate of Southern California. Due to the small site, there were limited options for building placement. Therefore, the architects' analysis focused on the placement of building components to take advantage of abundant natural ventilation and light, and to control heat gain and heat loss.

The biggest challenge was to overcome the year-round substantial temperature differential between day and night. To compensate for this condition, concrete floors and some concrete walls were strategically placed and used as thermal heat sinks. Furthermore, the solar panels are building integrated and form canopies that shade the building. Overhangs are provided at south-facing glazed areas to control and regulate summer and winter heat gain. Dual-glazing with a low-e film was utilized in aluminum frames that have thermal breaks to control the indoor thermal environment.

Operable windows and a perforated-steel stair are strategically placed so that as hot air rises, it passes through and out of the house. The rooms are kept cool with a combination of window placement for cross-ventilation; double-

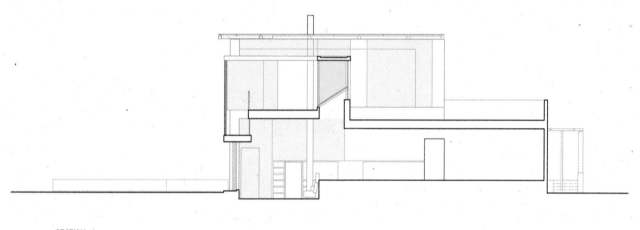

SECTION A

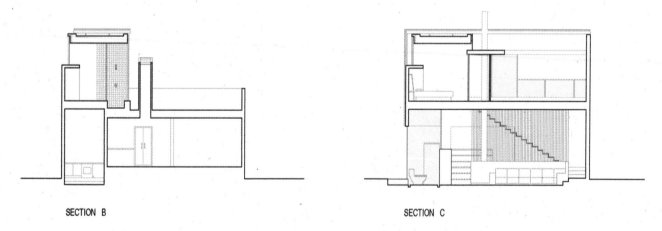

SECTION B

SECTION C

Building sections

glazed, krypton-filled, low-e windows with stainless steel spacers; and recycled insulation that boosts the thermal value of the wall to 75 percent above a conventional wood frame wall construction and reduces envelope infiltration.

Operable skylights are used in both the kitchen and a bathroom for natural light and ventilation and to maintain privacy. One hundred percent of the building area is day-lit and 92 percent of the building can be naturally ventilated.

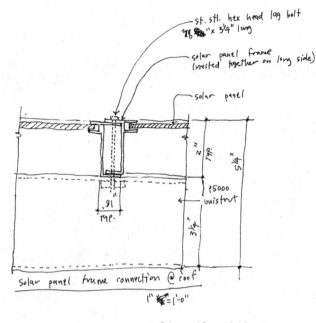

Solar panel frame sketch

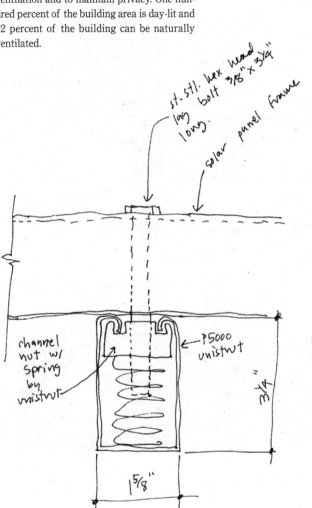

Solar panel detail sketch

Above: The home combines the California modern aesthetic, with its blurred relationships between interior and exterior spaces, and twenty-first-century technology. The result is a powerful collection of interlocking spaces that use recycled and sustainable materials in unconventional ways.

Right: The designers chose to take advantage of the through-lot, rotating the addition 180 degrees from its former orientation. What was previously the main entry at the north became the rear, as the new design restructured the home to face toward the south.

Above: Detail view from the casement window toward the open dining space.

Opposite: The casual dining table rests atop a cantilevered piece of steel pipe.

The stair tread and risers are constructed of perforated metal panels to allow additional natural light to penetrate into the main living space.

The stair tread and risers are supported by a singular steel pipe to complement the "language" of the dining table.

The large couch in the living space serves multiple functions. It provides storage, and a portion of the couch can be converted into a queen-size bed.

WATER CYCLE

The landscaping is native and drought-tolerant planting with a substantial amount of gravel, to allow water to percolate into the ground. A drip irrigation system with seasonal adjustments was installed. The roof stormwater is collected in a large scupper, which is directly above an underground retention basin (drywell) that allows a majority of the roof water to be retained on-site. The property is only six blocks from the beach, and retaining water on-site contributes to cleaning up the bay—the water isn't allowed to flow into the streets and collect oil, trash, and pesticides.

Appliances were chosen for both energy efficiencies and water conservation. The clothes washer (front-loading) and the dishwasher both use less water than traditional models. The kitchen faucet, showerheads, and toilets are all low-flow fixtures. The existing house toilet was replaced with a new low-flow type through a city rebate program and was provided at no cost to the owner.

Any rainwater that falls on the patio, pool, or the pond is retained using a collection and automatic overflow/recirculation pump.

Ninety percent of precipitation is managed on-site 31,280 gallons per year of water is used indoors and 4,600 gallons per year of water is used outdoors.

ENERGY FLOWS AND ENERGY FUTURES

A large part of the design of the house is the solar canopy, which provides 95 percent of the building's electric load through 89 amorphous silicon solar panels. This system is on a "net-meter" provided by the City of Los Angeles, which allows the grid to be used as a storage system and eliminates the time-of-use charges with traditional electric use. For the existing house, new insulation was blown into the walls, and roof and batt insulation was provided underfloor.

Heat is provided through a solar electricity radiant in-floor heating system for the concrete floors of the new addition. Heat through the floor is a more efficient mode of heating than through forced air: air temperatures can be lower and energy uses less. Because 100 percent of the house is day-lit, it requires no electric light except at night and on overcast days.

Appliances were chosen for their energy efficiencies: the clothes washer (268 kWh/year), the dishwasher (416 kWh/year), and the refrigerator (365 kWh/year) are ENERGY STAR–rated and use substantially less energy than other models. Lighting control systems are used inside and out to further reduce consumption. Because of the very low power demand of the building, thousands of feet of wire were saved.

The pumps utilized for both the pond and the pool are sized to be as small as possible and are on timers to conserve energy; they use nonchemical filtration systems.

Two solar hot water panels are used (and are on the roof): one to preheat the domestic hot water before it gets to the gas-fired hot water heater and the other to heat the pool. The domestic hot water solar panel has halved the house's natural gas use on a home 2.5 times the original size.

Payback for all energy system is anticipated in approximately 10 years. Renewable site generation includes 4.5kw of solar electric PV system and 94.3 percent of electricity. Three solar thermal collectors provide domestic hot water and swimming pool heating. The three collectors provide 81.7 percent of heat energy.

Energy Utilization Summary

This summary is based on a compilation of actual energy consumption data, as well as calculations per 2001 ASHRAE standard, given that the house consists of an existing building and a new addition and certain efficiency improvements have been made over a period of time to attain zero net energy consumption. The building is California Title 24 compliant.

Table 9.1 Baseline Building Energy Consumption and Power Demand

Electricity consumption	35.1 kWh/day
Appliances (refrigerator, dishwasher, washer and dryer, miscellaneous)	4.7 kWh/day
Lighting (interior and exterior)	10.4 kWh/day
Space conditioning (heating and cooling; heat pump, 3-ton)	6.9 kWh/day
Pool pump (3/4 hp/1.15 kw, 2 hrs/day)	2.3 kWh/day
Pond pump (1/2 hp/0.90 kw, 12 hrs/day)	10.8.kWh/day

Power Demand	
Plug loads	0.4 W/sf
Lighting	3.1 W/sf
Space conditioning	0.8 W/sf
Pool and pond pumps	1.2 W/sf
Natural gas consumption	2.24 therms/day
Domestic hot water	0.71 therms/day
Cooking	0.17 therms/day
Clothes drying	0.27 therms/day
Heater (165,000 btu/hr)	1.09 therms/day

Table 9.2 **Energy-Efficient Building Energy Consumption and Power Use**

Net Electricity Consumption	0.9 kWh/day
Electricity consumption	15.9 kWh/day
Appliances (ENERGY STAR refrigerator,dishwasher, washer, misc.)	2.9 kwh/day
Lighting (interior and exterior, daylight, controls, timers)	5.4 kWh/day
Space conditioning (improved envelope/glazing, radiant-heated floor; no cooling)	3.3 kWh/day
Pool pump (3/4 hp/1.15 kw, 0.5 hrs/day)	0.6 kWh/day
Pond pump (1/6 hp/0.21 kw, 12 hrs/day)	2.6 kWh/day
Solar water heater pump for swimming pool (1/6 hp/0.21 kw, 5 hrs/day)	1.1 kWh/day
Solar electricity site generation (4.5 kw system)	-15.0 kWh/day
Power Demand	
Plug loads	0.3 W/sf
Lighting	2.1 W/sf
Space conditioning	0.5 W/sf
Pool, pond, and solar pumps	0.9 W/sf
Solar PV	2.0 W/sf
Natural gas consumption	0.77 therms/day
Domestic hot water, assisted by 50 sf storage solar water heater	0.26 therms/day
Cooking	0.17 therms/day
Clothes drying	0.27 therms/day
Swimming pool heating, assisted by 2x 60 sf active solar water heaters	0.07 therms/day
Reduction in electricity use, from 35.1 kwh/day to 0.9 kwh/day	97.40%
Reduction in natural gas, from 2.24 therms/day to 0.77 therms/day	65.60%
Reduction in natural gas for water heating, from 1.80 to 0.33 therms/day	81.70%
Baseline electricity density—annual	24,986 Btu/sf
Design electricity density—annual	640 Btu/sf
Baseline natural gas density—annual	46,720 Btu/sf
Design natural gas density—annual	16,060 Btu/sf
Baseline energy use density—annual	71,706 Btu/sf
Design energy use density—annual	16,700 Btu/sf
Overall energy use reduction	76.70%

Approximately 65 percent of the site is covered with nonpermeable surfaces, including the porous gravel that allows for efficient water drainage.

MATERIALS AND CONSTRUCTION

Materials were selected based on their effects on indoor air quality. Indoor air quality was emphasized by minimizing offgassing. The designer's selection criteria were: to use materials that are durable/long-lasting and have low- or no-maintenance aspects, have some recycled content, have no formaldehyde content, and be obtained and transported locally. Although not required by the city, over 85 percent of the construction debris was recycled.

The major materials used were concrete, with 50 percent fly ash content, and recycled mild steel that was rusted and then sealed; wood products were constructed from composite recycled materials (MDF and OSB) for cabinetry, flooring, and structure (TJI composite members were used instead of conventional lumber). The stucco used on the exterior has an integral colored pigment so that painting is never required. All concrete forming materials and 20 percent of the framing material were from reclaimed sources.

Sealed OSB was used on the floor of the existing remodel and the kitchen cabinets. Formaldehyde-free MDF was used for the bedroom cabinets. Homosote (100 percent recycled newsprint) was used as a wall finish. All paint used was low-VOC, and the floors were left as a concrete finish.

Smaller "off-the-shelf" elements such as industrial broom bristles were used as design elements in lieu of a more costly virgin material. The designers avoided rigid or blown foam insulation made with an HCFC blowing agent, and sized electrical wiring properly.

These details, coupled with the qualities and character found throughout the Solar Umbrella, distinguish this project from similar projects and benefit not only each individual resident but also the community at large. The goal for the project was to create a beautiful, low-maintenance, high-quality architecture that is also sustainable. The Solar Umbrella, both beautiful and energy-generating, will continue to serve its purpose long into the future. Utility costs in the past have been relatively low in this country. As utility prices continue to rise, solar panels will become even more important. Showcasing solar panels in a way that lets people see they can be beautiful and serve a dual purpose has far-reaching, long-lasting effects.

Above: Detail view of the wood panel wall, storage, and complementary door, with the large window that merges the living space with the backyard.

Opposite: The open living space flows seamlessly from the kitchen, separated only by a low bookshelf.

Top: The built-in cabinets and bookshelves along the wall of the living space are an efficient solution for the need for storage space.

Bottom: The bookshelf revolves outward to reveal access to a full bathroom.

Opposite: The master bedroom incorporates a wall of storage; the built-in wall cabinets contain storage space and lighting for the bed. Clerestory windows above the built-in storage space allow additional natural light to penetrate into the bedroom.

The surrounding neighborhood has a density of about 14 dwelling units/acre, and most of the lots and houses are very small compared to the national average. Efficient use of space was seen as important: Some of the furniture is built in, as in the kid's bedroom, and the large couch in the living room and is sized so that a portion of it can be used as a queen-sized bed for overnight guests. In the master bedroom on the second floor, the wall becomes the storage: A built-in wall of cabinets conceals clothes and drawers and the individual lighting for the bed. The design also incorporates a relatively large garden space for such a small lot.

COLLECTIVE WISDOM AND FEEDBACK LOOPS

The most important intelligent design strategy was proper planning and orientation and making the structure as passively sustainable as possible. Active systems then became icing on the cake. An effort was also made to demystify the perceived complexity of sustainable design by demonstrating it can be accomplished with little difficulty, and to show the range of strategies that can be implemented with their respective costs and paybacks.

Another important aspect for the owners and architects was the education of others regarding sustainable design. Several tours and events have been held at the house: for other architects, design professions, contractors, community organizations, and institutions, such as the American Institute of Architects, the Boys and Girls Club, Venice Family Clinic, Los Angeles County Museum of Art and others. Within one year, more than 1,000 people visited the Solar Umbrella, including routine trips from the eight local area architecture and design schools.

Also important was to understand exactly how much energy is being used and generated and the life-cycle costs of the energy systems. The own-

Second floor bath view showing the use of natural daylighting.

ers have been diligent in recording how much energy the solar panels generate monthly. This and all project information is shared with visitors and has been made available to the public. Continuing collaboration is occurring with the solar consultant to fine-tune, monitor, and document the sustainable features. This information is continually compiled and adjustments are made.

The most important lesson learned was that a holistic approach to energy and environmental design must take into account the competing performance, cost, social aspects, and regulatory constraints associated with the implementation of a series of energy design measures on any sustainable project. This approach resulted in a highly efficient building that met even tougher standards for quality architecture.

PROJECT ECONOMICS

The city department of water and power provided a rebate of over $18,600 and the federal government provided a rebate of $4,000 for the solar system. Appliance rebates totaling $300 were utilized for low-flow and ENERGY STAR. The original house had minor dry rot in the framing of the walls so the owners were able to reuse most of the wall framing and all of the roof and floor framing; even the original stucco was retained: it was sand-blasted and skim-coated with a new color to match the new addition. Obtaining a variance to allow a carport in lieu of an enclosed garage also saved both money and space.

Another key strategy was to provide extra insulation (best return on investment!) and ensure minimal infiltration. A tight envelope resulted in a dramatically reduced demand for energy, thereby reducing the need and costs for systems that would have been necessary to produce more energy.

The remaining cost of the solar system was still substantial (taking into account the rebates just noted)—about $20,000. The payback time on this is estimated to be 12 years (the warranty on the panels is 25 years, although they should last a lot longer). The solar hot water, which preheats the gas-fired HWH, has a payback time of 10 years (equal to the warranty). Energy costs for the entire building are now less than $300/year. As utility costs increase the payback period will decrease.

PROCESS AND RESULTS

Predesign

The existing building location on-site was analyzed for proper orientation and heat gain and differences between the local and regional climate. The architects saw the potential of designing an addition that would reorient the home 180 degrees and dramatically change the relationship with the neighborhood as well as its passive and active solar orientation while conserving precious open space. This also included an analysis that would result in saving the original 1923 bungalow to conserve building resources and save time and money.

Design

Numerous environmental considerations were incorporated in the early planning and design stages of the project. The architects and energy consultant collaborated from the outset to minimize energy use and best utilize natural features such as the sun and prevailing winds.

The orientation and shape of the building and the placement of windows maximized natural daylighting and natural ventilation and provided shading where needed. The building's design and technologies allowed it to achieve a level of energy efficiency that exceeds both the State of California Title 24 Energy Code and local area standards set by the City of Santa Monica's Green Building Design and Construction Guidelines by more than 50 percent, resulting in annual energy bills of less than $300.

Construction Process

The construction process was managed to be as resource efficient as possible. The architects provided the contractor with a waste management plan that resulted in over 85 percent of the construction waste being recycled. A waste removal company sorted and recycled construction debris; however, contractors were also required to recycle their own personal waste such as soda cans and so on. Reclaimed wood products from another construction site were used for all concrete forming. Any remaining materials in good condition were then used for structural framing.

Construction was anticipated to take nine months. Actual construction lasted 13 months due to many innovations and experimental applications and programs. Inspectors were not familiar with the solar system and many materials associated with green building, and the learning curve caused delays. The service planner for LADWP (Los Angeles Department of Water and Power) had problems locating the service due to the solar system causing further delays. The contractor had to be continually educated about sustainability, and it took considerable work to explain, for example why they had to wait four days to get 50 percent fly-ash concrete when they could get a normal load of concrete the next morning.

Operations/Maintenance

The home was designed to significantly reduce operation and maintenance costs. An operation and maintenance program was designed and an operation manual provided to the owner. All systems are currently being monitored for performance. It is important to coordinate rebate requirements with actual product and installation warranties.

Materials, such as Homosote, oriented strandboard, concrete, natural stone, and natural solid woods were used, all of which have homogeneous solid cores. When scratched or damaged, it is easy to repair, or is unnoticeable. Landscaping requires almost no maintenance and is drought tolerant. Exterior finishes are natural pigmented stucco, recycled and rusted cold-rolled steel, and concrete, requiring no painting. After a year of occupancy there no maintenance on the building was required, other than adjusting and tuning the active solar, pumps, and irrigation systems, and cleaning the gutters. In the first year of operation, the utility cost for the building was less than $300.

Commissioning

The architects had previously completed a number of LEED-certified buildings, including pioneering certification in sectors of the building industry where the USGBC had not yet developed certification standards. At the time of construction of this project there were no certification criteria for SFR or existing buildings. The architects had previous success at getting the USGBC to accept applications for certification for projects that had no LEED certification criteria, so they attempted several times to have the USGBC use the Solar Umbrella as a pilot project for SFR LEED Certification; to no avail. Nonetheless, the architects independently commissioned and fully documented the building following LEED criteria and methodologies developed in-house and with the sustainability consultant.

Postoccupancy Evaluation

Detailed records have been kept and performance has been measured against design criteria. Even though the building was designed to be a net zero energy user, it is currently generating only 95 percent of the energy used. Initially, energy generation was only at 80 to 85 percent, until adjustments were made to pool and pond pumps and automatic timers, and some solar panels were added. Energy generation is lower than anticipated due largely to accumulation of dirt on the panels and the coastal fog. The panels are now cleaned every four months, which has increased energy output significantly. Stormwater retention, thermally broken glazing, in-floor heating, and ENERGY STAR appliances are all performing as planned. Water usage was also initially high. Sensors have been added, landscaping has been established, and usage has decreased substantially.

A number of unusual sustainable materials were used, such as cabinetry and flooring made from oriented strandboard (OSB), wall made from Homosote (recycled newsprint) and recycled rusted steel siding. These sustainable materials, as well as many others, have proved to be durable materials and are performing well.

Initial payback for all sustainable systems was anticipated to take seven years. Current projections now anticipate 10 to 12 years. The entire sustainable items, including the solar system, solar hot water system, and thermally broken glazing, had an incremental cost of $35,000 most of which was recovered in state and local rebates and federal tax credits.

The Solar Umbrella provides a direct benefit to design, development, and building professionals and students on an ongoing basis. Through comprehensive documentation, publication, and outreach, the project teaches valuable lessons on overcoming barriers to green, affordable development and showcases new strategies and technologies for others to build upon.

The master bath is slightly elevated over the master bedroom space; the openness of the bathroom creates the illusion of a large master bedroom suite.

Beals' Residence, Atlanta, Georgia

Architect/Designer: William Carpenter, FAIA, PhD, Lightroom Studio

■ By William Carpenter and Ric Nardin

WHEN JUSTIN AND JENNIFER BEALS first consulted Lightroom Studio, they described themselves as "urban pioneers." The owners of a successful media company and die-hard sustainable-design enthusiasts, they had moved to an area of Atlanta that was then in an early state of renewal. There they built a concrete tower of their own design. As their company prospered and the area's revival continued, they began to desire more openness and light for their growing art collection.

OVERVIEW

Adjoining the original tower, the L-shaped addition contains a 1,200-square-foot art gallery, a 1,000-square-foot guest suite, and a spacious kitchen. Both "legs" of the addition open onto a courtyard with full-height glass, allowing for maximum interpenetration of interior and exterior space. In addition to the modernist principle of spatial transparency, the hearth has been pulled to the center of the courtyard, in an echo of Wright's Barnsdale House. Indeed, the L shape of the addition itself is derived from Wright's Usonian houses, with their separation of public and private spaces.

View of the entrance through the steel trellis. Note the overhang facing south.

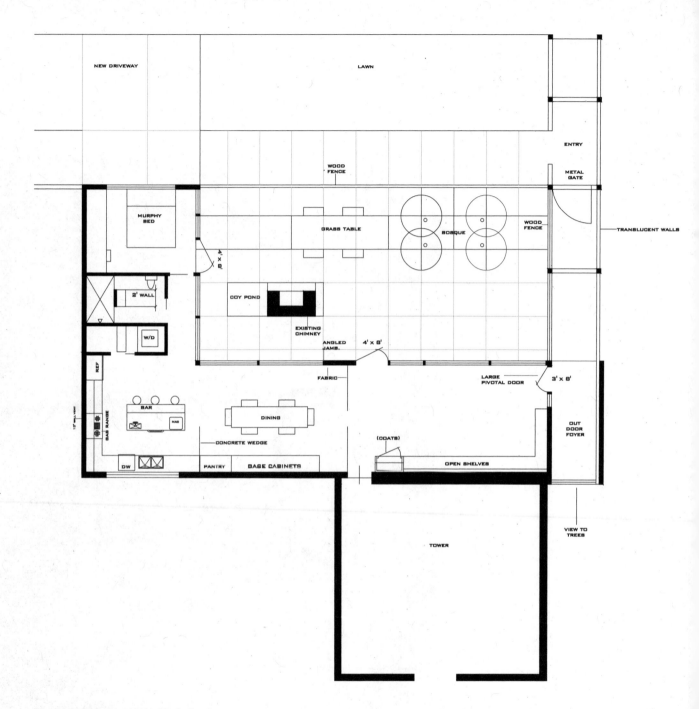

NEW DRIVEWAY

LAWN

ENTRY

WOOD
FENCE

METAL
GATE

MURPHY
BED

GRASS TABLE

BOSQUE

WOOD
FENCE

TRANSLUCENT WALLS

2' WALL

4' X 8'

COY POND

W/D

EXISTING
CHIMNEY

ANGLED
JAMB.

4' X 8'

LARGE
PIVOTAL DOOR

3' X 8'

REF

FABRIC

GAS RANGE

BAR

MAG

DINING

(COATS)

OUT
DOOR
FOYER

CONCRETE WEDGE

DW

PANTRY

BASE CABINETS

OPEN SHELVES

VIEW TO
TREES

TOWER

Floor plan of the Beals' residence, Atlanta, Georgia.
Note the exterior fireplace and shaded glazing.

Overall views showing the layering of elements and the private courtyard.

DESIGN DETAILS

Clerestory windows in the "public" walls of the new areas help create well-lit interiors while preserving privacy. Spaces opening onto the courtyard have full-height glass. The rooms are variously sheltered from the sun by roof overhangs and by a large curtain running the length of the gallery. The curtain is made of Tyvek, which can develop a silken flexibility and drape.

A bright-green metal armature projects beyond the covered entry passage, on axis with the door of a building across the street and referencing nearby railroad trestles.

CONSTRUCTION DETAILS

Selected materials include recycled concrete block and corrugated metal cladding for the tower. The preexisting tower had developed structural problems, which were repaired in the course of the project. In addition to redesigning the tower's structural supports, Lightroom also added a roof terrace.

SUSTAINABILITY

Interpenetration of interior and outdoor spaces encourages the use of unconditioned living areas. Passive solar strategies include overhanging eaves for the southern exposure. Recycled and sustainable materials include low VOC paints, Argon filled and UV inhibiting glass, Georgia Cypress, selected recycled interior doors, Tyvek interior sheers, and recycled steel entry trellis.

Side view of the trellis showing the existing tower constructed in 1999 by the owner.

Above: Entry view of the trellis showing the relationship between interior and exterior rooms.

Left: Courtyard view showing the transparency of interior and exterior spaces.

Detail view of the hearth placed as an anchor in the koi pond.

Detail view of the entry trellis, with the warehouse shown in the distance.

Overall view from the street showing the relation to the existing residence.

Above: Detail view from the dining space to the gallery.

Opposite: Interior view showing the kitchen and dining area.
Note the translucent cabinetry and dark stained ebony oak floor.

Entrance view from the street showing the parking garages and terrace porch above.

Bush Residence, Atlanta, Georgia

Architect/Designer: William Carpenter, FAIA, PhD, Lightroom Studio

■ By William Carpenter and Ric Nardin

WHEN ARTIST DIANNE BUSH BEGAN to consult with Lightroom Studio regarding a design for her residence, painting studio, and gallery in Atlanta's Old Fourth Ward, her initial vision was relatively simple: a modern building with a loftlike feel. As the consultations progressed, however, and as Dianne began to recognize additional opportunities, a more dynamic vision emerged, one perfectly suited to the quickening energy of the surrounding neighborhood.

OVERVIEW

A longtime fan of the industrial modern aesthetic, Dianne knew the look she wanted as well as the basic set of rooms. Her visit to Lightroom's award-winning studio in Decatur ignited more detailed ideas, as well as confidence in a fruitful collaboration with me, the architect. The project's double-height living area, for example, is modeled on Lightroom's primary working space. But the organization of requested spaces was inspired by my fascination with the historic urban fabric of Savannah, Georgia. That city's celebrated ordering of residences in an urban grid punctuated by large squares drove the design development process. The result is a set of spaces constellated in a manner similar to those residences, arising separately from the street grid and in neighborly harmony with each other and with the surrounding area. Pavilions of varying heights are aligned along a central "street" and courtyard, a design that references both Savannah's urban fabric and a Sol Lewitt sculpture in a nearby park.

DESIGN DETAILS

Two rows of three pavilions each contain an orderly progression of spaces, beginning with an art gallery, which spans the central axis and faces the public street. Behind it are the artist's studio, the double-height pavilion containing the kitchen and master bedroom, living and dining rooms, a guest house, and, finally, a pair of garages, one surmounted by a rooftop terrace, which serves as a nod to the front porches of houses that once lined the street.

CONSTRUCTION DETAILS

Materials include recycled concrete block, corrugated metal, aluminum frame windows with tinted, argon-filled glass, garage doors of sustainable mahogany veneer, and polished concrete floors. Using foam-filled 12-inch blocks provided an R value of 11 in the walls. The Roof R value is R-40.

SUSTAINABILITY

The courtyard opens to the southwest, serving as a passive solar collector, its concrete slab providing the thermal mass.

Passive cooling is achieved through cross-ventilation strategies implemented with operable windows on the upper floors. The concrete block walls are filled with zonolite, providing exceptionally effective insulation, while the roof achieves an R60 rating through the use of environmentally friendly Icynene. The project is constructed of all recycled materials, including concrete block and steel. None of the surfaces are painted. Narrow-track driveways with grass strips provide areas to absorb rainwater and reduce runoff.

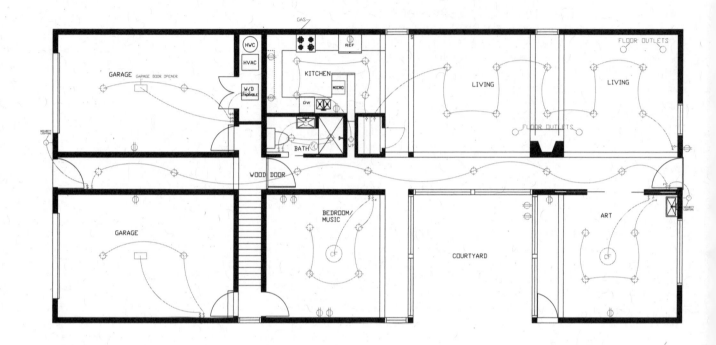

GAS

HWC

HVAC

W/D STACKABLE

GARAGE
GARAGE DOOR OPENER

REF

KITCHEN

MICRO

DW

BATH

WOOD DOOR

GARAGE

BEDROOM/MUSIC

CF

FLOOR OUTLETS

LIVING

LIVING

FLOOR OUTLETS

COURTYARD

ART

CF

LEVEL 1

Electrical plan

TERRACE

LOFT

EXPOSED TO BELOW

CF

BATH

CL

WP

220 OUTLET
(TO BE ADDED AFTER
INSPECTION)

UPSTAIRS
KIT/DIN/LIV

DW

KITCHENETTE

ROOF

ROOF

LEVEL 2

Finally, the guesthouse serves as a rental unit, helping the owner to afford a sophisticated and environmentally friendly design while providing an admirable example for others moving back into the once-decaying city center.

Dianne calls her new home "Casa Bob" after her father, who provided both enthusiasm and guidance during the design process and helped her realize her dream of living and working in an increasingly vibrant in-town neighborhood.

Study model showing central organizing courtyard and functions as separate buildings.

Front elevation view showing the art gallery and the view to the rear garden.

Entrance view from street showing the terrace porch.

View from the hearth to City Hall East and into the kitchen area.

View from the living room into the courtyard. Note the art studio space on the left.

Overall view of the living room showing the tall apertures that define the alley spaces and cross-axes.

View from the dining space into the kitchen area.

Dominey Residence, Atlanta, Georgia

Architect/Designer: William Carpenter, FAIA, PhD, Lightroom Studio
By William Carpenter and Ric Nardin

TODD DOMINEY, A CELEBRATED WEB-site designer, and his wife Heather are fervent admirers of the modernist principles promoted by the case study house movement. When they planned to expand their existing bungalow with a carport and outdoor living space, Lightroom Studio created an integrated design that satisfied both the couple's practical needs and aesthetic enthusiasms. Moreover, in accord with case study ambitions, the feat was accomplished within a tight budget.

OVERVIEW
The project consists of a deck extending out to a pair of pavilions housing a carport and an outdoor living room. Covered space totals approximately 1000 square feet. Modernist hallmarks such as the interpenetration of interior and outdoor spaces are readily evident as the design mediates between architecture and the surrounding landscape. Indeed, the project blurs boundaries between architecture, minimalist sculpture, and landscape. References to southern vernacular design also enrich the design, including the shotgun cottage and the dogtrot cabin. A primary "shotgun" axis within the existing house is continued across the deck and between the dogtrot of the two pavilions, terminating in a specimen tree in the backyard. Following a strategy promoted by Frank Lloyd Wright, a hearth is pulled out from the center of the house and placed in the outdoor living room. And part of the living room roof is a pattern of open joists, accommodating a large white oak that projects through it.

DESIGN DETAILS
The overall design builds on the lineage of case study houses, elegantly extending the interior spaces of the bungalow to outdoor living spaces

and the landscape beyond. The spare design of the stucco fireplace itself provides a piece of minimalist sculpture, while the unadorned back wall of the living room serves as a canvas for the lives that will inhabit it, as breezes blow through or a fire roars. A narrow slit in the wall of the carport playfully reveals the oak tree immediately behind it.

In addition to its modernist principles, the design thoughtfully integrates details of the existing house. The roof of the carport, for example, references and transforms the cornice of the existing structure.

CONSTRUCTION DETAILS
The existing oak presented challenges as well as opportunities. Arborist input was sought and implemented to care for it. While the program called for paving near its base, the root structure had to be carefully protected, as did its access to water. An organically shaped border was traced around its base, and porous concrete was selected for the surrounding paving. Materials include recycled concrete blocks, hard-coat natural stucco with metal galvanized bead edges, and Georgia cypress. All construction processes and materials choices follow the LEED process. The total cost of the project was $58,000 including architects fees.

SUSTAINABILITY
Unconditioned living space is inherently friendly to the environment. The project is built primarily of Georgia cypress, harvested from a sustainable forestation program in the south Georgia swamps. The roof of the living room is slanted to drain rainwater onto a bed of slate chips covering an underground tank. A manual pump connected to the tank is used for watering the landscape.

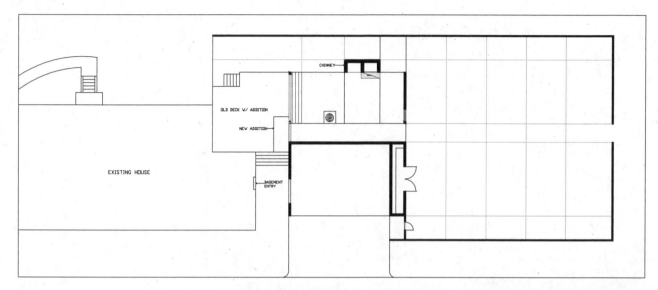

CHIMNEY

OLD DECK W/ ADDITION

NEW ADDITION

EXISTING HOUSE

BASEMENT
ENTRY

Above: Floor plan of the Dominey residence, Atlanta, Georgia.

Right: New stair entrance at side yard showing the deck area and stainless steel cable rails.

Detail view of the trellis that frames the existing tree. The roots were carefully addressed and porous concrete was used to maximize water infiltration to the roots.

View from the rear garden into the pavilion.
Note the hearth on the right and the clear
view from the existing residence evocative of
shotgun houses.

Street view of the new car park area. Note the free-standing sculptural wall that screens the outdoor living space from the parking. The vertical slot frames the tree and is uplit at night.

Right: Detail view of the existing pin oak and cypress trellis.

Opposite page top: Overall view of the pavilion showing the garden storage on the left.

Opposite page bottom: View from the existing residence.

Opposite page top: View from the existing residence.

Opposite page bottom: Carport shown from the street. Note cornice on the existing residence matches the new pavilion cornice.

Above: Detail view of the new hearth and rose trellis.

Lightcatcher, Atlanta, Georgia

Architect/Designer: William Carpenter, FAIA, PhD, Lightroom Studio
■ By William Carpenter

FOR TWO PROFESSIONAL ARCHITECtural photographers, a home designed to process light is a perfect fit. Lightroom Studio took advantage of a preexisting foundation on a wooded lot to create an environment that met the owners' living and working needs while appropriately channeling light into both these aspects of their lives.

OVERVIEW

When the owners first consulted Lightroom Studio, they had already purchased their property, which had a house on it, one clad in pink asbestos siding. Demolition soon followed, leaving just the foundation, oak flooring, and the front door, all of which were recycled into the new structure. Also remaining was their need for a home that contained living space, a darkroom, office/studio space, one designed to allow sufficient light in to showcase their growing art collection yet protect it from damaging solar rays.

During an initial phase of the project, I followed the two photographers as they went about their daily work. In doing so, I observed we had similar professional concerns, including attention to light, the value of perspective, and the critical importance of the size of the aperture through which to target a view. Accordingly, the notion of both buildings and cameras as lightboxes inspired the ensuing design, complete with various lenses, apertures, and filters directing the allowed illumination as well as the perception of place. The resulting 2,600-square-foot structure, with its windows designed to take advantage of different light sources and views, skillfully accommodates the owners' working and living spaces. A central atrium, two and a half stories tall, connects the two spaces, imbuing both with ample ambient light.

DESIGN DETAILS

Central to the design was a concern for the building's context. Careful attention was paid to how the new building relates to the scale, proportion, and fenestration of neighboring houses and to the street. The result is a house that fits in with those of its neighbors while still being distinct. In fact, the design is markedly different from the surrounding vernacular, but its presence is not jarring—which is why the "new kid on the block" has been welcomed.

The central atrium contains a 20-foot-high window of white laminated glass that diffuses harsh rays of the sun. Other windows open onto views of the wooded landscape. A large window in the master bedroom is trained on a water oak; in contrast, a tiny window in a bedroom closet makes a playful reference to an ancient pinhole camera and projects landscape images onto the back of the closet door.

CONSTRUCTION DETAILS

Early in construction, the general contractor disappeared, and I assumed that responsibility. In due course, I and the owners discovered the benefits inherent to the design/build process. As the structure rose, details of the design could be altered on-site and unanticipated opportunities seized.

As noted, the new house rises from the foundation of a preexisting structure. In some places, such as under an expanded fireplace, additional footings were installed. Maple flooring was used throughout the second floor.

SUSTAINABILITY

In addition to the foundation, oak flooring and other parts of the demolished house were recycled into the new building.

Recycled concrete block was used throughout. And passive solar strategies were employed in the fenestration, with large windows drawing in light from the east, with smaller windows opening to the west.

Detail view of the master bedroom exterior window, facing east. Note the corner window which dissolves the solidity of the room and opens the bedroom to the rear garden.

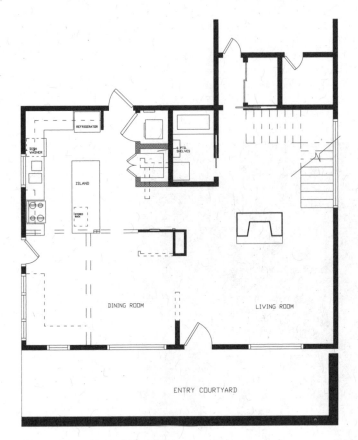

Floor plans of Lightcatcher, Atlanta, Georgia.

Front entry view of the new residence showing the entry courtyard.

Materials palette of hard-coat stucco, storefront, and Georgia cypress.

Entry view showing the existing door, which was left in its original location.

Entry view at new courtyard space. Note the reuse of the original 1930s door.

Lightroom Studio, Decatur, Georgia

Architect/Designer: William Carpenter, FAIA, PhD, Lightroom Studio

■ By William Carpenter

I N 2002, I RELOCATED TO AN OLD HOUSE in a deteriorating area of Decatur with the dream of erecting a modern architectural studio. A large tree-shaded lot stretched out behind the modest early twentieth-century house, which at the time was surrounded by boarded-up buildings. Within a year, as I lived and worked in the old house, I designed a new studio for the back lot, ground was broken, and the walls began to rise. Then, at the same time I was overseeing the construction of a client's new home, my own general contractor disappeared and I had to become my own contractor as well. What I learned in the ensuing months I eventually described in my book *Learning by Building* (Wiley, 1997). More important, what emerged from this experience was an award-winning 3,800-square-foot structure that helped revive the neighborhood and now houses a thriving, multidisciplinary practice. Notably, in 2006, Lightroom Studio was cited by the South Atlantic Region of the AIA for design excellence.

OVERVIEW

Lightroom Studio is designed to accommodate the rhythms of the workday; it provides spaces for concentrated design work as well as for client consultations, group meetings, and individual meditation. The design program called for two parking spaces, a model shop and utility room, an entry stair, a large studio space, kitchen, guest room, two baths, a loft bedroom/workspace, and a roof terrace.

The resulting design was fueled by my fascination with the compression and expansion of space. It can be described as a wooden volume placed within a concrete container; its materials play on the contrast between the utilitarian cool of an industrial loft and the warmth of colors in a jewelry box. As visitors come in and ascend the entry stairs, the space contracts and compresses, terminating in a wooden entrance hall. Reminiscent of Frank Lloyd Wright's studio in Oak Park, in which clients moved through a compressed corridor before emerging at the architect's office, the entry space at Lightroom expands into a double-height conference room and studio, with concrete block walls and enormous windows. Both clients and staff, and even the UPS deliveryman, say that entering this space inspires them. Moving on from there, another compression leads through a service core, composed of kitchen, bathroom, and guest room, to enclosed stairs, the confines of which expand again onto a loft workspace overlooking the studio. A third staircase ascends to a tree-sheltered roof terrace, revealing an 1870s-era building on an adjoining lot; and, beyond, a view of the town square of Decatur to the north and the Atlanta skyline to the west.

DESIGN DETAILS

The entrance is deliberately tucked away at the rear, reached along a path that helps both clients and staff transition from the hectic public street through a leafy courtyard to a protected, almost sacred, creative space. The open plan of the work areas encourages personal interaction and the exchange of ideas, central to the interdisciplinary, creative ethos of the practice.

CONSTRUCTION DETAILS

The materials for Lightroom Studio were selected to relate to the historic house next door, which is made of scored paint, stucco, and native Georgia trees, including cypress, maple, and pine. The exterior is clad in cypress and hard-coat natural stucco covering concrete block. Maple flooring is used throughout the second and third floors. In the wooden core, the walls are constructed of fin-

Opposite: **Entrance view to the courtyard.**

ished plywood. And because it is located in a fire district, the studio employs sprinkler systems and a sophisticated system of heat-triggered metal shutters that automatically descend over the windows when the internal temperature reaches a critical point.

SUSTAINABILITY

A passive system of cooling is achieved through ventilation patterns that channel air from the shaded courtyard up through the structure and out through a small pavilion on the roof terrace. Trees—which were protected during construc-tion—shade the structure to the south and west. Argon-filled glass was selected for the windows. A north-facing window is the largest; a slightly smaller one, facing west, is coated with UV in-hibitors. The roof is insulated to a rating of R60. The cypress cladding, from a sustainable foresta-tion program in the south Georgia swamps, is sealed with the UV inhibitors. Water-based seal-ers are used throughout the interior and exterior. Exterior walls are of recycled concrete blocks. Slabs around the perimeter are of porous con-crete, allowing water to penetrate to the roots of surrounding trees.

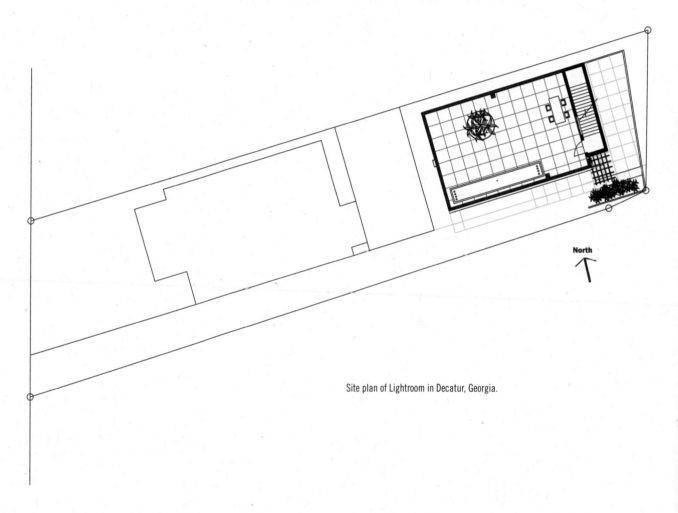

North

Site plan of Lightroom in Decatur, Georgia.

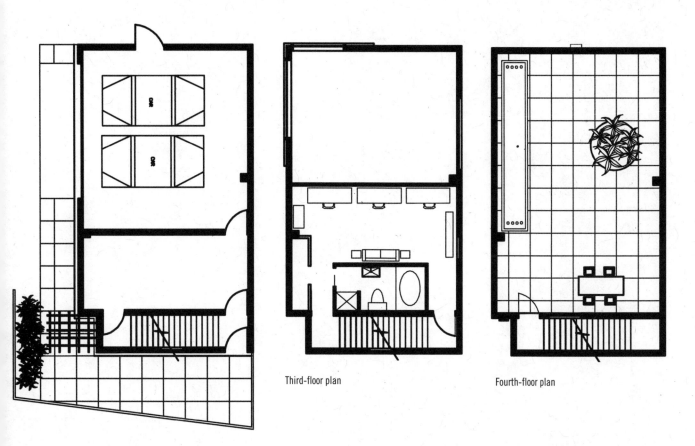

First-floor plan

Third-floor plan

Fourth-floor plan

View of the new residence in relation to the existing 1880s mansion.

Above: View of the residence/office from the existing mansion.

Opposite: Courtyard view showing the entrance garden.

View from the loft into the Lightroom Studio.

Sequence view of the entry stair
and lobby.

Detail view of the loft
and Georgia pine wall.

Detail view of the
entry window.

Carter Residence, Atlanta, Georgia

Architect/Designer: William Carpenter, FAIA, PhD, Lightroom Studio, and Timothy Nichols, AIA, LEED AP

■ By William Carpenter

THIS PROJECT, COMPLETED IN 2008, designed for Amy Carter, the daughter of former President Jimmy Carter, is located near the Carter Center in Atlanta, Georgia. Amy and her husband Jay Kelly, a new media designer, have an eight-year-old son. She is an illustrator and photographer and had often collaborated with her father on book projects.

Phase one of the project consisted of a new bedroom, bath, and art studio, Phase two consisted of a new rear garden, a home office, and guest room. Opening the home up to the views was an important consideration. Lightroom Studio opened up the rear of the house with a glazed wall, facing southeast.

DESIGN DETAILS

A cantilevered roof overhang, which glows at night, directs the family and visitors to the entrance, tucked away at the rear. The new addition features a digitally fabricated sunscreen that shades the glazing and creates leaflike shadows that change throughout the day, based on a random digital design. The pattern on the sunscreen was designed by artist and architect Timothy Nichols, AIA, LEED AP.

CONSTRUCTION DETAILS

Native Georgia materials, including cypress, oak, and pine, were used. The exterior is clad in cypress and hard-coat natural stucco covering concrete block.

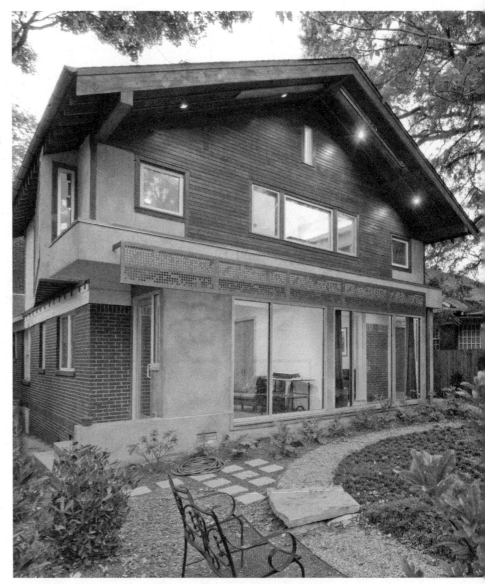

View of the digitally fabricated copper screen and rear courtyard.

SUSTAINABILITY

A passive system of cooling is achieved through ventilation patterns that channel air from the shaded rear yard up through the structure and out through operable window openings. Trees, which were protected during construction, shade the structure to the south and west. Argon-filled glass was selected for the windows. A north-facing window is the largest; a slightly smaller one, facing west, is coated with UV inhibitors. The roof is insulated to a rating of R40. The cypress cladding, from a sustainable forestation program in the south Georgia swamps, is sealed with the UV inhibitors. Water-based sealers are used throughout the interior and exterior.

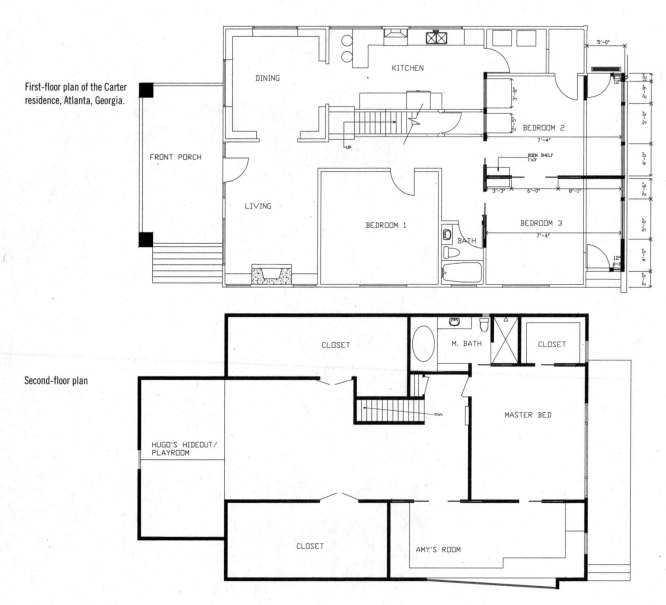

First-floor plan of the Carter residence, Atlanta, Georgia.

Second-floor plan

View from the new studio into the rear garden space showing new and existing red oak floors.

Shot–Trot House, Houston, Texas

Architect/Designer: Brett Zamore, Zamore Homes

■ By Lee Cuthbert and William Carpenter

THE HOUSTON, TEXAS, SHOT–TROT house truly offers something for everyone. Designer Brett Zamore combined the best of the vernacular Southern shotgun and dogtrot housing styles and made his hybrid energy-efficient, modern, and affordable. People took note in Houston, and nationally, too, as the house generated media interest in all quarters. It's not industrial and lofty; it's not too traditional; it is designed to cool itself naturally; and it's relatively inexpensive. Zamore rethought affordable home design and came up with a winning combination of price and style by using common-sense ideas like building on an 8-foot grid to minimize materials waste. (Since then, Zamore launched his own line of kit houses—www.zamorehomes.com—using the Shot–Trot as a foundation and updating it with several styles and sizes, smaller and bigger.)

OVERVIEW

While a graduate architecture student at Rice University, Brett Zamore helped improve Houston's Fifth Ward with his creative renovation of a vintage shotgun house. It impressed David Kaplan, who wrote about the project for a Rice publication; and when he later decided to buy a house, he contacted the young designer. At first, the two tried to find an existing home to renovate but soon they decided to build a design Zamore had been tinkering with since his university days. It combines the ventilation (and circulation)

The structure is constructed in such a way as to allow for ideal natural ventilation and air circulation, and is designed to be approximately 40 percent more energy efficient than a standard home.

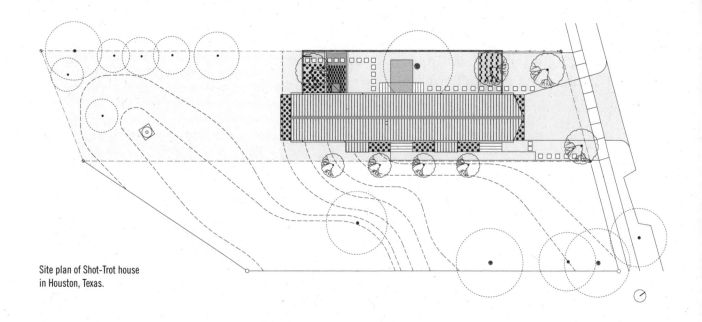

Site plan of Shot-Trot house
in Houston, Texas.

1. KITCHEN   2. DINING ROOM   3. LIVING ROOM   4. WORKSPACE/BEDROOM   5. MAIN BEDROOM   6. BATHROOM   7. PORCH/DECK   8. OPEN ABOVE TO LOFT

Floor plan

properties of the shotgun (front to back) and the dogtrot (side to side). Front and back porches connect the home to the landscape and the street (making it an "antideveloper" house, says its creator); and the centrally located side doors consist of inward-opening French doors and a sliding louvered barn-style door. For privacy or to block out sunlight, the big door can slide over the 8 foot by 8 foot opening provided by the hinged doors and still let the breeze through.

The 1,200-square-foot Shot–Trot is long and narrow (16 feet by 80 feet), and from the street looks like an updated shotgun, albeit with a tall, modern roofline fronted by a forward-leaning peak (to further connect the home to the street). This altered geometry makes it clear this shotgun is born of the twenty-first century, and it provides the interior spacious vaulted ceilings (workers on Kaplan's home likened the front elevation to a Whataburger). A galvalume roof both

adds to the home's modern appeal and recalls the older homes that inspired its design. Hardwood floors and clean finishes make the home feel cheery, if not downright cozy. And it can be done for less than $100 per square foot, says Zamore, depending on materials and finishes.

"It made me think a lot about how to minimize—during this time where there is so much waste," says Zamore. "Not just how to get the most out of construction materials, but also

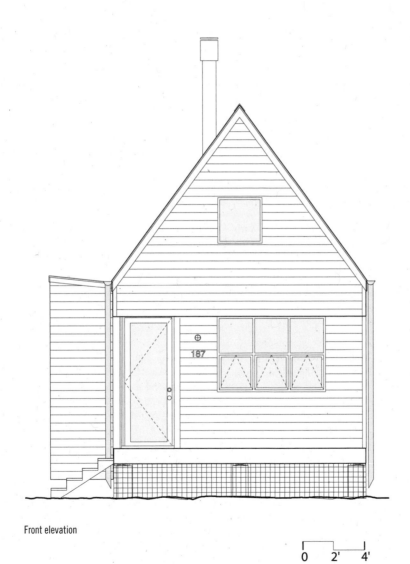

Front elevation

0 2' 4'

Side elevation

space. I think the Shot–Trot is a good example of how to get the most of a small house. It feels a lot larger than it actually is."

DESIGN DETAILS

Flow means a lot to a house that's only 16 feet wide, and the Shot–Trot is laid out for efficiency. The front door is on the left-facing side of the home, and it opens directly into the kitchen on the right and the open dining room and living space beyond it. Both bathrooms are "appendaged onto the side of the house," according to Zamore, to reinforce the open floor plan. He labels the center of the home where the French and sliding doors are the "transition zone," as a wall rises beyond it separating the office (or guest bedroom) and master bedroom. For Kaplan's home, he let the owner choose his own finishes, and elect to forgo a walk-in closet off his bedroom. For the kit version of the Shot–Trot, Zamore added the walk-in closet and a larger closet in the other work/bedroom. He moved the washer and dryer from back in the bedroom area

to an area along the hallway, and he eliminated a loft accessible via a ladder over the bedroom areas because it wouldn't meet the International Residential Code. That area is now a small attic with pull-down stairs. "It's now a more generic layout that would work for almost anybody," says Zamore. "It's very functional."

Buyers of the kit homes can choose from six floor plans (the Shot–Trot is Kit 02), and may select from one of three finish packages each for exterior siding, flooring, countertops, cabinetry, plumbing fixtures, appliances, fixtures, and accessories. With relatively little modification, Zamore says any of his kits can be constructed to meet LEED Certification standards. Alterations to insulation, windows, countertops, and landscaping must be made, plus specifying a tankless water heater and ENERGY STAR rated appliances, all increasing the up-front cost of the homes. The standard finish packages do not include all LEED-approved items, though Zamore notes that he does give customers a choice of IKEA kitchens, and their cabinets are formalde-

hyde-free. Without any modifications, the Shot–Trot and its kit counterparts are designed to be 40 percent more energy efficient than standard homes.

"It really is a hallmark of these houses, the way [they] are ventilated and how [they] breathe, even on the inside," says Zamore. In the hottest months, Kaplan's energy bills are below $100.

CONSTRUCTION DETAILS

Unlike prefab and modular housing, Zamore Homes are all site-built, with kit components shipped directly from the closest suppliers in the network to reduce transportation costs. Zamore uses off-the-shelf components; and, as with his first Shot–Trot, he has trusses, wall panels, roofing—as many pieces as possible—preordered and assembled at the manufacturer's facility, delivered ready to install. Home buyers can choose from standard wood framing, steel framing (excellent for hurricane and seismic activity–prone areas), or structural insulated panels (SIP) as the backbone of their homes. By joining rigid foam

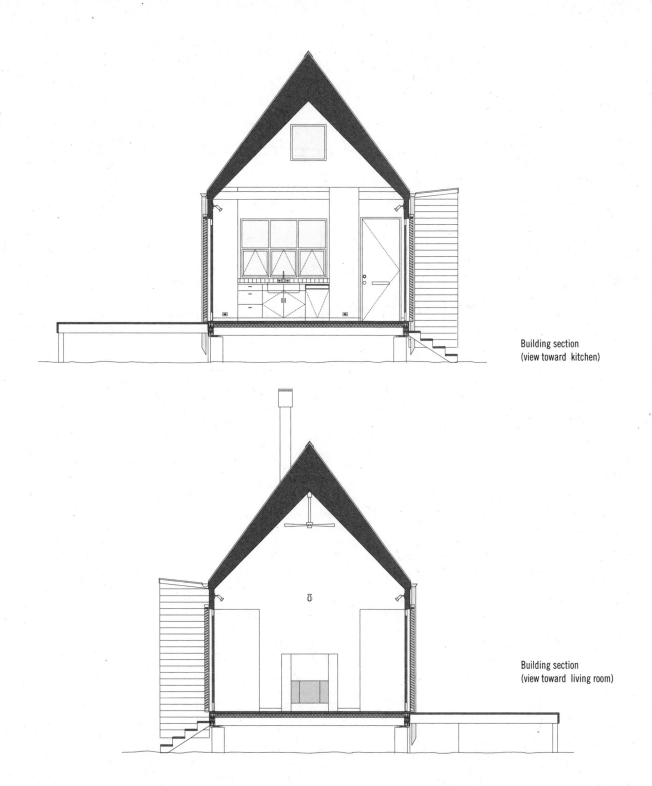

Building section
(view toward kitchen)

Building section
(view toward living room)

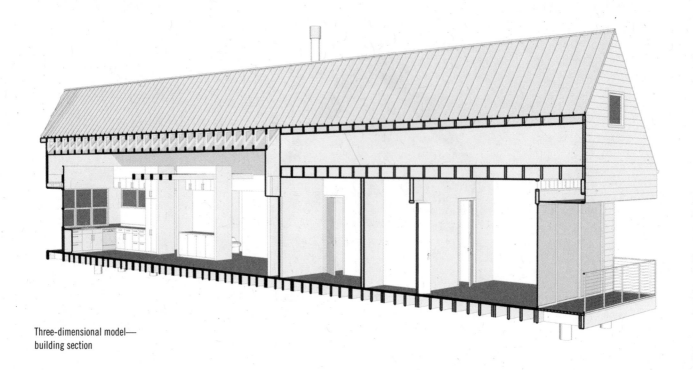

Three-dimensional model—
building section

insulation to oriented strandboard (OSB), SIPs enhance thermal performance, as gaps between the structural elements and insulation are eliminated. SIPs provide an especially well-insulated envelope, though Zamore says in the humid South it's better for houses to breathe a little. Building with steel framing or SIP panels adds a significant cost to the home's construction, notes Zamore.

Toward that end, Kaplan's home was constructed using standard wood framing to allow airflow from the base to the eaves beneath its hardiplank siding, allowing moisture and heat to escape. The home sits on piers 30 inches off the ground, better for ventilation and to protect the home from mold and moisture in an area prone to rain from tropical storms and hurricanes. Zamore says the kit houses may also be constructed on a perimeter wall foundation for extra warmth.

Like many of his ideas, Zamore's use of the 8-foot grid takes a simple idea and maximizes it.

"It's not that innovative," says the home designer, "because it's just utilizing an existing system." Plywood sheets come in 4-foot by 8-foot sizes; 2-by-4 or 2-by-6 boards come in 8-foot lengths. Framers can just go to work with their nail guns, and not take time to cut and size members. "I'm trying to minimize waste, and also the waste of time," explains Zamore. "Time in the field is more expensive than the building materials. The cheapest thing about a house is actually its framing. If you can reduce the work done in the field, then you're saving a lot of money."

The Zamore Homes concept resembles that of the old Sears, Roebuck and Company house plans, sold by the retailer through stores and catalogs. Thousands upon thousands of the retailer's homes were built across the United States, giving homeowners an architect-designed, built-on-site house for the least amount of money. Homebuilding eventually became an industry of customization, and the Sears concept was no longer valued. Perhaps now is the perfect time to revisit the idea; for those who want an energy-efficient, high-design home, built for them on-site at an affordable price, the modest little Shot–Trot is a portal to a new dimension.

Three-dimensional model—
exterior perspective

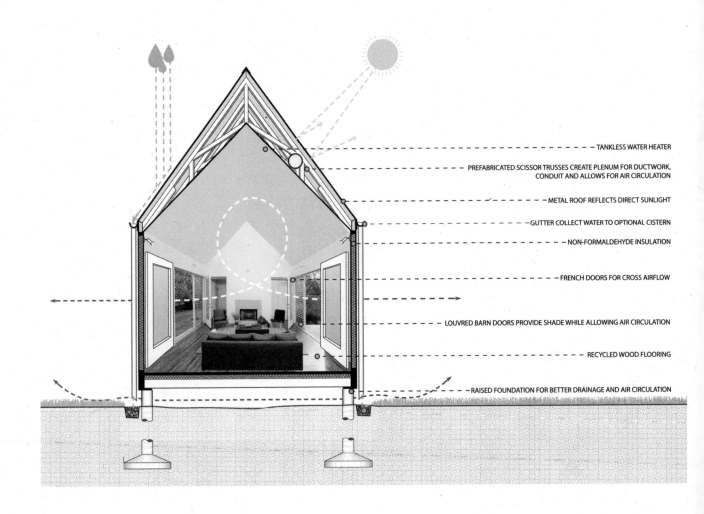

TANKLESS WATER HEATER

PREFABRICATED SCISSOR TRUSSES CREATE PLENUM FOR DUCTWORK, CONDUIT AND ALLOWS FOR AIR CIRCULATION

METAL ROOF REFLECTS DIRECT SUNLIGHT

GUTTER COLLECT WATER TO OPTIONAL CISTERN

NON-FORMALDEHYDE INSULATION

FRENCH DOORS FOR CROSS AIRFLOW

LOUVRED BARN DOORS PROVIDE SHADE WHILE ALLOWING AIR CIRCULATION

RECYCLED WOOD FLOORING

RAISED FOUNDATION FOR BETTER DRAINAGE AND AIR CIRCULATION

Above: Systems diagram

Opposite: The Shot-Trot house is one of six different kit homes that can be purchased online. The design can be modified slightly and constructed on-site in a relatively short period of time. These kits are reminiscent of the old Sears and Roebuck house plans of the past.

Top: The home includes both a front and back porch to make a connection between the home and the landscape and the street; this concept is further achieved through the forward-leaning peak in the roof facing the street.

Right: The design incorporates elements of circulation and ventilation derived from both shotgun and dogtrot home plans. This is achieved through front and back porches, combined with centrally located side doors.

Unlike typical prefab and modular housing, these kit homes are all site-built, with components shipped from the closest suppliers to reduce transportation costs. The homeowner can select from three different exterior siding choices.

Right: The two side porches consist of French doors and a sliding, louvered barn-style door. The barn door can remain closed while the French doors are open, to allow for shading from the sun while providing natural ventilation throughout the home.

Opposite: The Shot–Trot house is the result of the desire to achieve the most use from both construction materials and space. It was constructed with very little waste, and it feels much larger than it actually is.

Right: The main entry into the home is located on the left-facing side; it opens into a small hallway created by a wall, allowing for storage space.

Opposite: View of living area showing the cathedral ceiling and sculptural wall.

The kitchen, dining, and living spaces are all open to one another; the high ceilings create the illusion that the space is larger than it actually is.

View from open dining area into standard IKEA-furnished kitchen filled with natural light.

Johnson–Jones Residence, Phoenix, Arizona
Architect/Designer: Eddie Jones, Jones Studio, Inc.
■ By Lee Cuthbert and William Carpenter

I N 1999, ARCHITECT EDDIE JONES planned and built a 4,500-square-foot, four-bedroom home for his family at the base of Phoenix, Arizona's South Mountain. It holds the distinction of being the first home permitted in Phoenix using "alternative" building materials—in this case, rammed earth walls. More, it embraces a less-than-desirable site with a truly artful concept. Properly orienting a home on its property is the most important part of energy-efficient design, says Jones, and it is the most important element of a successful design. "If you're sensitive to what sites need, then theoretically there are no bad sites," he says. The Johnson–Jones home's other inhabitants are Jones's wife, Lisa Johnson, and her teenage children.

OVERVIEW
The home sits in the affluent Ahwatukee community on the south side of Phoenix, at the base of South Mountain and its surrounding 16,000-plus-acre South Mountain Park—the world's largest municipal park. A steady stream of joggers, hikers, and bicyclists passes the house daily. When rescue helicopters are needed inside the park, they use the cul-de-sac in front of the home as a helipad. More than one banged-up nature enthusiast in need of a

telephone has come knocking at the Johnson–Jones door.

Situated at the back of the lot is a large round-water chlorination tank built by the City of Phoenix. This imposition on the landscape allowed Johnson and Jones to buy the lot for about half the cost of surrounding properties, and it inspired a unique home design that uses a circular motif to great effect. Jones, who operates the architectural firm Jones Studio, Inc., in Phoenix with his brother Neal, says the house he initially sketched is largely the one that got built. Celebrating what others would consider to be an eyesore—the water tank—Jones designed an entry courtyard with a curved exterior wall, a round-water collection cistern, a tall cylinder containing an interior circular staircase, and round patio and pool in the rear. Even the stepping-stones to the door are round.

Several considerations dictated the orientation of the house on the lot, according to Jones: The best views of the mountain are toward the north; the home's focus should be away from the water tank; and a western exposure should be avoided. "If you forced a conventional house on this property, it would be a failure," he says. Facing a home toward the street would mean the rear would face west, and afternoon heat gain would be intensive.

The home is situated on a lot that adjoins a large, round water chlorination tank built by the City of Phoenix. Rather than try to hide or disguise the tank, it was used as the inspiration for the circular motif that is repeated throughout the home's design.

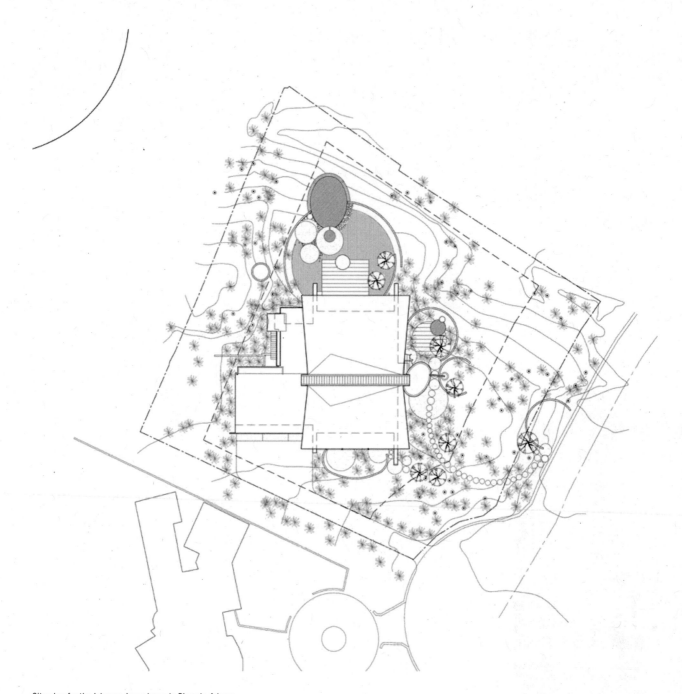

Site plan for the Johnson-Jones home in Phoenix, Arizona.

DESIGN DETAILS

The Johnson–Jones home features an 18-by-40-foot glass wall across the north-facing back, while the private east-facing entry consists of a large curved concrete block wall, enclosing a courtyard mostly covered by a large Palo Verde tree. The large rammed-earth walls stand on the east and west sides of the home, and contain minimal glazing, although they are intersected by a sky-lit glass roof hallway extending from the front door entry to the garage exit on the west side. Plenty of natural filtered daylight fills the house from the south glass wall, and through roofline windows and abundant use of glazing in areas that do not receive direct sunlight.

The large family room area consists of an open kitchen with cabinet doors of vertical grain fir and maple, a large entertainment center, a dining table, grand piano, and sectional seating largely selected by Jones's wife, a Knoll furniture dealer. She also persuaded her husband to use flagstone for the family room floor instead of concrete. The high-ceiling family area is open to the roof; a second-story balcony separates the upstairs living areas from the overlook. Adding to the ambience of the family room is the view of South Mountain through the glass wall, and in a near field, the patio area. Large doors open onto a recreational oasis, with a hot tub and deck area hugged by semicircular perforated concrete block walls, looking out onto an elliptical swimming pool, all inspired by the chlorination tank.

Across a hall from the family room are two bedrooms, one for each of the children, plus a study area, and a south-facing patio with a surround of metal louvers to keep sun exposure to a minimum. In the room designed for Johnson's son, a sliding bookcase reveals a small hidden room, just for the fun of it.

The second story, accessible via a curved staircase located inside the cylindrical concrete entry stair tower standing prominently near the home's entry, is home to the master bedroom and bath, and a work studio for Jones. The highlight of the upper volume is certainly the glass bridge Jones designed of two pieces of half-inch tempered laminated glass. From the top of the stairwell, the bridge separates the bedroom on the left

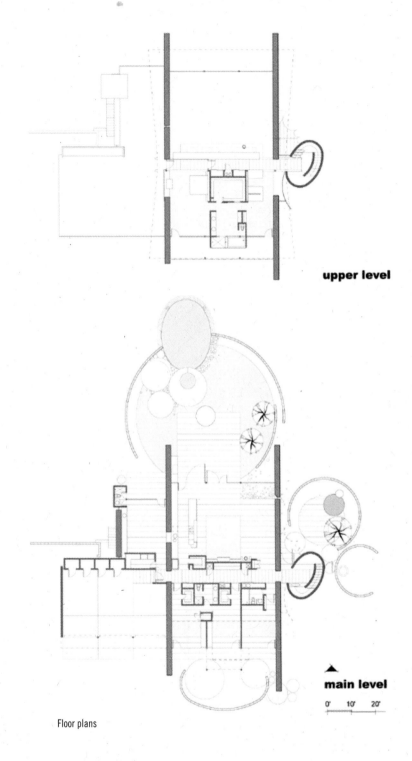

upper level

main level

0'   10'   20'

Floor plans

from the overlook to the family room on the right. It is covered by a skylight, and the diffused light adds to the brightness of the downstairs area. Jones says dropping a sledgehammer on the glass floor could not break it, yet there are those too timid to cross.

A lot that had been scraped clean of flora and fauna by the city now features a host of natural desert plants, watered by the open 18-foot cistern at the front of the home. Rainfall is annually low in the Sonoran desert, so Jones designed his house to make the most of it. His butterfly roof moves the rainwater to a scupper and ceremoniously down a set of chains into the cistern where it is al- lowed to slowly seep out into the surrounding landscape, which Tempe, Arizona–based land- scape architect Bill Tonnesen designed after sur- veying the vegetation nearby on South Mountain. He re-created the topography and plant life that would have been there naturally.

CONSTRUCTION DETAILS
Though the rammed-earth walls look like a se- ries of blocks stacked on top of each other, they are in fact totally monolithic; the joinery of the plywood formwork is debossed in the soil. These 4-foot-high forms are filled with 8 inches of mois- tened soil at a time, compacted by pneumatic ramming tools until the form is full. Every 4 feet the formwork is stripped and reset until the 18- foot wall reaches its full height. "There is no rebar or reinforcement from the foundation into the wall," Jones explains. "It's all friction. There is no mesh, or vertical or horizontal reinforcement, nothing in the wall but dirt and a 3 percent port- land cement content required by code, which is negligible."

Estimates show that rammed-earth walls can cost twice as much as conventional framed walls to build, but as Jones points out, rammed-earth walls comprise the structure, the insulation, and the exterior and interior finishes.

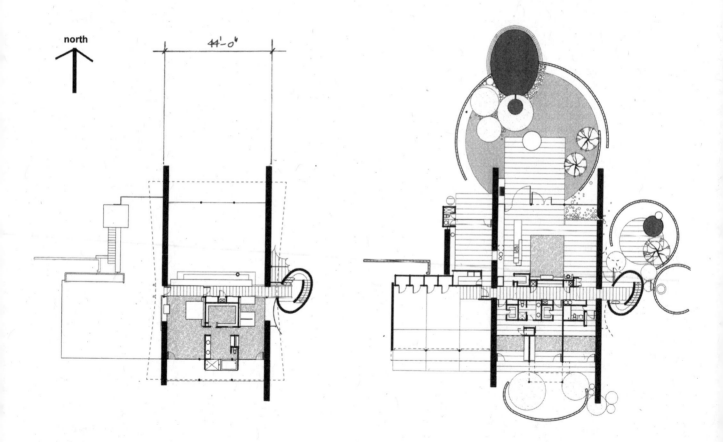

Floor plans

The benefits of rammed-earth construction have been known by builders for centuries. "Every country on the planet has earth architecture in some form," Jones says. Engineering tests, according to the architect, show it takes about an hour for heat to move 1 inch through a rammed-earth wall. With its 24-inch-thick monolithic walls, the surface temperature of the walls inside the house never changes. The energy savings are huge: Jones estimates a 4,500-square-foot house constructed conventionally would be twice as expensive to heat and cool each month. Plus, since most of the soil mixture came from the site, there was no transportation cost.

Local building code requires a concrete footer and stem wall of 8 inches; Jones made his 16 inches high and attached nearly all plumbing and electrical components to it, and not the earth wall above it. Although, like concrete, rammed earth can be channeled for subsystems, Jones surface-mounts his on the concrete at the base of the wall. Where a headboard sits against a rammed-earth wall in an upstairs bedroom, it contains its own switches and electrical components. Not only does this method keep the look of the walls clean but it helps reduce the cost of subcontractor work, which Jones says has risen in the past decade from about $18 per square foot to near $50 per square foot as a limited number of experienced subs look to cash in on the popularity of rammed-earth construction. "There are so few contractors that can do it, they charge whatever they want to charge," notes Jones. "Anytime one deviates from convention—around here that's a stucco house with mission tile—you're going to pay more because it's different. It's unfortunate that rammed earth has become an elitist material, because it's dirt."

SUSTAINABILITY

Though his firm, Jones Studio, Inc., is known for its environmentally conscious work, Jones says sustainable, or green, design is rarely discussed as a special or unconventional approach to a problem. In the desert, he says it is the only way to design, and his clients expect him to provide solutions that maximize energy efficiency and minimize heat collection. In his own home, Jones

not only used cool rammed-earth walls but he also specified highly efficient mechanical equipment and high-performance glass. Most of the materials used for finishes contain recycled content, and lush landscaping coupled with a pond inside the curved front entry wall provide instant cooling and relief from the desert heat on the approach to the house. Jones says he believes that environmental design is a moral responsibility, and hopes with a little education, the public will not settle for "dumb building."

He tells the story of a jogger who passed one day while Jones himself was working on the job site in jeans and toolbelt. He noticed the runner had stopped and was scowling at the home, so he walked over and asked him what he thought. "He told me it looked like a pump station," recalls Jones. When informed that the walls were not concrete but in fact compacted dirt, and that the roof sloped toward the center to capture rainwater and irrigate the property, the jogger broke into a big grin and asked question after question. "He couldn't wait to get home and tell his family what he had learned," recalls Jones. "I love that about architecture. It may be perceived as unusual or abnormal, but once it's understood, it's perfectly normal to the point that all the other examples of conventional housing become weird."

Large doors open onto a recreational oasis, with a hot tub and deck area surrounded by semicircular perforated concrete block walls, looking out onto an elliptical swimming pool, all inspired by the chlorination tank.

The 24-inch-deep rammed-earth walls appear as a series of blocks stacked on top of each other, but they are completely monolithic; the joinery of the plywood formwork is imprinted in the soil. The walls contain no reinforcement other than what is found in the foundation system.

The 4-Parts House, Seattle, Washington

Designer/Architect: Annie Han and Daniel Mihalyo, Lead Pencil Studio

■ By Lee Cuthbert

THE 4-PARTS HOUSE, THE SEATTLE home of architects Annie Han and Daniel Mihalyo, was built almost entirely by the couple themselves during 2001. The concrete and steel structure occupies what had once been a trash-filled urban infill lot. The couple overshot their initial $50,000 budget by $20,000, though Mihalyo estimates that had a general contractor built the home in 2001 it would have been a $275,000 project. Today, Mihalyo says, "It probably would cost $450,000, given Seattle's enormous construction inflation." The house includes office space for the couple's firm, Lead Pencil Studio, which won the Founders Rome Prize for 2007/2008.

OVERVIEW

After looking for existing buildings they could renovate into an office and residence, Han and Mihalyo decided to build their own structure on a 5,100-square-foot vacant lot eight blocks from the heart of downtown Seattle. After hauling away over 25 pickup-truck loads of garbage, the pair spent their free time for most of 2001 building a boxy 1,350-square-foot home and office with the commercial/industrial feel they had been searching for, but with a host of energy-saving features that make the house very inexpensive to operate, including radiant heat from the concrete floor. They also selected materials and fixtures for the home that saved money up front, like salvaged doors, sinks and bathtubs, and surplus aluminum from Boeing for trim.

The 4-Parts House was made sustainable in many ways, ranging from its small environmental footprint to the incorporation of salvaged doors and surplus aluminum from a Boeing plant into the cladding.

The couple take a long-term view of sustainability, not only choosing to design a home that is energy efficient, but one that inserts itself seamlessly into the recycling chain and that saves greenhouse gas emissions by also including their office space. There are many aspects to "building green" and these architects considered them all, choosing to leave a very small environmental footprint.

The 4-Parts House consists of a downstairs sleeping area (part 1), a 550-square-foot office, which is the entire upstairs of the home (part 2), the large, high-ceilinged living area including the kitchen (part 3), and the "portal" (part 4), containing a pair of vintage front double-doors, a small entry landing, and an operable 24-by-10-foot west-facing front window. Upstairs in the office area, two more round west-facing windows add to the flood of natural light in the home. Mihalyo says that in Seattle, facing west is a must "to capture as much of the low-angle winter sun as possible. Summer heat gain is rarely an issue in our temperate climate," he notes.

Typical of the neighborhood, the 4-Parts House was constructed on a long, narrow lot (40 by 125 feet). Instead of placing the house toward the front of the sloped lot, as is common, the architects built their home toward the back. Though it interrupts the continuous "flank of house fronts" on the street, Mihalyo says the benefit is great. "It creates a large front yard that allows privacy from the street," he says, "and keeps the windows of neighboring structures open to daylight." It also allows the couple to add a second structure in the front, below-grade, in the future should they choose. "Our lot is steeply sloped," says Mihalyo, "and it would be the easiest thing to do to preserve views and openness."

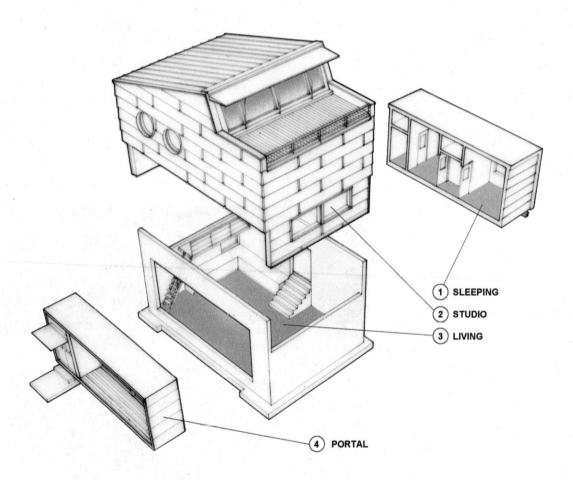

1 SLEEPING

2 STUDIO

3 LIVING

4 PORTAL

Axonometric diagram of the 4-Parts House in Seattle, Washington.

The kitchen space consists of unfinished plywood cabinet fronts and rolled-steel countertops that are lightly treated with beeswax for the purity of the aesthetic, as well as for environmental purposes.

Above: The stair detail demonstrates the desire to fuse clean, modern design with environmental ideals to maintain a small building footprint.

Opposite: The master bedroom and the home's only bathroom are located just off the living space; the stairs help to separate the two public and private spaces and make the space feel larger than it is.

DESIGN DETAILS

The loftlike home is defined by its concrete bottom level, constructed using material mixed with 30 percent fly ash, a waste by-product that increases strength and helps decrease harmful emissions. Upstairs, the wood-frame second story is clad in sheets of recyclable hot-rolled steel that the homeowners treated with a water-based clear coat to prevent surface oxidation. The couple splurged on extra fiberglass batting insulation in the walls and ceiling of the second story—to a level twice that required by local code—and Mihalyo says that investment has already "paid back handsomely." Upstairs, a canopy-covered 5-by-20-foot passive solar south-facing window helps regulate the home's temperature. "This has worked magically and is a feature that should be de rigueur for all house designs, particularly in northern climates," says Mihalyo. "We can't overestimate what a benefit this has been and what wonderful illumination it provides."

The couple concentrated on making the living area—the home's central space—"extraordinary," says the architect. The high-ceilinged room contains the kitchen, dining, and relaxing areas. "We put the most attention there by making a grand connection to the landscape with the large west-facing windows, making sure the proportions were harmonious, providing some nice details for the eye to focus on, and allowing for multiple perspectives within this space and to the outside," the architect explains. Inside the living space, plywood cabinet fronts are unfinished, and rolled-steel countertops are lightly treated with beeswax, not only for the purity of the aesthetic but for environmental reasons as well. Unfinished metals, for example, provide "low impact at the recycle stage," says Mihalyo.

When the time came to put up the poured-in-place concrete walls, Mihalyo and Han splurged a bit and hired a local company of five brothers to complete the installation. Other than that and some subcontractor work on the electrical and plumbing, the two architect/owners provided the labor. The savings, as previously mentioned, were huge. But Mihalyo says their choice of materials was not driven by budget as much as a desire for simplicity, efficiency, and low environmental impact.

SUSTAINABILITY

When discussing the ways in which the 4-Parts House is energy efficient, Mihalyo says, first and foremost, the size of the residence makes the biggest impact on its level of consumption. Because the entire upstairs is the office of Lead Pencil Studio, the couple lives downstairs in 800 square feet. "By most standards," Mihalyo explains, "800 square feet would be considered a very small house, but because the ceilings are 15 feet high and because the office is part of the house, it doesn't feel small." And typical of his long-term view of sustainability, he notes that this not only required fewer building materials but it also took less energy to produce the materials.

"By incorporating our office into the house, we are also able to save on heating and cooling a second space," says Mihalyo, "saving additional energy in eliminating a work commute." It also allowed the couple to double the utility of the rest of the home, which provides a work kitchen, bathroom, and occasional conference room in the living room. Because the home is small, the high-efficiency water heater can double as the heating unit for the radiant system, eliminating the need for a furnace. And choosing a salvaged sink, bathtub, front door, bathroom sink, and the aluminum from Boeing saved money up front, points out Mihalyo, "and consequently kept material out of the waste stream." This was a primary consideration for selecting the galvanized steel snap-lock standing seam roof. The unpainted steel can be easily recycled after its projected 60 years of service. "We try to use unpainted products as much as possible, and when paint is necessary, used low- or no-VOC acrylic paints," says Mihalyo.

As Mihalyo and Han grow their practice, they are now considering a move of the office out of the home, or perhaps into a second structure on the property. They also plan to install a rainwater collection cistern, and maybe storage shed in the back. Though Lead Pencil Studio is not a design/build firm, Mihalyo says building his own home was a great experience. "The highlight of the home has been the joy of building something with our own initiative and labor," he says. "We would encourage everybody who has the desire to try it someday."

The 800-square-foot lower-level living space feels spacious partly because the 15-foot ceilings give the sense of additional space.

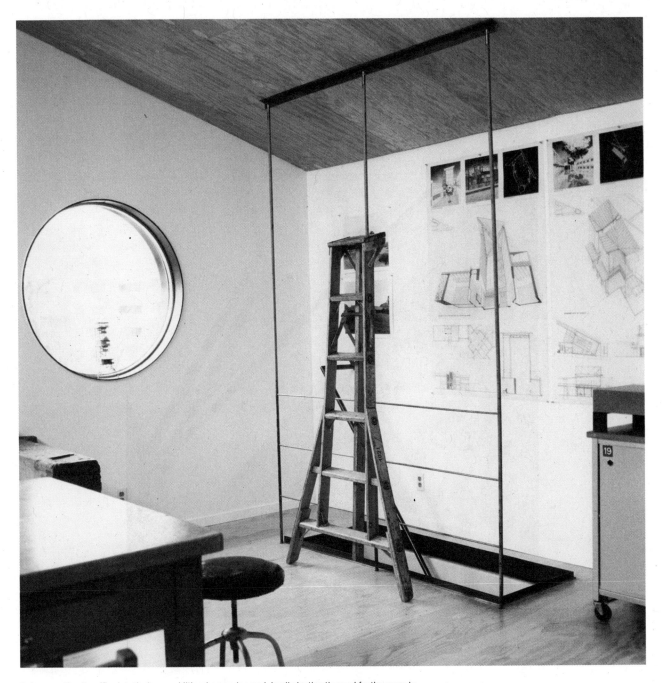

By incorporating the office into the home, additional energy is saved, by eliminating the need for the owner to commute to work. It also doubles the utility of the rest of the home, which includes a work kitchen, bathroom, and occasional conference room in the living room.

The western wall of the living area is framed by a 24-foot by 10-foot operable window, to capture as much of the low-angle winter sun as possible. Summer heat gain is rarely an issue in the temperate Seattle climate.

Capitol Hill House, Seattle, Washington

Architect/Designer: Jim Burton, Jim Burton Architects

■ By Lee Cuthbert

WHEN ARCHITECT JIM BURTON was engaged by clients Io Salant and Ophir Ronen to remodel their newly purchased Seattle split-level home, clients and designer had a meeting of the minds: make it clean and modern and, primarily, Make it green. "The homeowners, with a new baby on the way, did copious amounts of research on "smart home" products and technologies. With Burton, founder of the Seattle firm BLIP Design, a plan was fine-tuned to make the house light, open, structurally reinforced, and energy efficient. The Capitol Hill House was awarded a 2005 Built–Green Design Award and became a case study home for the city of Seattle, the Built Green program, and the Cascadia Region Green Building Council.

The original clients sold the home; Jim Burton is working on additions to the house for the new owners (including an underground rain collection cistern) and remodeling another Seattle home for Salant and Ronen.

OVERVIEW

Located in the Capitol Hill neighborhood of Seattle, Salant and Ronen purchased the 4,100-square-foot home (built on a 5,000-square-foot lot) and planned on a modern update that would include a roof deck for entertaining and hanging out with the baby. The home, as purchased, had been added onto and remodeled in the '70s and '80s. Traffic flow was awkward; spaces were unnecessarily obtuse. Armed with a wealth of knowledge on green concepts—from proper insulation to self-sustaining systems to the off-gassing of various materials—the homeowners presented a well-articulated want-list to the architect. Some ideas were deemed impractical—geothermal heating, all LEED lighting—but many were utilized.

The front elevation of the house prior to the renovation project.

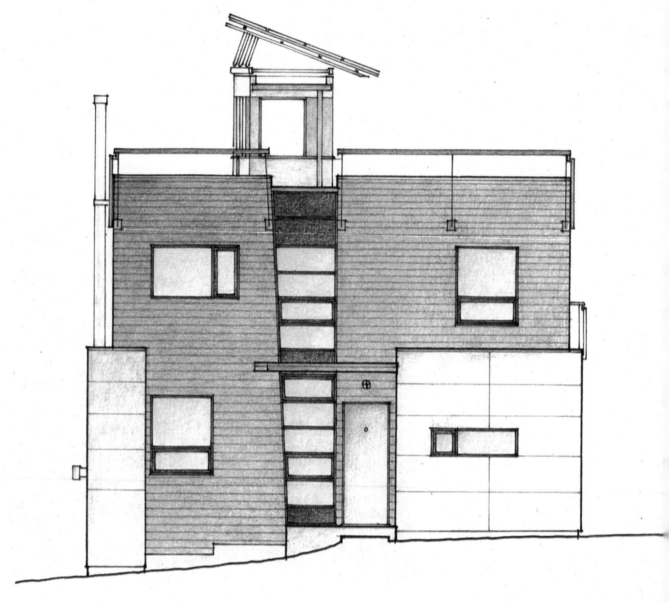

Front elevation of Capitol Hill House,
Seattle, Washington.

The signature feature of the home is a new small penthouse structure, which supports photovoltaic solar panels and solar hot water collectors. It also serves as an access point to a new large roof terrace with views of Lake Washington and the Cascade mountains. As part of the home's renovation, walls were removed and the stairs were relocated to the center of the structure, leading to the penthouse. Not only does air move efficiently throughout the house, but the penthouse acts, says the architect, as a "solar chimney," pulling warm air up and out and fresh cooler air in from below. Designed for efficiency, the house has no mechanical ventilation systems. Heat is supplied via a hydronic radiant heat system in the floors.

A wastewater heat recovery system allows warm waste water at the showers to preheat supply water. With the roof's solar hot water collectors, warmth from the sun is sent into the hot water storage tank, where it transfers its heat into water. A gas-fired boiler is only utilized when additional heat is needed. Architect Jim Burton notes that as with the photovoltaic system, the solar hot water system is most effective during the warm weather months. He estimates that in summer the PV solar panel system provides 100 percent of the home's power, and about one-third during the winter.

With the homeowners' desire for a roof deck, a structural analysis was done of the house and some deficiencies were found. The foundation had to be rebuilt, and a previous second-story addition had to be reinforced. It was constructed with the walls inset from those of the structure below. Burton and his team bolstered the undersized rafters' structural elements to existing stronger structural elements, resulting in a roof terrace that will easily support up to 70 people. In fact, the architect explains that of the original building, only the exterior walls, the floor, and the roof framing were kept. The interior was gutted and reconstructed using Icynene expanding foam insulation and 5/8-inch drywall to increase thermal mass. The result is a "super tight envelope," Burton says, yet one that uses solar capabilities and good airflow to naturally heat and cool itself.

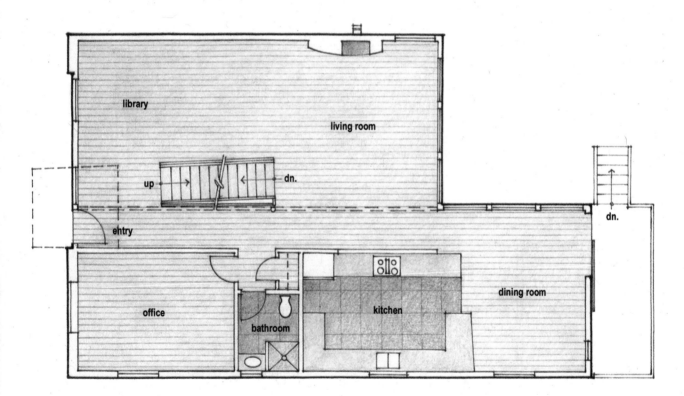

Floor plan

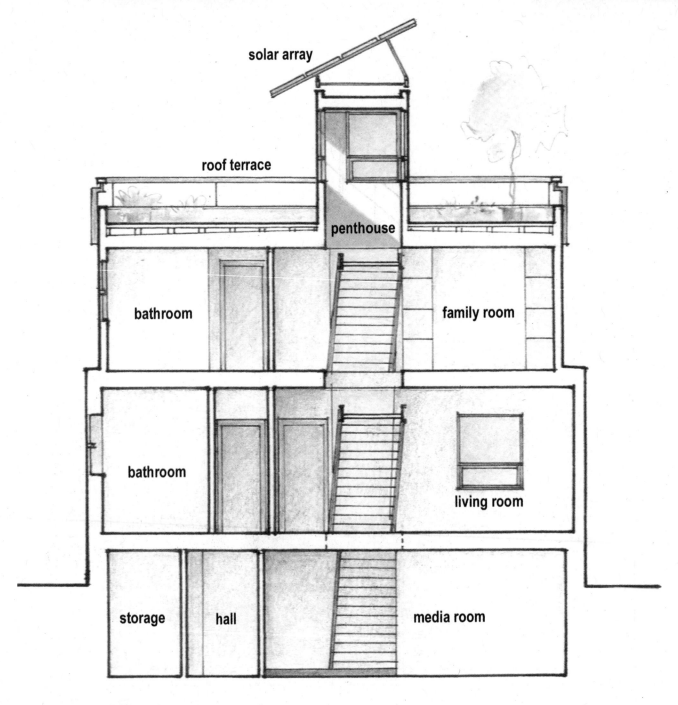

solar array

roof terrace

penthouse

bathroom

family room

bathroom

living room

storage

hall

media room

Building section

DESIGN DETAILS

Comparing the before-and-after photographs of the Capitol Hill House, it is remarkable how appropriate and unforced the new modern façade of the home appears. Where there had been windows there are now larger ones, including a central strip of floor-to-roofline glazing, contributing loads of natural light to the central section of the home. Light also falls down the stairway walls from the penthouse structure. Salant and Ronen painted the interior in light tones (using low-VOC paint, of course) and even kept finishes light to brighten the interior.

Outside the home, red cedar gives the house warmth that only wood can provide, but also a clean linear aesthetic. Most important, it provides great insulation. By situating the siding a few inches from the actual surface of the structure, a pocket of air is created to help regulate the temperature inside the home.

SUSTAINABILITY

Although the up-front cost was high, the owners of the Capitol Hill House elected to install BP photovoltaic modules on their penthouse roof. Even under gray Seattle skies, the units collect enough energy to provide power to the house, and occasionally feed back into the Seattle power grid for credit. The system is capable of producing over 3000 kWh/year. The city allows for up to 4 additional feet on its building height limit for solar collectors, and those on the Capitol Hill House just fit.

Seattle is home to the thriving chain of next-generation home improvement stores, Ecohouse. Here, Salant and Ronen were able to choose from a variety of green products, from flooring materials to double-flush toilets. For the kitchen, the couple selected ENERGY STAR appliances and Paperstone countertops. Made locally in Washington State, Paperstone is a composite of post-consumer recycled paper and water-based resin renown for its durability. Every item in the home was carefully considered. All lighting is either fluorescent or low-voltage. Flooring is renewable bamboo or reclaimed fir (for the stair treads). Even the landscaping was planned for native and drought-resistant plants.

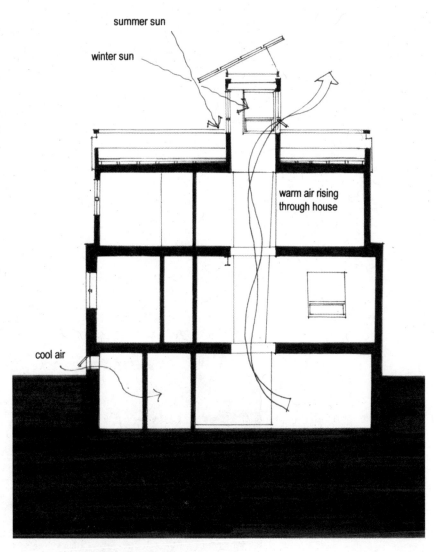

Solar chimney diagram

As chief technology officer for a Seattle technology company, it was only natural that homeowner Io Salant wanted to integrate "smart house" connectivity into his own abode. All major systems—lighting/fans, solar, electrical consumption, heating, security—are computer controlled via a NetSteams server and can respond to each other to increase efficiencies. That server also provides distributed audio, loaded with MP3 files that can be sent to speakers in any room of the house.

Right: The modern renovated front elevation improves energy efficiency by incorporating a central strip of floor-to-roofline glazing that allows for natural light to penetrate the central section of the home.

Opposite: The exterior of the home is clad in red cedar, for a warm look that only wood can provide; it also makes for a clean linear aesthetic and serves as excellent insulation. By situating the siding a few inches from the actual surface of the structure, a pocket of air is created to help regulate the temperature inside the home.

The penthouse roof incorporates photovoltaic modules . The units collect enough energy to provide power to the home and occasionally feed back into the Seattle power grid for credit; the system is capable of producing over 3000 kWh/year.

The stairs were relocated to the center of the home, to give access to the new penthouse addition. This lets air move efficiently through the structure, while the penthouse acts as a solar chimney, pulling warm air up and out, and fresh, cooler air in from below.

The completed redesign of the home resulted in a smart house, one in which all major systems—including lighting/fans, solar, electrical consumption, heating, and security—are computer controlled via a NetSteams server. The systems can respond to each other to increase efficiencies.

DESIGNhabitat 2 Initiative

The School of Architecture at Auburn University
■ By David Hinson and William Carpenter

S INCE 2001, THE SCHOOL OF ARCHI-
tecture at Auburn University has collaborated with Habitat for Humanity
affiliates across Alabama to improve the energy
performance and design quality of Habitat
homes. Building on the success of the first round
of this collaboration, David Hinson, director of
the DESIGNhabitat Program, approached the Alabama Association of Habitat Affiliates (AAHA)
with a proposal to study ways to integrate factory-based production into the volunteer-builder
culture of Habitat affiliates.

Initial research pointed toward modular construction as the most promising strategy, and in
2005 the DESIGNhabitat 2 initiative began. In
this initiative, a team of architecture students
and faculty (Hinson and Stacy Norman) at
Auburn partnered with a modular housing production company, Palm Harbor Homes, to design
and build a modular Habitat home.

The DESIGNhabitat 2 initiative was designed
with five objectives:

1. To capitalize on the systems-built industry's
   expertise re: production process, resource ef-
   ficiency/conservation, and quality control.

2. To build on the design-quality advances realized by recent designer-led/ academy-based
   modular design and construction initiatives.

3. To integrate the energy performance expertise
   developed in the prior phases of the DESIGN-
   habitat program into the DESIGNhabitat 2
   home.

This designHABITAT 2 home is not only
unique in its modular prefabrication but
it also incorporates an energy-conserving
design in its clearly laid-out plan.

4. To explore how this approach might benefit Habitat affiliates that struggled to build homes due to limited volunteer resources.

5. To immerse students in the challenges and opportunities associated with affordable housing design, and to cultivate an ethic of service and community engagement as an integral part of their strategy of response.

The students began the project with a semester-long predesign research effort intended to immerse the team in the specific design opportunities and constraints associated with factory-based construction. The students also sought to identify the "leading edge" of design innovation (including energy performance, materials and construction systems, and building configuration) relative to modular design and construction, both inside the industry and within the professional design community.[1] Perhaps the most important area of predesign exploration involved a careful study of how this approach could be integrated within Habitat's traditional site-built, volunteer-builder culture.

"The team began the next semester with a month-long charrette intended to generate alternative prototype home proposals incorporating the lessons of the fall research phase. In mid-February, five proposals were presented to a panel of project advisors (Habitat leadership, modular industry representatives, and faculty) who selected one of the schemes to advance to design development and construction.

The selected scheme was chosen by the advisors because of its energy-conserving design features, the clarity of its plan, and because the scheme offered the most clearly identifiable site-built features (the central connecting space and porches), an important consideration in Habitat's volunteer builder–centered culture.

As the project moved in to design development, Habitat for Humanity International was working to develop a viable strategy for responding to the impact of hurricanes Katrina and Rita. The impact of these two disasters on the Gulf Coast states of Texas, Louisiana, Mississippi, and Alabama dramatically reframed the DESIGNhabitat 2 initiative. Within the span of a few weeks, the condition envisioned in goal 4—small, often rural HFH affiliates with money but fewer human resources—became the reality for Habitat affiliates across the four-state Gulf Coast region. Facing a need for more than 20,000 homes and a human resource capacity of (at best) 1,000 houses a year, Habitat for Humanity International realized that this emergency demanded new ways of approaching the construction of Habitat homes. Modular production quickly emerged as one of the "alternative" strategies that Habitat's Operation Home Delivery (OHD) leadership wanted to evaluate.

With support from the OHD program, the DESIGNhabitat 2 project team partnered with a new Habitat affiliate in Hale County, Alabama, one of the western counties in the state most affected by hurricane Katrina. The Hale Co. HFH affiliate

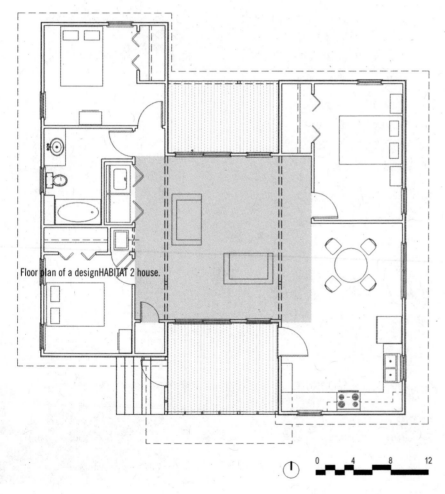

Floor plan of a designHABITAT 2 house.

0   4   8   12

quickly identified a family displaced by Katrina as the future homeowners for the DESIGNhabitat 2 home.

The student-designed DESIGNhabitat 2 home went into production April 18 in Palm Harbor Home's plant in Boaz, Alabama, and was shipped to the home site in Greensboro, Alabama, the following week. Under the direction of Hinson and Norman, the architecture students responsible for the design then began a two-week "blitz build," to complete the site-built components of the home. The keys to the DESIGNhabitat 2 House were turned over to Dorinda Crews and her three children on June 23, 2006.

The construction of this home was supported via a grant from HFHI's Operation Home Delivery program, in-kind donations from Palm Harbor and other product vendors, and a generous grant from a private foundation. The home was constructed for approximately $60,000 (including the value of donated materials and services).

While the DESIGNhabitat 2 program builds on the prior (and ongoing) work of professional designers and academy-based modular initiatives, it also moves this work forward. Most significant among these accomplishments are:

- The DESIGNhabitat 2 home is among the first homes completed for Habitat for Humanity in the region to integrate this particular mix of design quality and energy-performance objectives with the modular construction process. As such, it offers valuable lessons for Habitat regarding the integration of design quality objectives, climate-appropriate design features, and energy performance into their efforts to rethink their delivery model in the wake of the Gulf Coast disasters.

- The DESIGNhabitat 2 home is among the first academy-based modular home design initiatives to be built via direct collaboration with *a production modular builder,* integrating the industry's experience with prefabrication and the innovation and imagination of a faculty/student design team. Together with recent and ongoing academy-based initiatives involving prefabrication,[2] this project offers valuable lessons for future research and design.

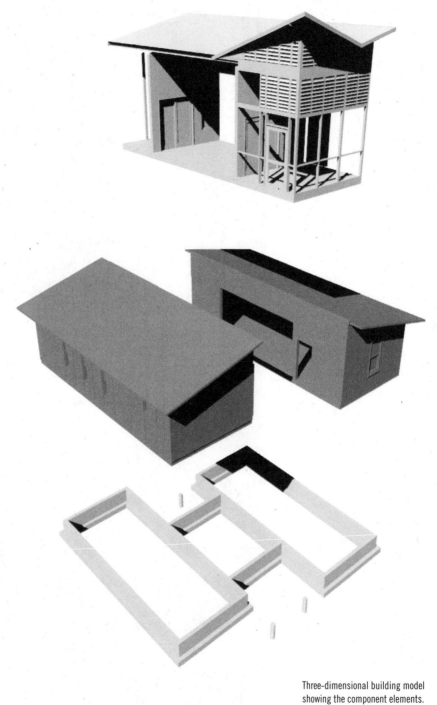

Three-dimensional building model showing the component elements.

The designHABITAT 2 home is prefabricated in a warehouse based on the finalized design proposed by the students of the School of Architecture at Auburn University.

The prefabricated modules are relocated to site, where the students spend approximately two weeks finishing the construction of the home.

• The DESIGNhabitat 2 home offers significant evidence that the gap between the design and energy performance potential of factory-based construction and the realities of affordable housing can be closed.

Beyond these accomplishments, the DESIGNhabitat 2 program's integration of design/build and service-learning teaching methods has pro-

vided the students involved with a powerful model for meaningful action in the face of a natural disaster of overwhelming magnitude. In the process of creating a building of high design quality for a client type rarely served by the profession, they have developed invaluable insights into the collaborative nature of effective community engagement and the critical competencies to become effective "citizen architects" in their professional lives.

The final scheme for the home was also selected because it included the most clearly identifiable site-built features in the central connecting space and porches.

The construction of this home was supported by a grant from the Operation Home Delivery program, donations from Palm Harbor, Alabama, and other product vendors, and a generous grant from a private foundation. It was constructed for approximately $60,000 (including the value of donated materials and services).

Clerestory windows let natural light flood the open-plan living space.

The screened porch was among the most important design features; it allows for natural ventilation through the home and lends a sense of community within its surroundings.

LivingHomes, Los Angeles, California

Architect: Ray Kappe, FAIA, principal, Ray Kappe Architects and Planners in Pacific Palisades, CA
Project Architect: Amy Sims
■ By Monique Birault and William Carpenter

OVERVIEW

Site: Dense beach community infill lot, no existing structure.

Program: Sustainable modern prefabricated homes of various sizes and stories. The model home is 2 stories, 4 bedrooms, 2500 square feet.

Project goal: "zero energy, zero water, zero carbon, and zero emissions" and to be priced lower than a conventional site-built house. Steve Glenn says he also wants to achieve "zero ignorance," educating homeowners about how best to live in and operate these houses.

Design start: 2004; building erection completed in one day August 2006.

Cost of house: 2,500 square feet x $250 square feet = $625,000 + foundation, $140 square feet; land cost: $950,000.

The model LivingHome was recently awarded the LEED® for Home Platinum, the first home in the nation to achieve the highest classification of the Leadership in Environmental and Energy Efficient Design program and one of only 20 LEED Platinum buildings in the USA. In April, 2007, it was named one of the "Top Ten Most Sustainable Buildings in the U.S." by the American Institute of Architects, the only residence in the country to be so honored.

The LivingHome architect/client team combined a unique client starting a modular home business and a world class architect with a longtime vision and passion for modular architecture. The client's love for the environment was a nat-

The model LivingHome was awarded the LEED® Home Platinum; it became the first home to achieve this classification.

ural outgrowth of his upbringing among the forests of North Carolina; this plus his brief experience in architecture school and exposure to developer Jim Rouse, uniquely predisposed him to create the LivingHomes company.

Ray Kappe, FAIA and founder of SCI-Arc, who had been exploring and designing sustainable modular projects as early as the 1960s, has used, in many of his buildings over the years, modular prefab principles in design and construction. Glenn and Kappe share their love for architecture and commitment to make the world a better place; in this case they set forth to do so via modular sustainable housing.

On a typical Santa Monica beach community residential street surrounded by an eclectic collection of one and two story homes, single and multi family, the exposed steel and glass building envelope immediately sets this home apart from the rest.

Upon entering the front door on the ground level one is overcome by the beauty and inviting feeling of this Kappe open plan home filled with natural light. Each room gracefully flows into the next across a concrete floor plane of varying levels; ones path through the great double height core space is guided by warm wood surfaced built-in cabinets while the eye is drawn through full height glass perimeter walls to the fountain in the homes entry level city garden. The double height first floor core is surrounded by the private spaces of the open second floor mezzanine where movable partition walls allow for visual continuity to the sky. The temperature is as comfortable as the feeling of the space, the primary full height glass perimeter walls facing south east and south west are shaded by overhangs that double as decks extending from the second floor plate; the glass continues to the roof level with overhangs where necessary. As one ascends, the building views beyond the garden come into focus. The uppermost level has the hidden surprise of a partially covered rooftop terrace garden with spectacular views. This LivingHomes model is a good balance of open and private spaces, perfect for feeling a sense of togetherness as a family occupies the various connected areas as well as optimal for feeling the energy of entertaining.

THE LOT

The residential infill lot was particularly well suited for the project as it was one of the few empty lots remaining in the area; it has great views and is close to retail. The sloped site triggered theoretical grade code requirements whose goal is to provide parameters for determining maximum building height. This resulted in conditions that drove Kappe to creating several levels changes on the ground floor, which resulted in double height spaces, the mezzanine/loft spaces and walkways open to the lower levels, visually and spatially enlarging the house. Adding to the open feeling and efficiency of the house are the freestanding wardrobe closets that serve as space dividers; bedrooms can be closed off with sliding partitions. The model house structural system allows for an additional room to be added on the second level. A home that can adapt and change with the needs of its occupants is another successful facet of the sustainable equation that LivingHomes sets forth to achieve. Kappe's design and organization balances the privacy needs of a home with close residences on three sides and full height glass and desire for an abundance of natural light through the placement of core elements, such as the kitchen and bathroom and the use of opaque glass where neighbors would be most likely to have views into the house, on the northern portions of the house. The garden is also surrounded by a wooden fence which minimizes direct views into the first floor. The site design on the hillside site also helps. design sensitivity of to provide an abundance of natural light and privacy, the vehicles being the polycarbonate window.

With Kappe's natural design inclination, something he adopted through his forays into modular building and sustainable systems in the 60s, to design in modules is clearly seen in the exposed steel construction interior and exterior. Steel, the darling of modern home design for the structural flexibility it provides in planning and its aesthetic, also has multiple sustainable benefits particularly applicable to modular homes due to its ease of assembly and transport. Also natural to Kappe's award-winning design is the extensive use of glass perimeter walls allowing for 100% day lighting, solar heating via reaction of winter sun and

concrete floors, and natural cooling by opening the sliding glass doors. The home heating system is hydronic heating, there is not an air-conditioning system in place nor needed. Outdoor spaces integrated into the home experience add 200 square feet of additional space. The home is extended by the garden which some call the outdoor living room and the open connecting decks projecting from the second floor plate (doubling as trellis first floor overhang); they connect each end of the house in some cases on a utilitarian level, a la indoor/out-door California living experience per the modern era of home building.

For Kappe, the architectural design process was basically the same whether the building was certified sustainable or not. The sustainability aspect for his type of architecture was driven by the specifications and material selections. There were a few material selections that Kappe might have preferred such as panelized wood for the wall systems, but a more sustainable material was selected. As time went on, the team's understanding of sustainable architecture grew exponentially and the client became an increasingly stronger champion for making sustainable choices. Kappe credits and appreciates Steve Glenn's championing leadership and interest in having a LEED Platinum project led to many sustainable materials being specified in the project.

INTERIOR MATERIALS

Amy Sims, Project Architect and Interior Designer, brought years of experience to the project. When design started in 2004, there wasn't as much information and research resources available on the internet as there is now. The internet is her chief research resource and she is constantly educating herself since the field of options is developing and expanding so fast. To reduce the adverse environmental impacts of conventional materials, the home features Forest Stewardship Certified (FSC) wood for the millwork, ceiling, siding, and framing, along with a variety of recycled materials including 100% post-consumer recycled paper based countertops; recycled glass tile, recycled porcelain tiles; and 100% recycled denim insulation and formaldehyde free, low VOC fiberglass encapsulated insulation.

The home is constructed of a combination of steel and glass building envelope, residing in the residential neighborhood of Santa Monica, California.

It is important for the architect to work closely with vendors when altering their specifications to install products in ways that are typical. Due to the relatively new focus on adapting specifying a sustainable building, close coordination with the manufacturer is required, especially when it's new product. It goes without saying that every material chosen for this project had to meet the high standard of modern aesthetics. Amy spent a lot of time searching for the right materials that would not only meet the LEED criteria and her criteria but also appealed to the Client and Architect. Cost was a consideration, although in some cases material costs were higher than desired because of the small quantity of the order for the model home.

It was essential to the team that the project had the warm feeling of natural materials throughout in the bigger expanses, such as the use of woods and in areas such as the cork kitchen floor with radiant heat below, while the outer perimeter remains concrete slab, including the selection of accent pieces, such as a trio of pendant fixtures made from hand-blown recycled glass that hangs over the kitchen island.

When queried on the notion that first cost of a sustainable home is typically higher than a non-sustainable home, Amy responded by pointing out that once a client desires the level of finishes exhibited in the model home, these finishes would cost about the same as sustainable finishes. Hydronic heating is more expensive than forced air, without a doubt, but once the clients start to understand what they are gaining in terms of health benefit and carbon footprint reduction, they begin make it a priority and it's no longer an issue. Vendors can also become consultants such as Bosch kitchen appliances provider, who was contacted and sent the LEED platinum standard and asked to recommend the appropriate appliances.

WHERE'S THE SUSTAINABILITY— THE TECHNICAL SIDE

The majority of the home's energy is produced by on-site photovoltaic panels. Most of the materials in the home are re-used, recycled, non-toxic or sustainable created. The two-story, 2,500 square foot prefabricated home was built in one day. Fabricated in Santa Fe Springs, California, the eleven 12' x 8' steel-framed modules were trucked to the site and hoisted into place by a giant crane. Low water consuming landscape and rooftop garden to divert storm water and alleviate the heat island effect of conventional black roofs; super resource efficient appliances; low-e exterior glazing and Polygal polycarbonate glazing; LED lights that use a fraction of the power of conventional lights; an integrated storm water management system and grey water recycling system; special fans that exhaust moisture from the bathrooms; and a house fan that automatically vents hot-air; a 175 CFM fan in the garage tied into the garage door that automatically exhausts carbon monoxide from the garage.

The home features low-emitting finish materials, low-Volatile Organic Compound (VOC) products, and also has an indoor garden as a way to produce and cleanse indoor air. The garden is filled with plants that filter indoor pollutants and are prolific oxygen creators.

In discussing her efforts to achieve sustainability, aside from site design that is responsive to the elements and microclimate, Amy frequently refers to the importance of the specifications. Sustainability is in the specification. LEED guidelines tell you what must be achieved and the architect is responsible for the research to achieve it. As Amy Sims says "it's not a mystery."

Contractor selection: Searching for a general contractor with sustainable experience doesn't come into play because it's prefab. Otherwise for site prep contractors will do what she specifies.

Construction waste/economy: According to LivingHomes, their steel-framed pre-fabricated house process is remarkably efficient in reducing waste. Only 2% ends up in landfills in contrast to the 40% for conventional construction. Factory assembly is also an excellent way to manage qual-

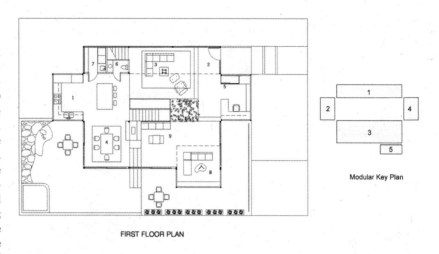

FIRST FLOOR PLAN

Modular Key Plan

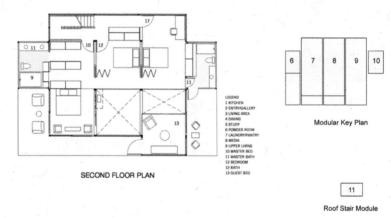

SECOND FLOOR PLAN

LEGEND
1 KITCHEN
2 ENTRY/GALLERY
3 LIVING AREA
4 DINING
5 STUDY
6 POWDER ROOM
7 LAUNDRY/PANTRY
8 MEDIA
9 UPPER LIVING
10 MASTER BED
11 MASTER BATH
12 BEDROOM
12 BATH
13 GUEST BED

Modular Key Plan

Roof Stair Module

The efficient floor plan shows the clear demarcation of public and private zones and the emissivity of interior and exterior spaces, perhaps inspired by Neutra and Wright.

ity and streamline production. The home was produced with 75% less construction waste than traditional home construction.

BUILDING MATERIALS/SYSTEMS

Structural system (steel): Steel was chosen because "it's considered the most recycled building material. It's also an extremely healthy material, because you have no mold or mildew issues, no infestation, no moisture issues," Glenn said.

When asked about claims in the early days of steel construction in residential applications

where occupants complained of popping sounds from expansion and contraction of materials, Steve Glen said he doesn't notice anything.

WALLS (TRANSPARENT/SOLID— WINDOW SYSTEM)

Transparent/translucent wall systems: 73% of the two-story double-paned exterior glazing is insulated using low-e Solarban60 film on the doors and windows, that combined with overhangs significantly reduces heat gain in the house during summer months.

Above left: The main living space on the first floor contains a double height core bounded with a second floor mezzanine with movable partition walls.

Above right: The home incorporates several levels changes on the ground floor, this resulted in double height spaces, that both visually and spatially enlarging the house.

Right: The open plan kitchen features Forest Stewardship Certified (FSC) wood for the millwork, ceiling, siding, and framing.

Large sliding doors allow for cross ventilation through the media room.

Wall system made primarily of large Fleetwood sliding door/windows with a few small operable windows to aid in air flow in the house: Amy Sims explained that because Initially Title 24 calculations were failing, we realized it was the glass. Polycarbonate, with three times the insulating properties of glass, and double-paned glass is used throughout the house.

All exterior and interior cedar paneling and tiger wood desks are made of certified Forest Stewardship Council which promotes sustainable forestry. These woods are formaldehyde free and urea free.

BUILDING ENVELOPE / INFILTRATION

Insulation: Wall insulation made from blue jeans fibers, ceiling insulation of blown-in cellulose and formaldehyde free, low VOC fiberglass encapsulated insulation.

The "green roof" garden insulates the house in the winter and absorbs solar radiation to reduce the heat island effect during the hottest months of the year.

LEED certification includes an air tightness test. A machine blows air into the house from inside and leakage around the house is measured. There were some surprises, but otherwise, once they are discovered, you seal them. Air tightness is key in the energy efficiency and effectiveness of building systems.

Flooring: Fly ash concrete, cork, and recycled glass tile.

Energy: The home's energy use is 80% more efficient than a conventional residence of similar size.

Glass envelope: This is another natural partner of sustainable design when managed well.

The electrical life of the home is significantly influenced by the building envelope. There are several important components to sustainable building envelope from the management of air flow to the management of natural light. In the case of the model LivingHome, the envelope is composed primarily of windows that are large sliders, and some small operable windows as well. To achieve this, the design team worked with the manufacturer and carefully specified the door components. The benefit of glass walls, aside from the clean look, is that electrical usage is lowered significantly due to availability of natural light. During the day the entire LivingHome is lit by natural light; there is no need for artificial light until the sun does down. The other benefit is solar heat interacting with the concrete

To make better efficient use of space many of the home's interior walls dually serve as storage space.

floors in the winter when the sun is low to heat the home during the day.

Heating: Originally she considered forced hot air but upon further research, Amy found many contaminates, so a radiant heating system in the concrete floor warms the space when the concrete heat absorption by the low winter sun is not enough.

An active solar system on the roof heats the water with a 50 gallon gas fired back-up boiler; the boiler uses the water from the solar system so it's not heating the water from cold to hot, it comes in already warm. There are sensors to monitor the water temperature and regulate the boiler. There are monitors on everything so we know how much water we are using.

Solar panels had to be adjusted several times to get to optimum energy production.

Air conditioning: "The house is designed in a way so that lots of air can get through and shaded in ways so the sun doesn't wreak havoc on interior spaces," says Glenn. He should know, having spent the entire summer working and living in the house. "The house fared much better than I expected. I never was hot if the windows were open."

The fan at top of the stairs is a very small vent fan. It's a natural heat vacuum.

The model home's combination of overhangs providing shade and openings for cross ventilation plus the use of a an exhaust fan at the top of the stairs (to the roof) creating a natural heat vacuum to draw out hot air, keeps air moving so the house can remain at a moderate temperature during hot summer days.

Electricity: Most of the electricity used in the house is produced by rooftop photovoltaic cells. The solar panels used on the roof would normally have a black back. However, since they are used on the roof garden canopy to provide shade over part of the terrace, a glass backed panel was specified to accommodate the double function. Although it added cost the benefit was worth it. The process of cost-benefit analysis is no different for sustainable design, although the criteria may shift. Amy found that driven by the Platinum guide.

When asked why the house wasn't more eclectically self-sufficient. Glenn said they didn't choose to do that because of cost.

Learning from Amy Sim's conversation, there may also be a design issue such as is there enough room for panels on the roof? In this case, how much of the roof do you want to cover with panels vs. have it open to the sun and sky?

LIVINGHOMES INSTALLS ONLY ENERGY-EFFICIENT APPLIANCES AND LIGHTS

Lighting: LED lighting was the primary light source. "We're only the second home in the country to have them," Glenn points out. He adds that they were chosen for their energy efficiency and longevity. "They use one-tenth the power of incandescent lighting."

The house has a battery back up should the electricity be compromised.

Appliances: Bosch recommended Evolution refrigerator that uses sensors to constantly measure temperature to provide consistent cooling and control the frequency of the defrost cycle.

A 700 Series Single Convection Oven is also featured in this area of the kitchen.

The NGT Series 30" Four-Burner Cooktop, manufactured of 98% recyclable materials, is topped by stainless steel vent hood.

The Bosch Evolution 800 Series Dishwasher features Sensotronic technology, which checks soil levels and adjusts water and temperature levels, saving water and energy. A Condensation Drying system in the dishwasher uses the final rinse's latent heat stored in the stainless steel walls to dry the dishes.

NATURE MILL COMPOSTER

Plumbing: The Kohler sink with Kohler faucet was chosen for its low-flow capabilities

Systems such as solar heating on the roof, a gray water system, and equipment located in the garage to recycle water are simple ways to be environmentally friends.

Landscape and irrigation: Permeable paving materials were used around the house with the native plans and low water planning scheme.

Rainwater is collected and held in a 3,500-gallon (13,000-liter) cistern along with "gray water" from sinks and showers. It is then used to irrigate the patio and rooftop gardens and perimeter plantings of drought-tolerant plants and trees. The roof garden uses an internet telemetry to determine when it needs watering. The LivingHome was the first residential project in Santa Monica to use gray water in irrigation.

Due to codes, the use of a gray water system is limited to an underground watering system. The firm is involved in a process trying to influence code for more expansive use of gray water watering practices in a residential application such as is used in commercial projects.

Sustainability goes beyond the qualities of design and materials related to structural, formal, functional, and aesthetic, it holds equally important the less tangible qualities that affect and reflect the occupant's quality of life, the creators desire, and our global need to be socially responsible.

Indoor E Q: The home features low-emitting finish materials, low-Volatile Organic Compound (VOC) paints and stains and a steel structure that does not allow mold growth.

Materials and Resources: There are also a variety of interesting recycled materials including a countertop made from 100% post-consumer recycled paper. Amy said "I spent a lot of time looking into the countertop material. Aesthetically, I was looking for something that was appropriate for the home, and functional as well. Paperstone can withstand a lot of heat, such as the heat coming off of the oven, and aesthetically I like it because it has a monolithic look to it. It cuts like wood, and when you cut through it, it's like a solid surface material."

Paperstone is from Kliptch, a post-consumer paper product made with cellulose and newsprint; resembles matte black granite.

Transport: The impact means of transportation makes is not always as simple as distance and needs to be taken into consideration. When re-searching the impact of receiving products across the globe, Amy found that receiving shipping via sea has a lower carbon effect than trucking products over the continent. However, when trucking in wood, carbon offset is dealt with by selecting other products that are closer.

Code challenges / busters and other issues: Roof garden proportions of garden to open terrace space were driven by code, regarding quantity of square feet triggering number of exits.

One of the challenges to building sustainable homes in some areas is that codes sometimes have not caught up with the building industry, such as the LivingHome's pioneering use of gray water for irrigation.

Note that most banks will not lend for manufactured homes (industry term for mobile home) so they have to be reassured that it won't be one of those. Disbursement schedule is different than a typical home—more money is needed upfront and the bank can't inspect the way they like—because the home is being built in a factory

While many customers desire a LivingHome primarily because of its superior sustainability achievements, that is not always the case. For those who are drawn by the opportunity to have the great modern home design of award-winning architect Ray Kappe, at good cost, Steve Glenn finds it easy to bring people to a position of desiring a sustainable home. He says the conversation usually begins with an explanation of how

Table 9.3 LEED Valuation Table

VALUATION CATEGORIES	POINTS AVAILABLE	POINTS ATTAINED
Location + Linkages (LL)	10	10
Sustainable Sites (SS)	14	14
Water Efficiency (WE)	15	15
Indoor Environmental Quality (IEQ)	14	9
Materials + Resources (MR)	22	8
Energy + Atmosphere (EA)	29	32.5
Homeowner Awareness (HA)	1	1
Innovation + Design Process (ID)	4	1.5
Totals	**109**	**91**

Certified: 30-49 points / Silver: 50-69 points / Gold: 70-89 points / Platinum: 90-109 points

LL: Located in a dense urban beach community close to retail and transportation the home was able to score all the points possible in this category.

SS: The inclusion of Southern California native landscaping only and minimizing demand for water usage LivingHomes achieved a top score.

WE: The 3,500 gallon cistern to collect all the rainwater run-off and the use of a gray water system for irrigation purposes garnered the highest points possible and a largest grant possible from the city to offset the cost.

EA: The highly efficient heating system that uses a solar hot water collector and a gas fired boiler backup for the hydronic system rather than a conventional forced hot air system to heat the house earned bonus points for the LivingHome.

IEQ: The cooling system based on natural ventilation and hydronic radiant heating greatly reduces the risk of indoor pollution and resulted in a high score.

MR: The factory built home significantly reduces the amount of waste involved in construction as compared to typical stick built homes as well as the fact that the steel frame design reduces the amount of materials normally used in on site structural framing which reduces the amount of material in general.

ID: The use of high performance environmentally preferable products and energy efficient appliances by Bosch, furniture by Design Within Reach, and water-efficient fixtures by Kohler are the point winning aspects of this category.

Above: The bedroom incorporates a wall of glass with a large sliding door that allows for sunlight and natural ventilation to flow through the space.

Right: Detail view of a small office tucked inside the home's interior containing built in book shelves and a desk.

Opposite: The large freestanding hearth spans the double height living area to further the relationship between the living room and the loft space.

homes are traditionally built and how unhealthy that can be from a perspective of what is in the materials and their effects on the inhabitants' health (carbons, formaldehyde, the mounting research that links repertory issues and cancers with these chemicals) to the manufacturing and transport of those materials, and how unhealthy that is for the environment. The conversation also includes water consumption and the differences between traditional planting and sustainable. The LivingHome deserves the applause it's receiving for successfully merging form and function, and style and substance.

A small reading nook tucked inside the roof garden space allows for natural shading though the series of exposed beams.

Teaching Design/Build: Studio 804

■ By Dan Rockhill

S TUDIO 804, WHICH TAKES ITS NAME from the final design studio within the graduate architecture program at the University of Kansas, compresses every aspect of a design/build practice into an intensive five-month experience. In the 10 years since the studio began, we've progressed from small-scale projects to creating affordable housing for the city of Lawrence to the point at which students now design, build, and install prefabricated homes for entry-level buyers in Kansas City. As a not-for-profit corporation that's associated with the university but receives no funding from it, we begin each year with nothing but the bank balance left by the previous graduating class and end with a completed design/build home, a satisfied client, and an invaluable learning experience.

If there's a difference between Studio 804 and most other design/build academic programs, it's that we are, as I like to say, a one-stop shop. That means the students work, not only with clients, neighborhood associations, and community development corporations (CDCs), but with uniform and international building codes, structural engineers, and inspectors who look twice at everything because of our nonprofessional status. While I greatly admire those programs that produce simple projects that don't have to stand up to real-world scrutiny, I'm pleased that Studio 804 gives students a chance to experience how complex the process of building for the marketplace actually is. Indeed, when

Once a design has been finalized, the students in the Studio 804 architecture program construct the modules in a warehouse.

they depart after five months, our alumni can actually produce a building, thanks to a comprehensive design experience that enables future architects to deal aggressively and immediately with issues they'll confront as professionals.

In fact, this approach may well represent an important paradigm shift in the way architecture schools teach studio. In the course of my 36 years as a professor, I've met with many former stu-

After all of the modules are completed, they are moved to the site via a flatbed truck.

dents who, after several years of work, expressed disappointment in the difference between the rarefied environment of the studio experience and the challenges posed by practice. While studio offers many positive opportunities to work on problems related to design, the absence of such powerful connections to reality-as-budget means that young people are deprived of the essential tools required to produce work in today's market. As many of us have come to recognize, this does a disservice, not only to our students, but to the firms that employ them, and to the building industry in general.

That's why our need to find our own funding, and the multifaceted way in which this enables us to engage with our clients, has proven so important. Since 2004, Studio 804 has produced modular prefab homes for urban infill lots in Kansas City, which we design and build in our off-campus warehouse and truck to their sites. (Prior to that, we erected five site-built houses in Lawrence, where the university is located.) Shifting our focus to Kansas City has delivered a number of benefits. The change has enabled us to provide much-needed housing stock for poor,

underserved neighborhoods in which property values have remained depressed for decades. It has connected us with CDCs that are eager to experiment with modernist typologies that can attract the urban-hipster homesteaders who will form the bedrock of the city's future. And it has allowed us to acquire properties for as little as a few hundred dollars and to enter into contracts that provide us with tight yet workable budgets, amounts that positively challenge students as both designers *and* builders. Best of all, working in Kansas City has generated gratifying results: Each of our prefabs has been sold by the CDC to an owner—*before* leaving the factory.

So how does it work? We begin the two-week design process in January—usually before there's a site—with each student bringing in and presenting a new three-dimensional model every day. Within half a week, I begin to cluster designs with similar characteristics, and these groups of students work to develop and refine ideas, which are ultimately combined into a single scheme. I try hard to keep the process democratic, by not favoring a particular student or concept; if unreconcilable proposals emerge, the

class takes a vote, and all commit to the outcome.

Once the design is complete, we present it to the CDC and further refine it based on the corporation's input. Construction documents are completed within days, and we typically have a building permit in hand by the end of the month. That leaves the students February and March to physically build the house, and six weeks for site and finishing work after the modules (typically, there are five or six of them) have been moved and assembled in early April.

As for the construction process, it's a bit like building a ship in a bottle—the whole house is finished inside and out in our warehouse, with only the plumbing, electrical, and heating work subcontracted out of necessity. Prefab, I've found, imposes a helpful discipline on both the design and construction processes. When Studio 804 first began, the entire experience was more fluid and experimental, and while this encouraged the students' imaginations (and egos), I often found myself arguing with 15 or 20 Gehry wannabes about why one or another superfluous aesthetic flourish had to be jettisoned. Now, the restrictions imposed by such immutables as the

The modules are lifted from the flatbeds by a crane.

size of the warehouse door, the length and width of the flatbed truck, and the dimensions of the infill lot leave less room for argument and help to focus and mature the students' abilities. (The fact that, at the moment, prefab also happens to be hip helps make up for the perceived lack of a creative big bang.) My students do nearly all their own sitework, as well, pouring concrete, erecting garages and tornado shelters, and putting down lawns. In every way that matters, the class is truly the author of the end result.

To my way of thinking, the benefits of exposing students to the design/build ethic are incalculable. In a conventional process, where the lines are drawn between them, responsibilities can be uncertain; in design/build, students learn to be responsible for everything, and not to make excuses. Similarly, Studio 804 alumni find themselves strongly connected to nearly every aspect of the design and construction industries, with a deep-seated understanding of process that militates against buck-passing, of the "Oh, the builder can figure it out" variety. Most of all, students learn the value of working and communicating with others to achieve a result—which lies, of course, at the heart of the design/build model.

The proof, I might add, is in the pudding. Studio 804 has been the recipient of approximately two dozen awards, including two Home of the Year prizes from *Architecture* magazine. The synthesis of design and craft achieved by our students is gratifying and impressive, and bodes well for the profession in general and the future of design/build in particular.

Once the house is completed, the students are responsible for installing the landscaping.

Above left: Detail view of the wood slat exterior wall system.

Above right:Detail view of the wood slat exterior wall system with outdoor recessed lighting.

Right:The home is ideally situated under a large tree.

Opposite: The students are required to do construction on most of the home's interior, typically subcontracting work only on electrical and mechanical systems.

Above left: Once again, the students construct the modules in a warehouse.

Above right: The modules are moved to the site and placed on the foundation with cranes.

Right: Another home under a large tree is ready to welcome its inhabitants.

Above left: Detail view of the translucent window surrounded by a metal frame.

Above right: View of the metal railing system and shading screen on the side of the home.

Left: Detail view of the wood siding exterior wall system.

Above left: The extended screen over the window allows for natural shading inside the home.

Above right: Built-in storage, complete with doors, provides a clean aesthetic.

Right: The translucent window lets in indirect light to the room.

Above: The flatbed trucks loaded with the completed modules, ready for relocation to the site.

Left: Using cranes to place the modules.

Entry view showing the dramatic new concrete entry stair. The students do all landscaping and concrete pouring for the homes. The deep recess at the front of the house provides an outdoor space as well as sun shading for the interior.

Above: Detail views of the wood slat exterior wall system and shallow stair entry.

Left: View of the home's storefront metal and glass assembly with operable windows that allow for natural ventilation.

The home's exterior is clad in a combination of wood slats and metal wall panels.

The doorway to the private rear balcony is virtually invisible along the wood slat wall.

Detail view of the interior translucent pocket door.

The seam along the floor, wall, and ceiling reveals the connection point between the two modules.

Endnotes

CHAPTER 1

1. Carson, Rachel, *Silent Spring*, Boston: Houghton Mifflin, 1962.

2. Hines, Thomsa S., *Richard Neutra and the Search for Modern Architecture*, Oxford University Press, New York, 1982.

3. Mazria, Edward, The Passive Solar Energy Book, Rodale Press, 1979.

4. Olgvay, Victor, *Design with Climate*, Princeton University Press, 1966.

5. Sargeant, John, *Frank Lloyd Wright's Usonian Houses*, p. 83. Billboard Publications, New York, 1984.

6. Wright, David, *Natural Solar Architecture: A Passive Primer*, Van Nostrand Reinhold, 1978.

7. Wright, Frank Lloyd, *The Natural House*, Horizon Press, 1954.

CHAPTER 2

1. Donald Schon, *The Reflective Practitioner*, New York: Basic Books, 1982, p. 103.

2. T. J. Williamson, Helen Bennets, and Antony Radford, *Understanding Sustainable Architecture*, London: Taylor & Francis, 2002, p. 70.

3. Ibid., p. 3.

4. Ibid., p.14.

5. Alan J. Brookes and Dominique Poole, *Innovation in Architecture,* London:Taylor & Francis, 2004, p. 41.

CHAPTER 4

1. Energy Information Administration Statistics (Architecture 2030).

2. Southern States Energy Board.

3. www.eere.energy.gov/buildings/building_america

4. www.energystar.gov/index.cfm?c=new_homes.hm_index

5. "America's Homes Get Bigger and Better," *ABC News*, December 27, 2005.

6. www.epa.gov/watersense

7. www.southface.org/web/resources&services/publications/factsheets/30_radonresistantconst.pdf

8. www.energystar.gov/ia/partners/bldrs_lenders_raters/downloads/ThermBypassGuide.pdf

9. www.southface.org/web/resources&services/publications/collateral/airseal_poster%20-%20for%20offset%20repro.pdf

10. www1.eere.energy.gov/consumer/tips/insulation.html#chart

11. 2005 ASHRAE Handbook Fundamentals, Inch-Pound Edition (2005) American Society of Heating, Refrigerating and Air-Conditioning Engineers, Inc.

12. www.energystar.gov/index.cfm?c=roof_prods.pr_roof_products

13. www.earthcrafthouse.com/documents/factsheets/AWF-Advanced_frame%2000-770.pdf

14. Energy Federation Incorporated.

15. Draft, April 23, 2008.

16. *Consumer's Guide to Radon Reduction*, EPA, 1992.

17. www.epa.gov/radon/zonemap.html

18. www.dsireusa.org

CHAPTER 6

1–3. Beveridge, Charles E., and Rocheleau, Paul. *Fredrick Law Olmsted Designing the American Landscape* (New York, Rizzoli International Publications, Inc. 1995).

4. Heeger, Susan, "Jen Jensen at Sklands" *House and Garden.*

5. McHarg, Ian L., *Design with Nature* (John Wiley & Sons, Inc. 1992).

6–8. Thompson, J. William and Sorvig, Kim, *Sustainable Landscape Construction, A Guide to Green Building Outdoors* (Washington, D.C., Island Press, 2000).

9. McHarg, Ian L., *Design with Nature* (John Wiley & Sons, Inc. 1992).

CHAPTER 8

1. "Multiple Chemical Sensitivity: A 1999 Consensus," *Arch. Environ. Health* 54 (3): 1999, pp.147–9.

2. Miller, C.S. "Toxicant-induced Loss of Tolerance: An Emerging Theory of Disease?" 105 (2):1997, 445–53. *Environ Health Perspect*, University of Texas Press.

3. Understanding and Accommodating People with MCS, Pamela Reed Gibson, Ph.D. (2005).

CHAPTER 9

1. The DESIGNhabitat 2 team student team included: Joey Aplin, Samuel Bassett, Cayce Bean, David Davis, Danielle Dratch, Joey Fante, Betsy Farrell, Russ Gibbs, Jennifer Givens, Simon Hurst, Walter Mason, Bill Moore, Matt Murphy, Ryan Simon, and Mackenzie Stagg.

2. The work of Daniel Rockhill and his students at the University of Kansas and the work of John Quale and his students at the University of Virginia exemplify the excellent modular design research underway in architecture schools. The work of these design/build studios provided a valuable source of predesign insight to the DESIGNhabitat team.

About the Contributors

WILLIAM CARPENTER, FAIA, PhD, is a nationally recognized architect and educator. A founder of Lightroom, an interdisciplinary design firm in Decatur, Georgia, he is a Professor of Architecture at Southern Polytechnic State University. He is a recipient of the National Young Architects Citation and the national ACSA/AIAS Educator of the Year Award. In 2000, he became one the youngest people ever to be elected as a Fellow in the AIA. He earned his doctorate (in Architecture and Education) at the University of Birmingham in England, and is the author of the acclaimed book, *Learning by Building: Design and Construction in Architectural Education* (Wiley, 1997). His work in independent film includes a production shown at the Cannes Film Festival (in collaboration with Vennila Films) as well as the First Prize winner (in collaboration with Shadowligh Pictures) of the International 48 hour Film Festival. He has two daughters, Esme (14) and Mirette (12), and a soulful dog, James Brown.
www.lightroom.tv
www.spsu.edu

LEE CUTHBERT is owner and founder of Victory Vintage, a modern design and furnishings shop in Decatur, Georgia. Lee is an experienced writer on architecture and design and has written extensively on a local and national level.
www.Victoryvintage.com

RIC NARDIN is a freelance writer and architecture enthusiast. He writes frequently on a variety of subjects including design, international finance, and healthcare. A screenwriter of independent films, his work has appeared at the Cannes Film Festival (in collaboration with William J. Carpenter and Vennila Films). He is based in Decatur, Georgia, where he lives with his wife Diane.

LYNN SAUSSY, ASLA, has been practicing landscape architecture for over 20 years and is principal of L.F. Saussy, Landscape Architects in Atlanta, Georgia. She is passionate about caring for the earth and loves educating clients on sustainable landscape practices for their gardens. When she is not working, she can be found visiting her daughter (21) at college, hiking in the north Georgia mountains, studying plants at the Atlanta and State Botanical Gardens, designing new products, and volunteering in her community parks. Her work recently appeared on an episode of HGTV's Ground Breakers.
www.lfsaussy.com

JIM BURTON, a principal with Carter + Burton Architecture, has been experimenting with sustainable building systems and technologies in his own homes with the construction of Studio Loggerheads and Boxhead. His personal time is spent raising Catherine (7) and Gordon (5) with his wife Cynthia while trying to find time for mountain biking, volleyball and painting.
www.carterburton.com

MONIQUE BIRAULT, AIA, a project manager for the University of Southern California's Campus Architect and Capital Construction Development Department, is interested in incorporating sustainable design and economical building techniques in the University planning and building environment. Previously, Monique has managed design and construction on the Getty Center, and long range planning for Pepperdine University, to name a few. She has also sat on numerous Board of Directors. Otherwise, she can be found immersed in her passion for jewelry design and fabrication. She creates commissioned pieces as well as jewelry lines sold by museums and her Los Angeles gallery.

ROBERT SOENS has been in the construction business as both a Commercial general contractor and homebuilder for over 20 years and has specialized in "Green" building practices for over 10 years. Robert shares his construction expertise as both a Community volunteer and leader while running Pinnacle Custom Builders in Decatur, Georgia. Robert also serves on the executive committee of the local home builders association and co-chairs the local USGBC Residential Green Committee.
www.pinnacle-custom-builders.com

DAN ROCKHILL is the J. L. Constant Distinguished Professor of Architecture at the University of Kansas and the Executive Director of Studio 804. He and his students have been producing modern prefab housing in the Kansas City urban area and most recently completed the first LEED Platinum building in Kansas. This work, along with his work as a Principal of the design firm Rockhill and Associates, has appeared in nearly 200 international books and journals, has been exhibited at the Venice Architecture Biennale, and was recognized for the 2006 Cooper-Hewitt National Design Award. The book *Designing and Building: Rockhill and Associates* (Tuns Press) is available from Amazon.
www.studio804.com
www.rockhillandassociates.com

ROBERT M. CAIN, AIA, has had a pioneering interest in passive solar design, energy-efficient design, and utilization of sustainable building materials and concepts for over 30 years. Virtually every project of his design utilizes aspects of sustainable technology. In practice since 1975, Mr. Cain continues to seek and promote advances and innovation in sustainable design.
www.Robertmcain.com

DR. SYDNEY G. ROBERTS is the home services program manager at Southface Energy Institute, a green building consulting nonprofit in Atlanta, Georgia, where she is researcher, trainer and consultant on energy efficiency, high-performance building and sustainable policy development. Specifically, Dr. Roberts manages the Southern Energy Efficiency Center, Building America and Home Performance with ENERGY STAR programs. She earned a doctorate from Stanford University in mechanical engineering. Sydney enjoys cooking for friends, designing and building furniture, and working out at the gym.
www.southface.org

Index

Numbers in *italics* refer to illustrations. Numbers in **boldface** refer to illustrated case studies.

WILEY BOOKS ON Sustainable Design

For these and other Wiley books on sustainable design, visit
www.wiley.com/go/sustainabledesign

Alternative Construction: Contemporary Natural Building Methods
by Lynne Elizabeth and Cassandra Adams

Biophilic Design: The Theory, Science, and Practice of Bringing Buildings to Life
by Stephen R. Kellert, Judith Heerwagen, and Martin Mador

Contractor's Guide to Green Building Construction: Management, Project Delivery, Documentation, and Risk Reduction
by Thomas E. Glavinich and Associated General Contractors

Design with Nature
by Ian L. McHarg

Ecodesign: A Manual for Ecological Design
by Ken Yeang

Environmentally Responsible Design: Green and Sustainable Design for·Interior Designers
by Louise Jones

Green BIM: Successful Sustainable Design with Building Information Modeling
by Eddy Krygel and Brad Nies

Green Building Materials: A Guide to Product Selection and Specification, Second Edition
by Ross Spiegel and Dru Meadows

Green Roof Systems: A Guide to the Planning, Design and Construction of Building Over Structure
by Susan Weiler and Katrin Scholz-Barth

The HOK Guidebook to Sustainable Design, Second Edition
by Sandra Mendler, William O'Dell, and Mary Ann Lazarus

The Integrative Design Guide to Green Building: Redefining the Practice of Sustainability
by 7group and Bill Reed

Land and Natural Development (Land) Code
by Diana Balmori and Gaboury Benoit

A Legal Guide to Urban and Sustainable Development for Planners, Developers and Architects
by Daniel Slone, Doris S. Goldstein, and W. Andrew Gowder

Materials for Sustainable Sites: A Complete Guide to the Evaluation, Selection, and Use of Sustainable Construction Materials
by Meg Calkins

Modern Sustainable Residential Design: A Guide for Design Professionals
by William J. Carpenter

Packaging Sustainability: Tools, Systems and Strategies for Innovative Package Design
by Wendy Jedlicka

Sustainable Commercial Interiors
by Penny Bonda and Katie Sosnowchik

Sustainable Construction: Green Building Design and Delivery, Second Edition
by Charles J. Kibert

Sustainable Design: Ecology, Architecture, and Planning
by Daniel Williams

Sustainable Design: The Science of Sustainability and Green Engineering
by Daniel Vallero and Chris Brasier

Sustainable Healthcare Architecture
by Robin Guenther and Gail Vittori

Sustainable Residential Interiors
by Associates III

Sustainable Urbanism: Urban Design With Nature
by Douglas Farr

 ENVIRONMENTAL BENEFITS STATEMENT

This book is printed with soy-based inks on presses with VOC levels that are lower than the standard for the printing industry. The paper, Rolland Enviro 100, is manufactured by Cascades Fine Papers Group and is made from 100 percent post-consumer, de-inked fiber, without chlorine. According to the manufacturer, the use of every ton of Rolland Enviro100 Book paper, switched from virgin paper, helps the environment in the following ways:

Mature trees	Waterborne waste not created	Waterflow saved	Atmospheric emissions eliminated	Solid Wastes reduced	Natural gas saved by using biogas
17	6.9 lbs.	10,196 gals.	2,098 lbs.	1,081 lbs.	2,478 cubic feet